3302381702

DENAZIFICATION

DENAZIFICATION

*Britain's Enemy Aliens,
Nazi War Criminals and
the Reconstruction of
Post-war Europe*

HELEN FRY

For James Hamilton
a creative voice and my co-author in fiction

*The reading of all good books is like a conversation with
the finest minds of past centuries.*
René Descartes

First published 2010

The History Press
The Mill, Brimscombe Port
Stroud, Gloucestershire, GL5 2QG
www.thehistorypress.co.uk

British Library Cataloguing in Publication Data.
A catalogue record for this book is available from the British Library.

ISBN 978 0 7509 5113 5

Typesetting and origination by The History Press
Printed in Great Britain
Manufacturing managed by Jellyfish Print Solutions Ltd

CONTENTS

Acknowledgements   7

Introduction   9

One   His Majesty's Most Loyal Enemy Aliens   15

Two   Hunt for Nazi War Criminals   38

Three   War Crimes Investigations   62

Four   War Crimes Trials and Courts   83

Five   Interpreters, Interrogators and Translators   94

Six   Military Government   110

Seven   Media and Newspapers   131

Eight   POW Camps and Re-education   143

Nine   Civilian Life   168

Postscript   177

Bibliography   181

Index   185

ACKNOWLEDGEMENTS

Six years ago I embarked on research which has unexpectedly led to the publication of an extraordinary number of books, all centred on the theme of refugees from Nazism who fought for Britain during the Second World War. The initial research resulted in two books: *Jews in North Devon during the Second World War* and *The King's Most Loyal Enemy Aliens: Germans who Fought for Britain during the Second World War*. Two further books followed during 2009 called *Freuds' War* and *From Dachau to D-Day*. In January 2010 *German Schoolboy, British Commando* was published. Now this book, *Denazification*, is a direct spin-off of the ever-widening research, and covers what the ex-refugees from Nazism did from the end of the war in May 1945 until their demobilisation. Many were seconded to the Intelligence Corps or Interpreters Corps to carry out their final duties in British army uniform. In many cases it involved top-secret work, making use of their fluent knowledge of German.

This book could not have been written without the help of the veterans themselves. My first thanks are to these exceptional veterans, many of whom have become close personal friends over the last few years. They have given up their time to be interviewed, which is often a lengthy process. They have entrusted me with their private stories, often painful memories of a time that formulated their young lives and a period that hides deep scars. They were proud to serve in British army uniform but have terrible recollections of the loss of comrades in action on the battlefields of Europe. Little did they or I realise when I embarked on my first account of their stories that it would lead to several years of writing and research and nearly a shelf of books! During the writing of these books I have received unprecedented support from Colonel John Starling and Norman Brown of the Royal Pioneer Corps Association. Many thanks to you both. Much material has been given to me by the veterans themselves, often in the form of unpublished memoirs. Upon completion of this book I am looking to deposit material that I have acquired into the Imperial War Museum so that future historians and researchers can have access to them.

Work on this book would not have been possible without the dedicated help and support of staff at the Imperial War Museum, London and the Jewish Military Museum in Hendon, north-west London. My grateful thanks for all their help with archival material. The Association of Jewish Refugees has given me exceptional support – with special thanks to Michael Newman, Howard Spier, Esther Rinkoff, Myrna Glass and Hazel Beiny. Huge thanks are due to Alexia Dobinson for typing up many of the interviews for this book. Her support is so much appreciated. To my friend and mentor Mary Curry, I owe an enormous debt of gratitude for her commitment and support of all my writings, this book being no exception. She has read and commented extensively on every draft of the chapters at every stage of writing and found research information which I would have missed. I am indebted to Sophie Bradshaw, Peter Teale and Simon Hamlet at The History Press for making this book possible. A special word of thanks to Mick Catmull at BBC South-West, who produced a miniature documentary for BBC South-West's *Inside Out* programme, screened in October 2006 called *The King's Most Loyal Enemy Aliens*. Also huge thanks to Mark Handscombe and Mark McMullen of True North Productions for making a one-hour documentary for National Geographic Channel entitled *Churchill's German Army*, screened regularly across Europe, Central Asia and America in 2009 and 2010. The documentary is based on my research, especially my paperback book *Churchill's German Army*, and is drawn upon other books that I have written about the German and Austrian refugees who fought for Britain during the Second World War.

My grateful thanks go to my writing partner in fiction James Hamilton for his loyal friendship and continued support. Under the pseudonym J.H. Schryer we have co-authored *Goodnight Vienna* and *Moonlight Over Denmark*. I am also indebted to the following friends for their encouragement: Richard Bernstein, Daphne and Paul Ruhleman, Jon Russell, Frank and Brana Thorn-Gent, Louisa Albani and Colin Hamilton. Huge thanks to Marian Stranavsky of Kenwood House for the red carpet! Special thanks to my family: to my husband Martin who has supported me since the early days of my writing career. Thanks to our three boys Jonathan, David and Edward for their interest and help with computer technology at crucial points. As ever my mother Sandra has been a tower of strength and practical help.

INTRODUCTION

History marks the end of the Second World War as 8 May 1945, the day that Germany surrendered unconditionally to Allied forces. The four occupying powers, Britain, America, France and Russia, had a huge task ahead of them in restoring democracy: to reconstruct post-war Germany and Austria, and remove adherents of Nazism and Nazi ideology from every facet of public life and employment. This process was termed 'denazification'. At the Yalta Conference in February 1945, the Allied leaders had already met to set the agenda for post-war Germany and Austria. This included dividing the countries into four zones, administered initially by occupying military forces who were to be gradually replaced by the Control Commission. The Allied powers did not underestimate the challenges. At the fore of everyone's mind was the need to hunt down and bring to justice the perpetrators of the most horrendous crimes against humanity. Eleven million people had been mercilessly murdered in the death camps, 6 million of them Jews, a million children.

One group of veterans, whose contribution to the denazification process is largely unknown, are the refugees from Nazism who fought for Britain during the war. Having served in various regiments of the British forces, they transferred in their thousands to the British Army of the Rhine (BAOR) and British Control Commission for work that required a fluent knowledge of German. This book is about them. At the outbreak of war on 3 September 1939, these men and women were termed 'enemy aliens' because of their enemy nationality. Later they anglicised their names in case of capture during combat, so tracing precise numbers is difficult. However, it is estimated that 3–4,000 German-speaking refugees were assigned to the Interpreters Corps and Intelligence Corps to undertake a range of duties. Their invaluable asset was their fluency in the German language. Their role became critical at this time for rebuilding the once Nazi-occupied countries of Europe. That work included the hunt for Nazi war criminals, 'Odessa' escapees, gathering evidence for war crimes trials, interrogations, intelligence duties, military government and all manner of work which required their knowledge of German. They were often sent back to the towns and cities of their birth because of their knowledge of the area and language. In the concluding chapter of *The King's Most Loyal Enemy Aliens* (in paperback as *Churchill's German Army*), I went so far as to argue that the enemy aliens became a vital, even indispensable, workforce for the occupying Allies. Much of the stability and successful reconstruction of post-war Europe is owed to their work in the British army.

Europe had seen six years of war. The beginning of the end for the Nazi regime really came with Operation Husky, the invasion of Sicily and Italy in the summer of 1943. It could only be a matter of time before a mass invasion force landed elsewhere. The place was to be Normandy; D-Day, 6 June 1944. Germany was the ultimate destination for Allied forces as they pushed through France, Belgium and Holland. The refugees amongst their ranks did not see this as the liberation of their former country, but the invasion of it. 'This is an important distinction,' comments ex-refugee from Bonn, Willy Hirschfeld, who as Willy Field fought with the 8th King's Royal Irish Hussars. 'We liberated France. We liberated Belgium and Holland, but we *invaded* Germany. The German people had readily accepted Hitler in 1933 and therefore we were not liberating Germany from an occupying force.' Many cities and towns in Germany were decimated by Allied bombing. The challenge that faced the Allies was not limited to rebuilding the country, but also involved avoiding the mistakes made at the end of the First World War, as ex-refugee Colin Anson (Claus Ascher), who served in the commandos comments:

> Smoldering resentment was the main engine which created the situation for Hitler to come to power in Germany in 1933. The First World War was often referred to as 'the lost war'. Germany was humiliated and Europe was to pay a heavy price for it twenty-one years later. The Second World War had to go to total destruction before Germany could be built up again.[1]

This time there was the added complication of denazification – the total restructure of a society that had seen thirteen years of tyranny, brutality, mass murder, and lack of freedom and civil integrity. In that task the German-speaking refugees in British and American army uniform came into their own. It tended to be the male refugees serving in the army, rather than the females, who were assigned to denazification work in Germany, Austria or in POW camps in Britain. Unlike their British colleagues, these refugees in uniform faced a number of emotional traumas. Firstly, they had to bear the impact of the recent war and that included the loss of comrades on the front line or injuries they themselves suffered in battle. Secondly, they had to cope with the loss of their families in horrific conditions in the concentration camps across Europe. News of that was often slow to filter through and it sometimes took years to establish what had happened to their families. Thirdly, they had to concentrate their minds on the tasks ahead in their new roles in the army: reconstructing the country which had unceremoniously thrown them out. And finally, they had to absorb the shockwaves of seeing their former German countrymen now subject to absolute surrender and defeat. They returned to find much of the country reduced to rubble and the infrastructure in chaos. Harry Rossney (originally Helmuth Rosettenstein, b. Königsberg) reflects:

> We witnessed the degradation of those once considered upright and honest people in German society: the doctors and teachers who were once admired and respected prior to the reign of Nazism. All this required tremendous adjustment. Past hatred and compassion for the present state of the people had to be resolved. That was not so easy for the 'King's most loyal enemy aliens'.[2]

Hitler had committed suicide in his bunker and the leading Nazi war criminals had gone into hiding.

Gideon Behrendt (Günter Behrendt), who enlisted in the Pioneer Corps before volunteering for the Parachute Regiment in 1943, wrote in his privately published memoirs *The Long Road Home*:

> And then the guns went silent. It was all over. Germany's unconditional surrender was signed. But for me there was no jubilation because by that time I had already seen photos and heard about the atrocities committed at the concentration camps, Bergen-Belsen and others. Our division had passed close by Bergen-Belsen on our way to Lüneburg and I had not known about the existence of such a place. The extent of the horrors the Nazis and their henchmen had perpetrated in other places of Europe, particularly in the East, only came to light at the end of the war. I was as shocked as the rest of the world, but the hurt went deeper into my soul. Hitler was said to be dead.

The Nazis had surrendered. The German people seemed to have accepted their defeat. Large parts of Germany lay in ruins and ashes. I had achieved what I set out to do: I had helped towards the downfall of Hitler and his thugs. I had been one amongst the millions of simple people who fought for justice and freedom.

For the enemy aliens returning to the place of their birth, it was an experience that was bound to be full of mixed emotions. Peter Perry (Peter Pinschewer, b. Berlin) went with British forces to Berlin. The past was all around him:

> Suddenly I was transported back to my early childhood. Behind me were the ruins of my father's barber shop, and next to it the bakery which had supplied our fresh, crisp breakfast rolls. For a while I gazed up at our old flat on the second floor. Suddenly I became aware that the present occupants had appeared on the balcony and were looking down with some alarm at the uncertain outline of a soldier contemplating their residence in the moonlight. I should have gone in, introduced myself and used the opportunity once again to see the place where I was born and spent a happy childhood. Unfortunately, I missed that chance.[3]

Walter Eberstadt (b. Frankfurt), who had fought in the Oxfordshire and Bucks Light Infantry, reflects on his entry into Hamburg:

> What did I make of all this? Does it sound plausible that I arrived in Hamburg, consumed with hatred of everything German, determined to avenge my family and everyone else persecuted by Hitler, to teach those bastards a lesson once and for all? Or that I would let on to no one who I really was, that this was the town in which I had spent my adolescence, gone to school, where many still lived who had known our family well? ... I of course wandered around the streets, looked at our old house, but Hamburg was no longer all that familiar. I had spent ten years forgetting, suppressing my childhood, and quite successfully becoming English. I had spent almost half of my life in England.[4]

In the aftermath of the fighting, or when Allied troops occupied a town or city, denazification began immediately and usually meant the immediate replacement of the local bürgermeister (mayor) on the strength of local information. All Nazis had to be removed from positions of power or responsibility: from offices of government and political life, including those in leading economic positions, the judiciary and media. The term 'denazification' also came to mean the process of removing the stigma of having been a Nazi for those 'lesser Nazis' and led to restitution of full civil rights. This enabled lesser Nazis to vote again in general elections and to have their jobs restored. In the British zone the work was initially carried out by the British Army of the Rhine (BAOR), but as personnel were gradually demobbed, BAOR was replaced by the Allied Control Commission in Germany and Austria. Many ex-refugees served in one or both. As more and more responsibility was passed back to indigenous Germans and Austrians, the Control Commission could best be described as a kind of shadow government. No important measures could be implemented without its agreement. Its importance decreased the longer the occupation lasted, until it finally came to an end in 1955.

Historians have long debated whether the denazification process was successful; the majority conclude that ultimately it failed because many of the Nazi war criminals were never brought to justice.[5] However, the men who were interviewed for this book argue very differently. Their view is that in spite of some failings with regard to justice and not capturing leading war criminals, denazification was successful because it led to a free, democratic Germany which functions as such today. Of the arrests of leading Nazi war criminals that were successful, most were carried out by the German-speaking refugees serving in the British forces. This included the arrest of Himmler, who eventually committed suicide whilst in British custody; Rudolf Höss, the notorious Commandant of Auschwitz; and SS Obergruppenführer Oswald Pohl, who had built up the Nazi administration during the 1930s. Walter Freud, one of Sigmund Freud's grandsons, was assigned to investigate the case of the Hamburg-based company Tesch & Stabenow, which had supplied Zyklon B gas for mass murder in the concentration camps. Freud was also sent on the trail of Danish Nazi war criminal Christian Gustaf Jepsen, who was hanged in Hameln Prison in 1947 after a trial under a British court. When Prussian-born Erwin Lehmann enlisted in the Pioneer Corps in the autumn of 1940, little did he know then that under the name John Langford, but still as a German national, he would serve as Churchill's bodyguard at the Potsdam Conference in July 1945. So too, Berlin-born Geoffrey Perry (Horst Pinschewer) did not realise what fate had in store for him when at the end of the war he captured

Britain's most notorious wartime traitor, William Joyce, near Flensburg on the Danish border. It was, for example, a group of five ex-German Jewish refugees serving in British Counter-Intelligence in Germany at the end of the war who discovered and translated the last will and testament of Adolf Hitler.[6] These were extraordinary times, and the men from refugee backgrounds in the British forces found themselves involved in astonishing work for the Allies. Those who were not posted back to Germany or Austria remained in Britain for post-war military duties often connected to the denazification process. Some worked in German POW camps up and down the country where they were engaged in the interrogation of POWs with a view to denazifying them in their re-education programme. All played their part in the process, whether in Britain or abroad. It is fair to say that without the German-speaking refugees in the army, post-war Europe could not have been reconstructed in such a short space of time. Harry Rossney adds: 'The contribution of the enemy aliens to the denazification process and the rebuilding of post-war Europe has a birthright to be heard for posterity and history's sake.'

This book, *Denazification*, finally tells their story and gives them due recognition for their crucial part in the reconstruction and stability of post-war Europe.

Notes

1. Interview with the author.
2. Taken from several interviews with the author.
3. Peter Perry, *An Extraordinary Commission*, p. 84.
4. Walter Eberstadt, *Whence We Came, Where We Went*, p. 331.
5. Although 1,500 received summary justice from the Jewish Brigade. See Morris Beckman, *The Jewish Brigade*, pp. xiii–xiv.
6. See Herman Rothman, *Hitler's Will* and Hugh Trevor-Roper, *The Last Days of Hitler*.

One

HIS MAJESTY'S MOST
LOYAL ENEMY ALIENS

The contribution of refugees from Nazism to the British forces in the Second World War began in the latter months of 1939. To understand the background to the part they played at the end of the war, it is important to briefly outline their roles from the beginning of it. Eventually over 10,000 Germans and Austrians served in the British forces, but at the outbreak of war they were classified as 'enemy aliens' and as such had restrictions imposed on them. The country which had given them shelter, namely Britain, was at war with the country of their birth and they were acutely aware of this irony. As enemy aliens they could not be conscripted by the British government; all had to volunteer because they were not yet British nationals. Amongst them were some of the finest brains of Europe: doctors, dentists, lawyers, engineers, surgeons, artists and musicians.[1] They had no hesitation in volunteering to fight Hitler's regime as they wanted to play their part in the defeat of Nazism. This was *their* war. They were not going to sit back and allow others to do all the fighting. Their motivation was never in doubt, as Harry Brook (originally Heinz Brück) succinctly said: 'I wanted to fight. I was humiliated by the Nazis when I lived in Germany and deprived of an education. I was angry and this was my opportunity to hit back.' For Willy Field (Willy Hirschfeld, b. Bonn), survivor of Dachau concentration camp, his motivation for joining up was clear: 'I volunteered for the British Forces because I wanted to give something back to Britain for saving my life. Without it I would have perished in the Holocaust alongside my parents and other family members. I wanted to fight the Germans. It was my duty.' William Ashley Howard (born Horst Adolf Herzberg), half-Jewish in the eyes of the Nazis, served first in the Pioneer Corps and then in the Royal Navy: 'Having been in Germany and lived through what was happening, every fibre of my body suggested that I had to do something. The regime was so evil. I was aware of the plight of the Jewish people and I considered it unquestionably my duty to fight at the highest level.' Michael Sherwood (born Isi Schwarzbard in Leipzig, 1924) expressed similar sentiments: 'This was my fight. In Germany we were kicked, molested, beaten up and had our property confiscated. We had no way to stand our corner. Being in the British forces was an instrument for education and to fight back.'[2]

Peter Sinclair (Peter Heinz Jacob, b. Berlin) enlisted in the British forces because 'of a hatred of all that had happened to us in Germany. Seeing and experiencing the spirit of people in England was inspirational, quite fantastic, despite all the set-backs which occurred. My conscience wouldn't let me sit back and not participate in the war. My father died in Argentina and my grandparents perished in Auschwitz.'

Once in uniform, the refugees swore allegiance to King George VI and became affectionately known as 'the king's most loyal enemy aliens'. Their full story has been told in an earlier book of that title and also in a book by veteran Peter Leighton-Langer. In the early years the men who enlisted were deeply disappointed that the only unit in the British army open to them as 'enemy aliens' was the Pioneer Corps – essentially a labour corps. The majority spent up to two or three years doing manual labour. There was much essential, if menial, work to be done constructing coastal defences, building Nissen huts, mixing concrete, forestry and carpentry. In 1942 their chance to fight came when the British government realised the recruiting potential of German-speaking refugees for special operations. Because of their knowledge of German, the first transfers from the Pioneer Corps were made early that year when certain individuals were vetted to discover their motives and suitability for secret missions behind enemy lines. The first group formed for hazardous missions was the Small Scale Raiding Force (SSRF), a kind of early commando unit. They received specialised top-secret training at Anderson Manor near Blandford in Dorset. From there, small groups of five or six men, usually with one German-speaker, were sent on coastal raids into North Africa, Norway and Normandy. Their aim: to test out defences, capture German POWs for interrogation, gather intelligence and capture radio transmission stations. It was a highly risky role and one in which some lost their lives. The second group trained for special missions were formed into a commando unit called 3 Troop of No 10 Inter-Allied Commando. They received the best and most rigorous training that the British army could offer. Once trained, they were the only commando unit that did not go into action together. They were assigned to other commando units, including the Royal Marine Commandos and No 6 Bicycle Brigade, for special raids and operations involving their knowledge of the German language. Some took part in the invasion of Sicily and Italy, or raids into the Yugoslav islands of Brač and Hvar in the Adriatic. Others landed on, or just after, D-Day and were part of front-line forces as they pushed through France. Due to the nature of their duties, often with reconnaissance missions behind the lines, 3 Troop had some of the highest fatality and casualty rates of the refugees who served in the war. The final group that trained together for special duties consisted of around 25–30 mainly ex-Austrians as part of Special Operations Executive (SOE). Their brief was to be parachuted into enemy territory in southern Austria to establish an Allied presence there and to try to take the strategic airbase at Zeltweg in the Styria region of the country. It was a high-risk venture involving a 'blind drop', with no one to meet them at the other end. One of those parachuted back into Austria was Anton Walter Freud, a grandson of Sigmund Freud, whose story is told in *Freuds' War*.

From 1943, enemy aliens were permitted to transfer from the Pioneer Corps to all regiments of the British forces. Many took the opportunity to do so and transferred to the Royal Artillery, the Royal Armoured Corps, SAS, Royal Navy, RAF, Gordon Highlanders, Black Watch, Coldstream Guards, Argyll and Sutherland Highlanders and other infantry regiments, paratroops and airborne forces. They were involved in every campaign of the war, including action in Sicily and Italy, the invasion of Normandy on D-Day and front-line fighting spearheading the advance through France, Belgium, Holland and finally the Rhine crossings into Germany. Some were amongst the first wave of parachutists to be dropped into Normandy prior to D-Day to prepare dropping zones for the incoming airborne forces. Once in fighting units, the men anglicised their names in case of capture. If they had not done so they would have been killed as traitors rather than treated as POWs if captured by the Nazis. Amongst the highest casualties were suffered by those serving in infantry regiments. These crack regiments, with a long and proud tradition of their own, were called upon to lead the main offensive, including the major campaigns into Belgium,

Holland and Germany. The knowledge of several European languages was used by reconnaissance patrols behind enemy lines ahead of their regiments and later to interrogate German POWs. They led major advances, often at night, into enemy territory and at a slow pace. Conditions were tough, sleep in short supply, and casualties and fatalities high as portrayed in the official war diaries. Sometimes, after an advance or capture of a village or town, hundreds of POWs would be taken in a short space of time. All had to be confined, fed and interrogated. Interrogations required a fluent command of German which is why the enemy aliens became so valuable. Some remained in Britain, where they were assigned to German POW camps or intelligence centres like Latimer House and Wilton Park. There they eavesdropped on the conversations of Nazi servicemen of differing ranks to glean useful information.

Refugee women made their own contribution to the British forces. It is estimated that just under 1,000 ex-German and ex-Austrian refugee women volunteered, most of whom were drafted into the Auxiliary Territorial Service (ATS). Here their skills and knowledge of German was largely undervalued or not used. Most were assigned to domestic duties and served in the Officers' Mess. Others served in the Women's Auxiliary Air Force. A handful of ex-refugee women were stationed at special listening posts like Bletchley Park. Some were recruited by MI6 to work at a top-secret propaganda station at Milton Bryan, a complex on the edge of the tiny Bedfordshire village just a few miles from the cipher school at Bletchley Park. Here the female refugees were involved in a clandestine German propaganda radio station, named *Deutsche Kurzwellensender Atlantik*, transmitting German radio broadcasts. It housed the latest technological equipment and included direct telephone lines to the BBC and Air Ministry. This complex later expanded its work to include another radio station, *Atlantiksender*. They made use of the most recent British military intelligence, thus providing credibility for their propaganda cover. However, the stories of the contribution made by ex-refugee women to the British forces during the war are among the least recorded. Very few have come forward to tell their tales, believing their contribution to be not particularly significant. Sadly, their testimonies are significantly under-represented.

Some German-speaking refugees, having risked their lives on the front line for the country that had saved them from Nazi tyranny, were captured during action. They spent time in POW camps in Germany and

Austria. Stephen Dale (Heinz Günther Spanglet, b. Berlin), survivor of Sachsenhausen concentration camp, served with the SOE. He was taken prisoner and survived a number of different POW camps before being transferred to Kaisersteinbruck camp (Stalag 17a), then Oflag 79 near Brunswick, the latter being from where he was liberated by the Americans in the late spring of 1945. Martin Werner Goldman (Martin Goldmann, b. Leipzig, 1918) served with the Royal Corps of Signals and was captured in Greece where he spent two years in a POW camp. He was later transferred to Villach, 30 miles from Klagenfurt in Austria (Stalag XVIII), where he was forced to build railways for the Nazis until the lines were bombed by the Allies in 1945. Fortunately, most of the enemy aliens taken prisoner whilst in action managed to disguise their German or Austrian origins and were successfully released at the end of the war. But inevitably there were casualties and fatalities, with some of the highest losses being from members of 3 Troop, No 10 Inter-Allied Commando. The men gave their lives on the battlefields of Sicily, Italy, northern France, Belgium, Holland and Germany. Those who survived headed with their respective regiments for the invasion of Germany. When they finally crossed into Germany, they were returning with the victorious Allied forces, but were still faced with resistance from die-hard Nazis. Many were setting foot on German soil for the first time in at least six years, in some cases longer. Geoffrey Perry (Horst Pinschewer) comments: 'Being back on German soil was like having goose-bumps but much more. It was a strange feeling, but was soon mingled with the reality of the horrors perpetrated by the Nazi regime in the concentration camps.'[3]

The full extent and horror of Hitler's Final Solution to exterminate European Jewry became a graphic reality for the Allied forces that entered the concentration camps. On 15 April 1945, British soldiers liberated Bergen-Belsen and found unspeakable conditions. The first Jewish chaplain to enter Belsen was Rev. Leslie Hardman, followed shortly after by the Rev. Dr Isaac Levy, both British-born Jews. They began ministering to the needs of the desperately ill survivors and burying the thousands of bodies of those who had died of starvation and disease. Piles of thousands of rotting emaciated corpses lay in hastily dug open pits. Those who had survived were in a terrible condition, with thousands dying in the days that followed. For the medical staff and army personnel there was often little they could do to save them. Rev. Levy wrote home to his wife Tonie in Britain:

I have just returned from my first visit to the death camp of Belsen ... I went to find Jews. And God, did I find them. And how I found them and what specimens of humanity they are after the treatment they have received. I am certain that 90 per cent of those who survived will never really be normal. They have suffered too much.[4]

Nazi war criminal Rudolf Höss, the infamous Commandant of Auschwitz, had visited Belsen concentration camp just before the end of the war. Later, after his arrest by the British, he described conditions as he had found them in Belsen on that visit. In his sworn statement, a copy of which survives in the Imperial War Museum, he wrote:

The Belsen camp, especially, was in a chaotic state. Thousands of dead bodies were lying around un-incinerated in the vicinity of the provisional crematorium. Sewage could not be disposed of. Orders were given to start immediately with the erection of temporary latrines. Obergruppenführer Pohl gave the order to Kramer that big squads of men had to collect all edible herbs in the nearby woods in order to contribute to the diet. Another increase of food could not be affected as the Regional Food Office refused to make greater contributions of food to the Belsen camp. I personally gave Kramer the advice to cut wood in the nearby forest (NB to expedite incinerations). Some time later when I visited the camp I found certain improvements concerning accommodation and drainage but the arch-evil, the lack of food, could not be met. Shortly afterwards, arriving transports from KZ [concentration camp] Mittelbau made everything illusory.[5]

Arnold Horwell (b. Berlin), who had been in 93 Company Pioneer Corps, carried out relief work in Belsen after its liberation. Correspondence to his wife back in England and other notes of his difficult work there survive in the archives of the Imperial War Museum. Horwell also acted as interpreter at the surrender of the Wehrmacht (the German army) in northern Germany. Amongst Horwell's papers there is a typed report on the conditions in Belsen, which states that at its liberation there were an estimated 50,000 people in the camp, about 10,000 lying dead in the huts or around the camp. Those still alive had had no food or water for about 7 days, after a long period of semi-starvation. Typhus was raging, filth everywhere, the daily death rate high: 'The tasks which faced the first comers must have appeared insurmountable. Nevertheless they were tackled with amazing success when one considers the resources available.'[6] A short time later the adult population of Belsen was made to file through the camp to see for themselves the crimes that had been perpetrated there. The Allies wanted to ensure that no German could claim that he or she knew nothing of what had gone on there. The local population saw for themselves the extent of the mass extermination programme and the state of the survivors. This was the first important step towards the re-education of German people by the Allied forces.

At the end of the war ex-Berliner Sir Ken Adam (Klaus Adam), the only German-refugee fighter pilot in the RAF, was assigned to a POW camp in Germany in charge of Luftwaffe pilots. He visited Belsen. The horror left its indelible mark. He insisted that the Luftwaffe pilots under his control pass through Belsen to see the horror. 'It shook them to the core,' says Sir Ken. 'One of them tried to commit suicide two days later.' In the coming days, many of the ex-refugees serving in the British army entered Belsen with their respective regiments. Nothing prepared them for the utter horror of what they saw there – images which continue to haunt them over six decades later. Rolf Holden (Rolf Hirtz), a survivor of Buchenwald prior to coming to England, was amongst the first liberators into Belsen:

> I was amongst the first British troops to enter Belsen, and from that moment, I was aware of exactly what had been going on in Germany since my departure. I had seen some horrible things in Buchenwald, but what I saw there … I'll never forget the first night of the liberation of Belsen. Six of us sharing a tent and we all had different religions. We talked about our beliefs all night. After what we had seen that day, we all asked the same question: how could God tolerate such things. We came to the same conclusion: that there can't be such a thing as God. From that moment, I was disillusioned with religion. Belsen profoundly affected every soldier who was there. We all had one priority – to try to alleviate the suffering of those who were still alive. For most of them, there was no hope. We caught many of the SS who ran the camp. Some of them dressed themselves as inmates but they were too well-nourished. It became an important matter to us to bring these people to justice.[7]

In his autobiography, *Whence We Came, Where We Went*, Walter Eberstadt graphically described the conditions as he witnessed them in the camp. A short extract is reproduced:

When we got to the mass graves, the SS had just arrived there with their huge death carts and trailers. They were carrying the dead to their graves on the double, forward and backward, body after body all the same dead faces, the sunken-in eyes, the shaved heads, the bony fleshless bodies. The most dreadful of all was that there was desperately little difference between the looks of the dead and the living. It was absolutely true to say that the living were just living dead. The slightest shock would take the last spark of life from them ... I talked to the SS men. They knew they were going to die. We had shot two of them already while they were trying to escape. One committed suicide and one was buried alive when he collapsed into one of the mass graves. At the end of their day's work the SS men were drilled on the double until they literally collapsed. From what they said I realized what brutes and animals they were, that they still did not realize the enormity of their crimes, that they were completely accustomed to what they saw around them.[8]

Garry Rogers (Gunter Baumgart), who served in the Pioneer Corps and the Royal Armoured Corps, was amongst those who entered Belsen. In his memoirs he writes:

We were advancing towards a town, Soltau, via the small German town of Bergen. We had come across mass graves before and we were not immune to the horrors of the Third Reich. The concentration camp of Bergen-Belsen opened our eyes to the real horror and atrocities Hitler and his henchmen had perpetrated. Much has been written about the horrors of the death camps and the Holocaust. At the time nothing was known to us while fighting was still in progress, although we had come across mass graves and other indications. Nothing could have prepared us for what we were about to see. Most of the guards had fled and all we found were the inmates in a condition which defies description. These are memories I have blocked out all my life. My own feelings at the time were that of shock rather than drawing any conclusions. Hate for the perpetrators, pity for the survivors, horror for the inhumanity of men, disbelief for the enormity of the crime, love for those I lost in the Holocaust. We tried to feed and comfort the inmates, but then had to pass them on to the medical staff and proceed with the war. Did it change me? Of course it did, and will always be a part of me.[9]

Herbert Landsberg, who entered Belsen with his Pioneer Corps company just days after its liberation, came unexpectedly face-to-face with the past:

We arrived at Belsen and could not believe our eyes when we saw the survivors in the camp. They were walking skeletons, having been systematically starved by the SS guarding them. We had orders to find the Medical Officer Dr Fritz Klein who had performed operations in the camp on Jewish inmates without anesthetic to find out how much pain a human body could withstand. By the time we arrived, he was hiding but we eventually found him. When I saw him, his face looked familiar. It suddenly came to me where we had met before. It was in 1931 when I was reading Law at Leipzig University. He was the Medical Officer there and I had to see him when I was suffering from an inflammation of the kidneys. He had looked at my papers then and shouted, 'Go away, you bloody Jew boy! All you suffer from is a disease typical of your race.' Here in Belsen, he stood before us, wanted for war crimes of unbelievable seriousness. At his trial in Nuremberg he was sentenced to death although he claimed what he did was in the interest of science.[10]

Landsberg was then posted to the Psychological Warfare Branch of Montgomery's 21st Army as a staff-sergeant, attached to the Guard's Armoured Division in a special mobile unit, travelling in an armoured scout-car equipped with sensitive listening equipment, guns and eight loudspeakers. His work involved the interrogation of German military personnel, including a German general on the Lüneburg Heath in the summer of 1945, when the German army of the west surrendered to General Montgomery's 21st Army Group. Willy Field, tank driver in the 8th King's Royal Irish Hussars, was not permitted by his commanding officer to enter Belsen, as he explains: 'My commanding officer knew of my German-Jewish origin and wanted to protect me from the trauma of seeing the horror of the camp. My comrades went in, but I didn't. I still did not know at this point the whereabouts of my own family. I began to fear that they might have suffered the same fate or that they were even in Belsen.'[11] At the end of the war Rudi Oppenheimer, a one-time member of the Pioneer Corps and RASC, was a sergeant in the Intelligence Corps. He learnt of the survival of his brother's three children, Eve, Paul and Rudi in Belsen, but their parents had perished in the camp only months before its liberation. Rudi Oppenheimer was granted permission to travel to Holland to collect Eve. Paul and Rudi returned to Britain later.[12]

As Allied forces entered Germany, attempts were made by the SS to cover up the evidence of the camps. In the last days of the war the SS were determined that prisoners in the concentration camps should not fall into the hands of the British and Canadian armies. They began moving prisoners, but the inmates were barely in a fit state to be taken anywhere. They were transported by cattle truck or taken on death marches to Sandbostel and Lübeck, where they systematically starved to death. Dr Hans Engel (originally from Hamburg) joined the Royal Army Medical Corps. On D-Day he was based on a British ship off the coast of Arromanches dealing with casualties from the Normandy landings.[13] In mid-April 1945 his unit already knew about conditions at a concentration camp in Sandbostel where an outbreak of typhus had occurred. On 27 April Dr Engel drove with the director of medical services through the Lüneburg Heath to relieve the camp. His eye-witness recollections are an important testimony:

> I entered the camp on 29 April with 3 medical captains and 100 medical orderlies. The horror we encountered simply cannot be described. I have seen a great deal of misery in the field through France and Belgium, cared for seriously injured and sick soldiers and experienced the terrible hunger which the Dutch population suffered through the winter, but this camp was so horrible that one can hardly describe it. On the first day there lay some 3,000 dead prisoners in the open, unnamed and unburied. Some 4,000 men from all countries of Europe had been transported there from Hamburg's Neuengamme concentration camp, the survivors of death marches, mostly non-Jews, and those the SS had already murdered. In the barracks lay the men, like skin and bones, suffering from hunger, thirst and infectious disease, many close to death, some on a wooden 'bed' next to a dead man whom he did not have the strength to throw out. They all lay in their excrement and vomit, and the dirt and stench were indescribable. It was an Augean stable, which I have never been able to forget. With Jewish poet Heinrich Heine, banished to France, '*When I think of Germany in the night, all thought of sleep has taken flight*'. Even today when I think of it, I lie awake and may weep quietly.

> The medical authorities of the British army had had fourteen days' experience of Belsen, so that we could start the relief immediately. The insect killer DDT had only recently become available and we covered all personnel and patients with the powder from head to foot three times a day and thus soon got rid of the typhus lice. All military personnel had been inoculated against typhus and typhoid every year, and we began to inoculate the patients and conscripted helpers. The next urgent measure was to give the sick intravenous infusions of glucose-saline and plasma in big quantities. Many had collapsed veins, which gave us trouble in inserting the needle. Fortunately

anaesthetic teams became available, with the cessation of fighting and injuries, who were expert at inserting these. As soon as the patients' diarrhoea and vomiting had ceased we could give warm sweet milk drinks, the only suitable food for these starved men. The British POWs were immediately repatriated, and their Red Cross food parcels could be diverted to the camp. I appointed two orderlies who produced milk drinks all day in a huge cauldron from dried milk, chocolate, Horlicks and Ovaltine. I am convinced that the infusions and milk drinks saved many men in their last hours. We also organised water tankers until a clean water supply could be restored. Next we brought in field kitchens and military cooks, and then a field laundry into the camp, and thousands of boots and blankets, which had to serve as clothing for the time being. All the clothes of the prisoners were destroyed.

We sent lorries to the big hospitals in Hamburg and Bremen to collect nurses. When these arrived, very cross, the matron said to me: 'We are not going to risk our health for these sub-humans.' Thereupon I gave them the 'curtain lecture' of my life; that my British soldiers were working day and night to save lives, which to us seemed more valuable than theirs, and that I expected them to work just as devotedly. This indeed they did after that. After three weeks in this purgatory, the matron came and said: 'Herr Hauptmann, I want to tell you that I have never been so ashamed to be a German as the day you gave us your talk.' The medical treatment was in the first days carried out with French and Russian POW doctors, who came voluntarily from the liberated Stalag XB with our Field Dressing Station. The army medical doctor brought another Field Dressing Station from 30 Corps on 2 May with doctors and medical orderlies to the camp, and on 6 May a CCS [Casualty Clearing Station] with 600 beds which was immediately overfilled. It was not till about 20 May that we could say we had done what we could and only a few prisoners were still dying, mostly from tuberculosis. You can scarcely imagine the rage the British troops had against the SS men. As Capt. Barer wrote: 'These monsters should be annihilated.'[14]

The difficult work carried out by soldiers and medics like Dr Engel in Sandbostel and Belsen left a lifetime's imprint of pain and trauma in both their conscious and subconscious. It is still hotly debated how much the German people did or did not know about the death camps and murder of 11 million people in the gas chambers, over half of whom were Jews. As Dr Engel concludes:

I can believe that the German population did not know or did not want to know exactly what was happening in these concentration camps on the hunger marches. But everybody knew that people were arrested daily and never seen again. That was common knowledge in 1935 when I still lived in Hamburg. What one can never forget or forgive are the SS murderers who systematically starved and dehumanised these men and women.

Amongst the utter devastation and knowledge that two-thirds of Central European Jewry had been murdered in Hitler's Final Solution, the German-speaking refugees in the British army feared for the survival of their own families. Many had received no news of them since the war. The painful and uncertain search for surviving relatives began. All too often confirmation came that they had perished in the Holocaust. George Rosney (Georg Jakob Rosenfeld, b. Karlsruhe) served in the Pioneer Corps, then REME and seconded to the Royal Horse Artillery. At the end of the war he travelled over 2,000 miles from Kiel on the Baltic coast to Theresienstadt in the Czech Republic in search of his parents. On 21 May 1945 he arrived at Theresienstadt where he was accommodated by the Russian commandant. In the camp he met Albert Steiner, his father's business partner, who had survived the war. Steiner broke the news to him that his parents had been sent east to Auschwitz. That terrible moment of truth was so unexpected and traumatic that it affected George Rosney for the rest of his life.

Willy Field, mentioned earlier, was stationed at the end of the war first in Berlin and then Lingen with the 8th King's Royal Irish Hussars.[15] He set about trying to uncover the fate of his family. From Lingen he was given a week's compassionate leave by his commanding officer to return to Bonn to look for his parents. Bonn was a city which had once had a Jewish community of nearly 1,000 people. Between 1933 and 1939 around 600–700 of them had managed to flee Germany and settle in England, Palestine or America, but the remaining 300 had perished in the Holocaust. Willy now feared the worst for his own family. He comments: 'When I first entered Bonn, it was a strange feeling but a very emotional one. I had said goodbye to my family from Bonn station back in April 1939. I had not returned since. Walking down the all too familiar streets brought back floods of childhood memories, both good and bad.' Willy spent seven days wandering around Bonn, desperately trying to find out something about his family. He visited all the places he and his extended family had ever lived. 'I could find out nothing,' he comments. 'Place after place yielded no information.' He discovered that in July 1945 only eight of Bonn's Jews returned from the concentration camps. All the others perished in the Holocaust. It was only years later that Willy and his twin sister Thea finally discovered exactly what had happened to their family. Through the Red Cross they learned that their father had died in Cologne awaiting transportation to a concentration camp. On 10 July 1942, their mother Regina, along with their brother Manfred, Aunt Henriette Moses and Uncle Markus Moses, were all taken to Minsk where they were murdered in a concentration camp.

For the lucky few who were reunited with family after the war there was a sense of unprecedented relief. Colin Anson (Claus Ascher), who had served in the commandos, asked to be posted back to Frankfurt so that he might find his mother.[16] Harry Rossney (Helmuth Rosettenstein) was amongst the fortunate ones who eventually found his mother: 'It took the Red Cross several years to locate my mother, who had left Berlin in March 1939 and returned to my home-town Königsberg. It was twelve years before we met again in London because at the end of the war she was trapped in the east under Russian occupation. It was then that I learned that three of my cousins had been killed in Stalingrad.'[17] Whilst Michael Sherwood (Isi Schwarzbard) was serving in Germany with 908 Military Government, he received a telephone call from a British soldier in Münster to say that his mother was still alive. Sherwood recalls:

> The soldier was stopped in the street one day by my mother and asked whether he could trace her son (me). The soldier was successful because he found my army address and was able to tell me the good news. I was given leave to go to Münster where I was reunited with my mother. She had survived a concentration camp but I was never able to glean which one. She never spoke about it, and it wasn't something I could ask her. It was only 60 years later when I wrote to authorities in Leipzig to try to find out, that I was told her name was on an original list of Jews, and against her name was written 'vanished'. But of course, I knew that she had survived.[18]

Gerry Moore (Gerhard Moses, b. Berlin), who saw front-line fighting with the Royal Armoured Corps, was notified through his guardian in London that his parents had survived the war in hiding in France thanks to a Catholic priest in Lyons. Now in the Intelligence Corps, he was granted leave to go and find them and was reunited with them.

Gideon Behrendt describes the emotion when, coming off duty one night whilst stationed in Germany with British forces, he had a surprise letter waiting for him:

> I opened the envelope but before I could read many words my eyes filled with tears. I could not believe my eyes, this was the handwriting of my brother Heinz, and I recognised it immediately. Unmistakably. Those lovely lines. My beloved brother Heinz was alive! The letter had been written in Bergen-Belsen, on the 15th June, 1945! I wasn't able to continue reading; the tears were streaming down my face. I don't remember much after that. I was out of my mind; one word only seemed to whirl though my head: Heinz is alive, alive … alive … alive! My feet carried me automatically while I still held the letter in my hand and the tears still flowed.[19]

By some miracle, Heinz Behrendt had survived the mass deportation to Minsk and stayed alive with only a handful of others from among the 85,000 Jews that had been crammed into the Minsk Ghetto. From the ghetto he was transferred from one concentration camp to another, finally ending up in Belsen, from where he was liberated in April 1945. But the joy at Heinz's survival was soon overshadowed by news of just how many members of the Behrendt family and school friends had perished in the Holocaust. Uncle Max from Berlin was deported to Auschwitz with his wife; so had Aunt Jenny with her husband Uncle Samuel, their daughter Lieschen and her baby boy and husband. None of them survived. Uncle Louis had been killed and Uncle Oskar had vanished, neither to be seen nor heard of again. Aunt Hertha committed suicide before being arrested by the Gestapo. Gideon Behrendt's father's last spouse in Germany, Tante Ottilie, was sent to Auschwitz, together with her 4-year-old son Michael, Behrendt's half-brother. Cousin Max Behrendt, the shoemaker, boxer and hero of the First World War, had also been killed in one of the concentration camps, whilst Hans Behrendt, the son of Uncle Louis, was gunned down in the streets of Berlin. The rest of the cousins in Berlin had escaped the fate of the other victims by living in hiding, or by pretending to be Aryans and working as labourers on remote farms. Aunts Rosa and Hedwig were sent to Theresienstadt but returned to Berlin at the end of the war. Multiple stories like these about the decimation of whole families were common for the refugees who fought for Britain.

One vital task which faced the Allies was the demilitarisation of the German forces, which went hand-in-hand with the denazification process.

It was a full-time job and one that would keep the Allied troops busy for weeks on end. German forces had disintegrated everywhere, apart from the last-ditch attempts by die-hard Nazis to defend Germany. The Allies had to bring order to Germany and deal with the disbanding of German troops. Part of that work included checking the soldiers for Nazi activities. If they had an SS tattoo, they came within the category for immediate arrest and interrogations as possible war criminals. In this respect, Ken Lincoln (Karl Ernst Levy, b. Grabow) was stationed with Field Security Disbandment Control and was involved in the interrogation of Germans released from the Wehrmacht.

Towards the final stages of the war, Commando Colin Anson was near Ravenna in northern Italy where masses of German forces were in disarray, their military vehicles out of diesel being towed by the only ones that had fuel left in their tanks:

> We fenced off fields on the Ravenna plain in this very flat part of Italy. The surrendering German POWs sat in row after row as far as the eye could see. I started by taking down names, took their money and gave them a receipt for it. They had Italian occupation money which was not worth anything anymore. I soon stopped making a list because it was impossible to cope with the sheer numbers. There was nowhere for them to escape anyway. I was amongst them all day and night; the first three days with virtually no sleep. We tried to lay on some rations for them; brought in water tankers so at least they could fill their water bottles. It was towards morning of one day that I got back to the bungalow where I was billeted. I stripped off, dashed straight across the beach and into the water. It was so refreshing. As I came back and opened the door, I recoiled because it was full of a pungent smell of Germans. I had been amongst the German soldiers so long that my clothes had begun to smell like them. It was a distinctive, rather acrid aroma made up of the smell of leather equipment, uniform material, sweat, *Jagdwurst* and other food from their diet. It was an unmistakable smell. In fact during the war, this distinctive smell saved lives because as soon as you got a whiff of it, you knew to take cover because there were Germans in the area.[20]

One of the men in Anson's troop who had been in a concentration camp before the war recognised a guard from that camp amongst the surrendering troops. 'He went ballistic,' says Anson. They checked the guard and found that he had the standard SS blood group tattoo, so he was handed to the military authorities for interrogation. He was on the run and had tried to hide amongst the mass of Waffen SS, ordinary soldiers of the German army. In those first few days, long hours in the heat meant that Anson soon became extremely tired and had no time to shave. It was whilst in this slightly dishevelled state that a significant incident occurred:

> Whilst I was rushing about, dealing with the POWs, trying to cope with the situation with my comrades, there appeared a small column of Kübelwagen, the open-top field command cars. It pulled into our field and stopped. In the front car there sat a German General, stony faced, looking over the heads of everybody. He didn't move a muscle. I was too busy to attend to him. He began to go a bright red colour, rising from his collar. It was the same colour as his red collar with the golden wheat sheaves symbol on. It rose into his cheeks and suddenly he shouted, in that peculiar crowing tone sometimes adopted by high-ranking officers: '*Ja, was ist denn hier los? Ist denn hier kein Lagerkommandant? Ich bin ein GenerAAAL!*' (which translates as 'What's the matter here? Is there no camp commandant? I'm a General'). And on the word 'General' he almost hit the top-C.[21]

Anson, in Denison smock (a parachute smock without badges of rank), green beret and a day's unshaven stubble, and in no mood for any nonsense, approached the German general. He said to the general, in a similar tone of command that the general may not have been addressed in since he was a cadet at Spandau: '*Abwarten! Ihre Leute kommen zuerst dran!*' ('Wait for it! Your men come first'.) It produced a reaction, as Anson explains:

> I have never seen a jaw drop quite so far so quickly as that general that day. He was horrified and indignant. I pointed out the camp commandant's tent a couple of fields away and asked them to report to him. Upon which one of them turned round to the front row of soldiers sitting in the grassy field and said: '*Feldwebel! Drei Mann zum Gepäcktragen!*' ('Sergeant, three men to carry luggage'). I quickly replied, '*Feldwebel, bleiben Sie sitzen.*' ('Sergeant, stay seated'). I then turned to the officers and said, 'Gentlemen, you will take such luggage as you can carry yourselves.' They looked deflated, took off their smart uniform jackets, and underneath they were wearing khaki shirts and breeches. They were no longer quite as impressive. They had to carry their own luggage. As I watched them, I felt slightly ashamed at being so rude to them, but on the other hand I really felt it was quite inappropriate

under the circumstances for a German general to start ordering me about. I was now in charge.[22]

Anson recalls another memorable incident at this time in which the German POWs feared their treatment by British soldiers:

I borrowed a motorcycle because I had to visit colleagues located further north who were looking after a surrendered Waffen SS unit. The transport NCO satisfied himself that I could manage the machine, though I had never ridden a motorbike before and I enjoyed the ride along the straight, empty road on a beautiful, sunny afternoon. I came across a group of worried-looking young German women who were the companions of the SS men. I overheard one of them saying to another: 'Oh, look – they are going to hang us!' pointing at some British soldiers erecting tall poles. I reassured them that we were not SS, that we did not hang people, but that the poles were for a chain link fence. Maybe I should have let them stew for a bit longer; but perhaps it may have helped them to understand the difference between the mentality of SS Nazis and normal, civilised people.[23]

In his memoirs, *The Long Road Home*, Gideon Behrendt wrote about his part in demilitarising the German forces. He recalls:

We didn't have to fight the enemies anymore but now had to disarm them, sort them out and separate them according to the following categories: Wehrmacht: soldiers and other ranks; Wehrmacht: officers and senior officers; SS-Personnel: other ranks; and finally SS-Officers and senior officers. It felt like cleaning up a shop or business after closing hours, after the customers had gone but the staff had to work on. Each of the above groups had to be registered and be sent to the appropriate POW camp. The initial groups were the first to be Denazified and released to become civilians once more. As each of the men stood before me for questioning and I filled the required forms as per instructions, the same question persistently haunted my thought: 'Did this man without a face actually kill any of my people?' The more I heard and learned about the Final Solution for the Jews, the extermination camps, the gas chambers and the Nazi obsession for killing, Jews in particular, the more my soul was torn and tormented. And yet, here I was looking at the same men who had until recently been very proud members of the 'Master-race', with raised arms in Nazi-salute, shouting 'Sieg – Heil – Sieg – Heil – Sieg –

Heil' at the top of their voices. Now they stood before me silent, their heads bowed – defeated. My heart ached and if possible I might have cried out in pain, but I was duty-bound to treat them 'fairly', as 'gentlemen soldiers', as a losing team after a football match, not as creatures that had destroyed cities and subjugated whole nations; not as murderers of innocent men, women and children.[24]

All services of the German forces had to be demilitarised, including the air force. Sidney Goldberg (b. Leipzig), who had been in the Royal Navy aboard HMS *Hilary* for the seaborne invasion of Normandy, was assigned at the end of the war to air disarmament duties, controlling large units of the German Air Force. He comments:

> We were in charge of German Luftwaffe POWs. They were kept in their own camps under their own officers minus their rank and insignia. We controlled them and intercepted their telephone wires and listened to their conversations. We discovered from the conversations that they were communicating with other Luftwaffe bases. Our task was also to de-militarise the German Armed Forces. We confiscated their equipment and ammunition. They were then formed into labour groups (*Dienstgruppen*) to carry out work for the British forces. The war was over. We didn't know what the future held for us, but we knew now that we were set for better things.[25]

The refugees serving in various regiments of the British forces were at least a year or more off demobilisation. They moved with their regiments through Germany for vital work in the reconstruction of post-war Europe. They witnessed the total defeat of their country of birth. How did it feel to be back on German soil? Geoffrey Perry reflects: 'I was very conscious of the British army uniform that I was wearing. Crossing back into Germany gave me a feeling like goose-bumps.' Walter Hirsch, who was born near Frankfurt, came to England on the Kindertransport and served in the Durham Light Infantry, and carried out interpretative duties in Göttingen and then Berlin. He comments: 'We walked for miles one day in Berlin and didn't see a single building standing.' So too Willy Field, who entered Berlin with the 8th King's Royal Irish Hussars and took part in the Victory Parade before Allied leaders. 'The destruction was absolute,' he says. What about feelings towards their former German countrymen? Willy Field is frank about that:

What annoyed me most about going back into Germany, especially in Hamburg and Berlin, was the attitude of the German people. When I spoke to them, they moaned and complained about their suffering and what they had lost from the Allied bombing. I could not be sympathetic. I told them, 'you brought this on yourselves. You were quick to say Heil Hitler in 1933.' They got what they deserved. I always made that quite clear to them. I was not sorry to see the destruction; however that does not mean that I would ever exact revenge. My motto is that you should forgive but never forget.[26]

Stephen Dale (Heinz Günther Spanglet, b. Berlin), a survivor of Sachsenhausen concentration camp, had served with the SOE and been taken POW in the war. He survived a number of POW camps. This is his reaction when returning to Germany with the British forces for post-war work:

I walked through Berlin and Hamburg, the places I knew best. There was a tremendous amount of destruction and disorganisation. I was pretty well unaffected, with no sentimental attachment. I was happy to leave Germany in 1939 but did not wish all the bombing and misfortunes on the German people. But it was inevitable. It was acceptable in the pursuit of the end of the war. I walked through the ruins of Berlin, with its heaps of rubble, the women were clearing up – this I didn't enjoy seeing, but accepted it as necessary. I harboured no feelings of vindictive pleasure.[27]

Mark Lynton (Max-Otto Ludwig Loewenstein, b. Stuttgart) wrote about the devastation of Berlin which he witnessed with British forces at the end of the war:

Nothing that I had seen in Hamburg prepared me for my first sight of Berlin. The city had not merely been bombed, it had been shelled and fought over, and it had literally ceased to exist. There was an occasional ruined, burnt-out shell sticking out from under mountains of rubble, and two huge concrete anti-aircraft bunkers still stood in the centre of town, which could have withstood an atomic blast. For the rest, there was nothing, no houses, no trees, no streets and – at first sight – no people – the abomination of desolation. The place was of course teeming with Russians and their equipment, everything from tanks to horse-drawn carts, and no one took the slightest notice of us. I spent the first few hours touring around that quite unimaginable heap of ruins, littered with broken vehicles, empty shells, burnt-out tanks, and all the aftermath of battle, all of which had been a city I had known intimately twelve years earlier.[28]

Peter Perry, who was born in Berlin, was appointed liaison officer and accompanied a British parliamentary delegation around the ruins of Hitler's chancellery and bunker. Amongst that group was Leslie Hore-Belisha, a former British secretary of state for war. Perry recalled:

This was my first opportunity to inspect the centre of the *Tausendjahrige Reich*, Hitler's 1,000-year German Empire, on whose ruins we were now standing twelve years after its foundation. The inner courtyard was still partly blocked by burnt-out armoured vehicles. We entered a seemingly endless, high-ceilinged corridor to the right of which monumental doors led to a succession of offices. Every conceivable space seemed to be decorated with the Nazi party emblem. The dimensions were vast, the shapes severely rectangular. Everything was clearly designed to convey a sense of Hitler's overwhelming power. His aim was to delight his supporters and to create a sense of fear in his opponents ... The floors were strewn with documents of every description. I found papers bearing Himmler's signature confirming the promotion of officers, as well as piles of Hitler's personal note paper and official telegram forms and batches of his Ex Libris labels.

We then found ourselves in the labyrinth of linked subterranean bunkers which had formed the command headquarters from which Hitler had tried to direct the final battle, and where his macabre wedding to Eva Braun had taken place prior to their and Goebbels' family's suicide. As a fitting end to our tour of inspection, we made our way through a tunnel back into the open. We found ourselves in a courtyard which contained a large open hole surrounded by some empty German army jerry (petrol) cans. Our Soviet liaison officer informed us that this was the grave in which the Russians had found the burned corpses of Hitler and Eva Braun.[29]

Colin Anson's emotional reaction on his return to Frankfurt shows how in the intervening years a 'brotherhood' had emerged from his training and combat in the commandos:

To walk these particular streets with the ghost of a German schoolboy walking ahead, with whom I had absolutely nothing in common anymore, was an almost schizophrenic psychological stress. To feel that I had to get back to my own people at The Mess, where I could relax again, showed me how I had changed. I hadn't really expected to survive the war in the Commandos, but there was a job that had to be done. I wanted to repay the debt to Britain for saving my life.

Anson visited the police headquarters in Frankfurt to look up his father's records. He discovered precisely who had betrayed his father to his death in Dachau. Anson stood at the crossroads of a moral decision:

I saw who had betrayed my father. It was a certain lock keeper called Herr Henkel who lived at Niederrad along the river Main, to the west of Sachsenhausen where I had originally worked at the Asbestos Works before my emigration. What should I do with this information? The knowledge produced a rather difficult psychological situation for me. I had a lot of discretion and authority at that time as a British Staff Sergeant and could pretty well do what I wanted. I could roll up outside his house in a staff car in uniform or I could go about on a bicycle in civilian clothes. I could also walk about with weapons. I *was* undoubtedly tempted to pay Herr Henkel a visit, invite him for a walk in the forest south of Frankfurt, from which only I would have come back. But I never took advantage of my situation. It was not my place to take his life. Why? Because my Protestant religious upbringing reminded me that 'Revenge is mine,' says the Lord. 'I will repay.'[30] I hated the Nazis, but I could not exact revenge on Herr Henkel for the death of my father. It was not my place to take another life in revenge.[31]

The vast majority of the enemy aliens in British army uniform were transferred from their existing units, including those still in the Pioneer Corps, to the Intelligence Corps or Interpreters' Pool. Their fluency in German was the reason for their transfer and became essential to the Allied Military Government. They were assigned to all aspects of military administration, the interrogation of POWs, Field Security, the gathering of evidence for the War Crimes Investigation Unit and the hunt for Nazi war criminals. Much of their invaluable work has remained unrecorded until now, often because they preferred not to speak about the war years. The next fifty years was to witness a wall of silence from survivors and those refugees who had fled Nazism prior to 1939. They were too traumatised to speak of their experiences and their loss, and that included their time spent in the British forces.

The silence extended to the part they played in the denazification process. It is only in the last ten years, at the turn of the twenty-first century, that they have felt able to articulate their stories and record their testimonies. With the passing of that generation many stories have been lost and not recorded either in official war diaries or papers at The National Archives, Kew. Prime resources for this book remain oral testimony through interviews with the survivors, the Sound Archive and unpublished archives at the Imperial War Museum, as well as published memoirs. The stories which unfold in the coming pages provide a snap-shot of what these refugees did for the reconstruction and stability of post-war Europe.

Notes

1. See Daniel Snowman, *Hitler's Emigrés* and Helen Fry, *Jews in North Devon during the Second World War.*
2. Interview with the author.
3. In discussions with the author. See also his autobiography, *When Life Becomes History.*
4. Isaac Levy's two books, *Witness to Evil* and *Time to Tell.* See also Viktor Frankl, *Man's Search for Meaning.*
5. IWM, ref: 05/14/1.
6. Papers of Arnold Horwell, IWM, ref: 91/21/1.
7. Rolf Holden, *One of the Lucky Ones*, p. 49.
8. Walter Eberstadt, *Whence We Came, Where We Went*, p. 323.
9. Garry Rogers, *Interesting Times*, pp. 152–3.
10. Letter to the author, 5 September 2006. Dr Fritz Klein was hanged on 13 December 1945 in Hameln Prison.
11. Interview with the author. See also Helen Fry, *From Dachau to D-Day.*
12. See Paul Oppenheimer, *From Belsen to Buckingham Palace*, Witness Collection, Beth Shalom Ltd, 1996.
13. Profile based on interviews with the author.
14. Correspondence with the author.
15. His story is told in full in *From Dachau to D-Day.*
16. The story of their reunion is told in Helen Fry, *German Schoolboy, British Commando.*
17. Interviews with the author. See also Harry Rossney, *Grey Dawns.*
18. Interview with the author.
19. Gideon Behrendt, *The Long Road Home*, p. 91.
20. Fry, *German Schoolboy, British Commando*, pp. 138–9.
21. Ibid., p. 139.
22. Ibid., p. 140.

23. Based on extensive interviews with the author. See also Fry, *German Schoolboy, British Commando*.

24. Behrendt, *The Long Road Home*, op. cit., p. 82.

25. Sidney Goldberg was demobilised in August 1946. Profile based on interview with the author.

26. Interview with the author. See also Fry, *From Dachau to D-Day*.

27. Stephen Dale, *Spanglet or By Any Other Name*, privately published memoirs, 1993, copy in the IWM.

28. Mark Lynton, *Accidental Journey*, p. 188.

29. Peter Perry, *An Extraordinary Commission*, pp. 128–9.

30. This is taken from St Paul's letter to the Romans 12:19, which is quoting Deuteronomy 32:35.

31. Fry, *German Schoolboy, British Commando*, pp. 153–4.

TWO

HUNT FOR NAZI WAR CRIMINALS

In April and May 1945, as Allied forces swept across Germany, the most wanted Nazi war criminals went into hiding, assuming false identities and disguises. A priority for the Allies was to capture them alive and bring them to trial. Adolf Hitler was said to have committed suicide with his new wife Eva Braun in his bunker on 30 April, escaping any accountability for his evil and murderous regime. His propaganda minister, Joseph Goebbels, and his wife committed suicide the following day. Now the highest echelons of Nazi government were on the run – fleeing from justice. Concentration camp guards and perpetrators of crimes against humanity were also in hiding, though some successfully fled the country in the coming months via the 'Odessa' escape network to South America and beyond.[1] Capturing and bringing them to justice was to prove one of the greatest challenges for the Allied forces. It was widely expected that the success of the denazification process hinged on bringing named war criminals to justice. The majority of high-ranking Nazis that were captured by the British were in fact arrested by the German-speaking refugees serving under anglicised names in the British army. Their fluency in German meant they were ideal for this undercover tracking work. It could take up to a year or more to investigate and track down the last known movements of a war criminal and find their secret hiding location. Himmler was eventually arrested and brought to Fallingbostel camp. He committed suicide by taking a cyanide pill whilst in British custody. Albert Speer, Dönitz and Jodl were arrested in the enclave of Flensburg, the final seat of the Nazi government. They all stood trial at Nuremberg for war crimes alongside Göring, Höss, von Ribbentrop, Keitel, Kaltenbrunner, Rosenberg, Frank, Streicher, Raeder, von Schirach, von Papen, Sauckel, Seyss-Inquart and von Neurath.

At the end of the war, one of the most sought-after war criminals who had gone into hiding was Rudolf Höss, the notorious Commandant of Auschwitz. He was responsible for the murder there of at least 3 million people, mainly Jews. He also sanctioned the most horrendous crimes in the camp. Höss had fled and was believed to be living under the assumed name Fritz Lang in a remote farmhouse near Flensburg, 100 miles north of Hamburg on the Danish border. A British team, consisting mainly of German speakers, was sent out to capture him. Initially having little success, they were assigned to track down Höss' wife, which they managed to do, and carried out surveillance of the area. One member of that team was ex-Berliner Gerry Moore (Gerhard Moses, b. 1923), who had transferred from the Royal Armoured Corps to the Intelligence Corps, his new role being the pursuit of Nazi war criminals in Germany. Before leaving for this new task, he was sent for three months' training in denazification to a castle in Britain, the name of which he does not now remember. 'It was at this castle,' he comments, 'that we received training on how to proceed with the hunt for war criminals and how to get information from POWs.' Moore was sent to Field Security HQ in Kiel on the Baltic coast to interrogate suspected Nazi war criminals. 'I was successful,' he says, 'at being able to find out whether or not they were lying during the interrogations.' It was during this time that Moore was assigned to the team that finally arrested Höss. It was early March 1946:

Höss was working under a false identity at a farm near Heide in Schleswig-Holstein, northern Germany, east of Kiel. A German man who wanted to save his own neck told us where Höss's wife and children were living. We tried to find out from her where Höss was hiding but she pretended not to know. So we turned up with a lorry at her place one day and told her to say goodbye to her children. We explained that she was being separated from them and she wouldn't see them again because she wouldn't reveal her husband's location. Initially she did not believe us until we ordered the children into the truck. It worked. She decided to tell us where her husband was living. This was enough for us. We were authorised in our roles to wear civilian clothes. We could go anywhere and ask for 10–20 soldiers to accompany us, which we did in the case of Höss. We drove to the specific farmhouse and our soldiers surrounded the place. We found Höss asleep in bed and got him up. He didn't resist. We drove him back to HQ where he stayed with us for one night in custody, but we weren't sufficiently high-ranking to keep him there. That one night he began to write out his testimony and how many had been gassed, etc in the camps. The following day he was transferred to Kiel and then Poland.[2]

German-born Howard Alexander (Hans Alexander), who served in 93 Company Pioneer Corps and returned to Germany as a captain in the British army, recalled their arrest of Höss:

> One night after the 11 o'clock curfew, we went to a farmhouse about five miles from the Danish border where we were reasonably sure he was hiding. We were accompanied by a medical officer in case Höss took a cyanide pill. We took him out of the building and he naturally protested that he was someone else. But we had photographs of him. He had put a lot of effort into changing his identity but he had kept his wedding ring with the date of his marriage inscribed on it. I interrogated him no end of times.[3]

After Höss' arrest he was interrogated by ex-refugee Fred Jackson (Jacobus). Coming into direct contact with such evil men was harrowing. Jackson could only get through the week by drinking large quantities of liquor. 'I was drunk for a week,' Jackson said in an interview. 'I just could not live with myself. He was the man who had killed my mother.'[4] A copy of Höss' sworn statement exists in the archives of the Imperial War Museum, donated by the family of Charles MacKay (Karl Krumbein).[5] Born in Austria, MacKay came to England on the Kindertransport in December 1938. In September 1944 he enlisted in the British forces and served for nearly two years in the Intelligence Corps. It is not known to what extent he was involved with Höss, but it would appear that MacKay may also have been part of the team that captured him. During the only night that the team held Höss, he was encouraged to recount everything he knew about the death camps. The sworn statement, taken in the presence of MacKay and his colleague Karl Abrahams (also an ex-refugee), makes chilling reading. The statement is a detailed account of Höss' involvement in the death camps and reveals the terrible crimes against humanity. In it Höss confesses that in 1935 he became Untersturmführer SS of Dachau concentration camp. Three years later in 1938 he was posted to Sachsenhausen as adjutant to the camp commandant, Uberführer Baranowski. The following year Höss was promoted to the rank of SS Hauptsturmführer and remained in Sachsenhausen until his posting to Auschwitz concentration camp on 1 May 1940. In his sworn statement he explains:

> My higher authority, the Inspectorate of Concentration Camps, instructed me to convert the site of the former Polish Artillery Barracks near Auschwitz into a quarantine camp for prisoners from Poland. After Himmler had inspected the camp in 1941, I was ordered to complete it as a big concentration camp for the east and especially to use the inmates for a greatly extended agriculture in order to make fertile the whole swampy and inundated territory on the Weichsel … The number of prisoners rose from day to day despite my repeated protests that accommodation was inadequate, and I continued to receive further influxes. As sanitary installations were in no way sufficient, epidemic diseases were unavoidable. In the year 1941, the first transport of the Jews from Slovakia and Upper Silesia arrived. Those who were of no use from a work point of view were gassed in the ante-chambers of the crematoria on the orders of Himmler given to me personally.

As early as June 1941 Höss had been ordered to appear before Himmler in Berlin and informed that: 'The Führer has ordered a solution of the Jewish problem in Europe.' Auschwitz was deemed ideal for the annihilation programme because, as Himmler told Höss, it had 'a railway junction of four important lines and also the district was not densely populated. The possibility existed of isolating the camp territory proper. It is for these reasons that I [Himmler] have decided to transfer mass exterminations to Auschwitz.' Höss was ordered to start preparations immediately and given charge, because, as Himmler confided in him, 'the task was so difficult and its implication so far reaching that it was one which he could not entrust to everyone'.[6] Höss wrote in his statement:

> I therefore received clear instructions to carry out the exterminations of all transports sent in by the RSHA [Reich Central Security Dept]. I had to consult SS Obersturmbannführer Eichmann of the RSHA Amt IV (commanded by Gruppenführer Muller) for the order in which the transports were of Russian POWs arriving from the areas of the Gestapo Leitstellen [control rooms], Breslau, Troppau and Katowitz which, on the orders of Himmler and the Gestapo Commandant concerned, had to be exterminated as well.

Later in the statement Höss explained in detail the nature and extent of the physical extermination programme at Auschwitz:

> As the crematoria which had to be built could not be finished before 1942, prisoners had to be gassed in provisionally erected chambers and burnt in earth holes. For this purpose, two old farmhouses situated slightly from the Birkenau area were made more or less airtight and strong wooden doors were installed. The transports of humans were unloaded at a side-line at Birkenau. Those capable of work were picked out and brought to the camp and all luggage was taken away and brought to the camp stores. Those destined for gassing were marched to the installation which was approx 1 kilometre away. Those ill or unable to walk were transported by lorry. In front of the farmhouses they all had to undress behind specially erected screens. On the doors were the inscriptions 'Disinfection Room'. The SS Subalterns on duty had the order to tell these people, with the help of interpreters, that they should take proper care of their belongings so that they might find them again immediately after de-lousing. These measures were intended to avoid any disquiet. The undressed walked into these rooms, two or three hundred at a time according to the size of the accommodation. Then the doors were screwed tight and two canisters of Cyclone B [sic] were thrown in through small holes. Cyclone B [sic] was a granulated substance of Plausaure and the desired effect was achieved, dependent upon the weather, in between three and ten minutes. After half an hour the doors were opened and the bodies extracted by a special squad of prisoners who were permanently employed on this job. The bodies were later burnt in earth-holes.

It was not only the extermination programme that was outlined by Höss. He also confessed to the medical experiments that were undertaken in Auschwitz:

> Of experiments carried out during my time as Commandant, and later in Amtsgrupps, the following have been carried out in Auschwitz: Sterilisation experiments of Professors Klauberg Karl, Chief of the Clinic for Women at Konigsghutte, Upper Silesia took the form of selecting apparently suitable persons in conjunction with the doctor concerned with the women's camp … In combating typhoid epidemics, various ways of exterminating lice were tried. Badly lice-infested but otherwise healthy persons were treated in various ways; amongst others, with Lausetto (a substance produced from the urine of

horses), the effects were noted. The Standartarzt Sturmbannführer Dr Wirths
selected women suffering from cancer in order to combat cancer by operating
at an early stage. He made use of the experience which his brother had gained
in a hospital in Hamburg. Dr Wirths also made experiments with the object
of killing persons by injections of Cyanide – namely persons who had been
designated for death by the Gestapo. The same doctor also made experiments
as to how long the human body could exist in cold water.

Höss confessed that he was personally aware that 3 million people were
murdered in Auschwitz. He estimated that of these, 2.5 million were
gassed. These figures were based on his personal experience but are also
identical to those given by Eichmann in a report to the Reichsführer SS
in April 1945. Most of the victims were Jews, but Höss reports that 70,000
were Russian POWs exterminated on the orders of Gestapo chiefs, con-
travening the Geneva Convention. The highest number of people gassed
in one day in Auschwitz was 10,000, which Höss comments amounted
to 'the utmost capacity of the then existing installations'. He continues: 'I
remember personally great mass transports of 90,000 from Slovakia, 65,000
from Greece, 110,000 from France, 20,000 from Belgium, 90,000 from
Holland, 400,000 from Hungary, 250,000 from Poland and Upper Silesia
and 100,000 from Germany and Theresienstadt.' In March 1945 Höss had
accompanied Obergruppenführer Oswald Pohl and Dr Lolling on an
inspection of a number of concentration camps. He describes his last and
most important inspection:

> We visited the camps Neuengamme, Bergen-Belsen, Buchenwald, Dachau
> and Flossenburg. Dr Lolling and myself left Obergruppenführer Pohl at the
> end of the tour in order to visit Leitmeritz near Aussig on the River Elbe
> where a big working camp was situated. The reason for this tour was an order
> of the Reicheführer SS which Obergruppenführer Pohl had to pass on per-
> sonally to all commandants. The order was, that no Jews must any more be
> killed in any way, and that the mortality amongst prisoners was to be com-
> bated with all the means at our disposal. At the same time Commandants
> received instructions regarding a possible evacuation of their camps.

Höss' knowledge of, and involvement in, Hitler's mass extermination
programme was clear. On 25 May 1946 the British handed him over to
the Polish authorities. He was tried, found guilty and sentenced to death.

On 16 April 1947 he was hanged at the Gestapo camp adjacent to the Auschwitz concentration camp.

★★★

The two veterans Gerry Moore and Howard Alexander, who were part of the team that arrested Rudolf Höss, also carried out interrogation work in Belsen. They arrived just a day or two after the liberation of Belsen to question the remaining guards. Moore recalls:

> The state of Bergen-Belsen was indescribable. I had seen people die in battle during my time with the Royal Armoured Corps, but this was the living dead which shook me to the core. Many of Belsen's survivors were too far gone to be saved and we knew they wouldn't survive. I was involved in the interrogation of the guards who hadn't fled the camp. I also tried to be helpful to the survivors; conversing with them, but the possibilities were limited.[7]

During this period Howard Alexander came face-to-face with another known war criminal, Irma Grese, dubbed the 'beast of Belsen'. She was deemed responsible for the most horrific cruelty, torture and shooting in cold blood of camp inmates whilst she was a guard in Auschwitz and Belsen. British soldiers arrested her on 17 April 1945, just two days after the liberation of Belsen. Howard Alexander was asked to act as interpreter whilst she was interviewed in British custody:

> We were unloading disinfectant at Belsen. We had no idea what we were coming to. I was to work as an interpreter. Then I was asked to be present as interpreter at the interrogation of Irma Grese. I travelled to Celle prison where she was being held. A British policeman interrogated her and I interpreted her responses. I told the policeman that it was a waste of time interrogating her – she was such a hardened woman who had committed the most horrendous crimes in Belsen. I would rather hunt for those who had not yet been captured.[8]

Irma Grese stood trial at the Belsen Trial and was found guilty of war crimes. She was transferred to Hameln Prison and hanged there on 13 December 1945. The British executioner Albert Pierrepoint was assisted by ex-German refugee Sergeant Major O'Neill, who had served in 3 Troop, No 10 Inter-Allied Commando.

Whilst on duties in Belsen, Howard Alexander extended a kind hand to one of the camp survivors, Anita Lasker-Wallfisch, who as one of the Jewish inmates was forced to play her cello in Auschwitz. It was Christmas 1945. Anita wrote about Captain Alexander in her autobiography *Inherit the Truth*:

We accepted an invitation to the Officers' Club on Boxing Day. One of my first dancing partners was Hans Alexander, Capt Alexander to be correct. He knew about our urgent need to get to Brussels, and as we were dancing he said: 'I hear you want to go to Brussels, I am going there tomorrow. If you like, I'll take you along …' Still dancing, I said to him: 'You know that we haven't got any papers …' He replied: 'That is your problem. If you want to come, I'll pick you up around 8 o'clock in the morning.' That was quite an offer. It goes without saying that I accepted. We had some very anxious hours that morning of 27 December. Capt Alexander had said that he would pick us up first thing. We waited endlessly but he failed to materialize. As time went by, we began to think that the whole plan was a figment of our imagination. Finally he appeared around lunchtime and was vaguely apologetic. We piled into the car, a chauffeur driven Mercedes, and rolled out of Belsen in style. We felt great. Capt Alexander never alluded to papers. We drove towards Holland, and I enjoyed the ride until we got to the frontier. There we were promptly stopped and asked to show our papers. I tendered my home-made document to the guard and was not altogether surprised that he did not wave us on. We were politely asked to step out of the car and follow him. Once inside the guard-room he told us that as far as he was concerned, Displaced Persons did not travel in private vehicles but only in large transports. He was very sorry but he could not let us pass. That was the cue for Capt Alexander. He took the papers out of the guard's hands – he outranked him naturally – looked at them for the first time and, without batting an eyelid, said brusquely: 'What's wrong with this! I have no time to hang around here. Put me onto HQ immediately!' Tense moments. I had seen myself being sent back to Belsen and having to start again from scratch.

As we were on Dutch soil, we went to a little restaurant to recover. I in turn apologised to Capt Alexander for having used his name on the paper. He just laughed. It was then that he told us he had only gone through with this charade for the hell of it. His plans for getting us over the frontier were as follows. He was a War Crimes Officer and it was his business to chase and arrest Nazis. If we had not succeeded in getting through at the first attempt, he would have driven onto another frontier post and taken us through as his prisoners. No one would have had the right to question him, or us. A most ingenious ruse; but I was glad we did not have to resort to it. It would have been somewhat preposterous to have had to pretend to be a war criminal in order to leave my 'fatherland'. The next frontier was easy. That was the one between Holland and Belgium ... Capt Alexander said he knew an old lady, a friend of the family, and he was sure she would put us up. We had a roof over our heads. Capt Alexander, his mission accomplished, bade us farewell. He had to attend to his own business. We had ceased to look like ex-Belsen internees and we definitely did not need any medical attention.[9]

Heinrich Himmler was top of the list of Hitler's government whom the Allies were desperate to catch. As Reichsführer SS he had overseen the police, security forces and Gestapo. He became overseer of the concentration camps, extermination camps and death squads, and was deemed ultimately responsible for the death of 11 million people. At the end of the war he too was on the run. He had assumed a false identity, fled to the region of Flensburg and disguised his appearance by growing a moustache and wearing an eye-patch. He was carrying the false papers of a sergeant major of the Secret Military Police. A British unit near Bremen became suspicious of his perfect papers when examined during a routine patrol. They arrested him on 22 May 1945. German-speaking refugee Ralph Parker was working in the Field Security Section at the time with British forces and was involved in the arrest of Himmler, but he, like many of his colleagues, did not immediately recognise him. Once in custody, Himmler's real identity was soon established. The following day, on 23 May, Himmler committed suicide by taking a cyanide pill whilst in Lüneburg, escaping any justice. Another ex-refugee in that unit was Mark Lynton (Max-Otto Loewenstein), who had served with the Third Royal Tank Regiment. Lynton describes the day that Himmler was in their hands:

Someone came bursting into the room, yelling, 'We've got Himmler! They're bringing him in.' Evidently my portly friend was the senior person in the immediate neighbourhood, and since this bit of news created predictable and instant pandemonium, neither he nor anyone else told me to leave. So I stayed, of course. Our breathless 'Paul Revere' turned out to be the security officer of some camp about thirty miles away, which had been set up as a catchment area for SS personnel. Two SS men had asked to see the commandant of the camp that morning indicating that they were speaking on behalf

46

of the Reichsführer der SS, Heinrich Himmler, who was in Hut 7! After everyone had recovered from near cardiac arrest, it was learned that Himmler had decided that the best way to avoid detection until such time as he was ready to be found was to hole up in one of our detention camps. He had provided himself with Waffen SS papers and, together with his two bodyguards, had been sitting quietly in that camp for the past couple of weeks while Germany was being scoured for the 'most wanted' Nazi left (with Hitler and Goebbels dead and Goering in custody). Screening techniques employed by the various ad hoc security officers, casually elevated to that occupation, were clearly on a par with Alien Tribunal practices, and the fact that this one spoke not a word of German was not helpful.

Himmler was duly led in a short while later and, though it was never clear why he thought this a good time to reveal himself, we very soon discovered what he had in mind. I became a major player in this extraordinary event by the mere fact that I happened to be there when Himmler, standing in the doorway with various guards hanging onto him like leeches, addressed the room, 'Sprechen Sie Deutsch?' When you had been in Third Tanks long enough you did not volunteer for anything, so first there was silence, then the man I had been talking with said to me, 'You had better stick around,' and so I stuck. Himmler looked even more colourless than his photos. He had shaved off his moustache and exchanged his pince-nez for horn-rimmed glasses, but otherwise had not attempted to disguise himself. He had papers indicating that he was a Waffen SS corporal by the name of Hitzinger, but he was also carrying various documents that left no doubt as to his true identity.[10]

There followed several hours of 'stand-off' because Himmler had decided he was not going to talk to anyone other than Eisenhower personally. Himmler was persuaded that Eisenhower was back in America; only Montgomery would be available but that would have to wait for the following morning. As Lynton comments: 'It turned out to be a splendid piece of improvised misinformation since, suitably embellished in translation, Himmler bought it.' Having secured the arrest of one of the most wanted war criminals, the unit did not anticipate the next turn of events, as Lynton describes. It was 23 May 1945:

It was decided to convert the office into sleeping quarters for Himmler by moving in a cot and posting double sentries at the door. The colonel, the staff officer and I were to sleep down the hall, and we would all get together with

Monty in the morning. By morning we hoped someone would have thought of the next smart move, or better still, would take Himmler off our hands. Himmler was fed, went under heavy escort to wash and clean up, and settled in for the night. And so did we, but not for long … Shaken awake by a sentry, we raced down the hall only to find Himmler on the floor, bluish in the face, making gargling noises: there was a distinct smell of bitter almonds. Standing in the room were several high-ranking bodies, brigadiers and up, looking foolish. Someone produced a doctor who pronounced Himmler dead, despite the gargling – death by cyanide comes within seconds and subsequent motor reflexes are just misleading. He also established that Himmler had carried a cyanide capsule in a back-tooth cavity and only needed to grind his teeth once to ensure departure. Everyone was to blame: the brigadiers for being idiots, the sentries for being intimidated, we for being careless. In the event, no fuss was made at all and everyone seemed just as happy to be rid of Himmler.[11]

Lynton then explains that he and four others buried Himmler's body in an unmarked location:

I was ordered to round up four of the sentries, sling Himmler's body in the back of a truck, drive out to Lüneburg Heath, and dispose of him. We did just that, without a coffin, not even a tree or bush in the vicinity. An hour later I could not have told anyone where we put him. No one ever looked for him, no one ever found him. He had been wearing a small metal swastika insignia on his tunic and I still have that. I guess that is all that is left of him. The sequel to the Himmler episode was that everyone in the whole zone became acutely cyanide conscious. A number of people arrested lost teeth by having flash-lights rammed into their mouths, to prevent their closing them. No one ever found another hollow tooth, but an amazing number of Germans did carry cyanide on their person.[12]

Admiral Dönitz, who was operating from a supposedly protected enclave in Flensburg, had taken over the reins of leadership after the death of Hitler. But Dönitz too was eventually arrested by British authorities, as Mark Lynton recalls:

Some of us participated in the 'capture' of Admiral Doenitz and his cabinet in Flensburg, just a few miles up the road. One of our infantry units was sent up to collect that crowd, and we went along just for the ride: not in our tarted-up tanks, needless to say. We all got our pictures in the London papers, which made it out to be the most dashing exploit since Prince Rupert last rode. It was about as exciting as watching grass grow: a bunch of elderly and very subdued characters, coming along meekly and without the slightest protest – all except Admiral Friedenburg, who swallowed cyanide in the lavatory.[13]

Dönitz stood trial at Nuremberg a year later and was sentenced to imprisonment. Whilst Lynton was in the region of Flensburg he was posted with five sergeants north to Denmark and finally to Copenhagen. It was here that they came into contact with the top Nazi in Denmark – Werner Best. Lynton and his interrogation unit spent five months in Denmark, setting up their HQ in Copenhagen's citadel: 'a forbidding Vaubanesque pile in the middle of Copenhagen, and daily processed truckloads of "suspects". Contrary to what our Danish friends may have believed, the overwhelming majority had nothing to hide and nothing to tell and it became so dull a routine, that we resorted to heartless little schemes to liven things up.' Things livened up for Lynton and his team when they had to interrogate SS Obergruppenführer Werner Best. Werner Best had been head of the German protectorate of Denmark during the German occupation. It was under Best's orders that Danish Jews were rounded up in the autumn of 1943. Due to the unprecedented action of the Danish people, the majority of Danish Jews were hidden just before 1 October 1943 and avoided the round-up. Over the course of several days Danish Jews were rescued from deportation to concentration camps by being taken in fishing vessels by night to the safety of Sweden.[14] Werner Best was eventually in British hands, and in spite of his part in the order to arrest Danish Jews, Lynton saw him as a moderate Nazi:

It was already widely known that Best was not only the most moderate among the German gauleiters or viceroys in various parts of Europe, but that he was a man of considerable culture and interests, insightful and sensitive, with a Hamlet-like streak of introversion and indecision. No one could ever quite explain how a man of his calibre and contradictions had risen in the SS hierarchy. He had been an early and convinced Hitler supporter but appeared to have grown disillusioned well before the outbreak of the war, yet had never been resolute enough to get off the bandwagon. Being named Gauleiter for Denmark certainly appealed to his ego, but he also seemed genuinely convinced that he could further understanding between the two countries ...

I had some long sessions with Best, during which not many matters relevant to Denmark came up, but we talked at great length about his views of Nazi philosophy, where it had gone wrong, and how it related to Germany and to himself. He was well aware of what happened to the Jews and to others whom Hitler wanted to exterminate. He deplored it, and I believed him. We talked a good deal about art, literature and other matters. He was an interesting, confused, tortured person and, in my view, deserved to be one of the few survivors among the top Nazi echelons.[15]

Werner Best was sentenced to imprisonment. After his release he became a businessman.

***

Another man on the Allies' list of most sought-after Nazi war criminals was SS Obergruppenführer Oswald Pohl, who had built up the Nazi administration during the 1930s. Towards the end of the war Pohl had been responsible for the administration of the concentration camps and SS industrial enterprises. A team of German linguists in the British army were assigned to find him. This included Captain Murdoch and Captain Eric Schweiger, both ex-refugees who had served with the Special Operations Executive. Pohl was on the run under the assumed name of Ludwig Gniss. For almost a year Murdoch and Schweiger tracked Pohl's last known movements until finally Schweiger discovered that one of Pohl's son-in-laws was living opposite the barracks of the Black Watch Regiment in Verdun, France. The building was placed under surveillance whilst Schweiger visited the local photographers. There he discovered a series of plates in the name of Ludwig Gniss. After a number of false leads, Schweiger discovered that Pohl (as Ludwig Gniss) was living in the tiny village of Armsen. The priority now was to capture Pohl before he committed suicide with a cyanide pill. On 27 May 1946 Pohl was finally arrested:

He [Schweiger] set out for Armsen in uniform, accompanied by a German policeman and a corporal in the Black Watch disguised as a Polish displaced person. On arrival, the policeman was sent into the village to ascertain that Pohl/Gniss was there, discovered him working in a garden. Schweiger then hid and the young corporal, who spoke broken German, went forward with the policeman and accused Pohl of having stolen his bicycle. Feigning anger, the corporal leapt at the unsuspecting Pohl and dived into his pockets – where two poison capsules were discovered.[16]

Pohl was arrested and taken to Verdun prison for a few hours before being transferred to 'Tomato', a small prison in Minden used by the War Crimes Investigation Unit. On 3 November 1947 he was sentenced to death by the Nuremberg Trials and executed at Landsberg prison on 7 June 1951, after a series of appeals. Obergruppenführer Glücks was also high on the list of wanted Nazis and, like SS Obergruppenführer Pohl, was responsible only to Himmler. Glücks had assumed a false identity and fled north. He was never brought to justice because in 1945 he committed suicide whilst his identity was being checked at a road block.

Whilst attached to No 2 War Crimes Investigation Unit, BAOR, Fred Pelican (Fritz Pelikan, b. Upper Silesia) received a phone call about the imminent lynching of an ex-SS guard of Neuengamme concentration camp. When Pelican arrived on the scene he discovered that the guard, SS Corporal Hans Barr, who had gone into hiding, had been spotted by locals in the nearby town. Pelican made several enquiries to locate Barr, who was wanted for war crimes committed in the camp. Within forty-eight hours Barr's whereabouts were given away by an elderly German. Barr was found in a basement of one of the local houses and arrested. At 2 a.m. that night Pelican escorted the van carrying Barr to prison in Hamburg. The following evening he was assigned to interrogate him.[17] Barr confessed to being part of the *Sonderkommando* (Special Command) at Neuengamme that injected Jews, and what he termed 'other sub-humans', with a phenol mixture by syringe. Within minutes his victims were absolutely stiff and lifeless. Barr explained to Pelican: 'You must understand sir, the process was completely painless and humane. Of course, you realise, I simply carried out my superiors' orders.' From the interrogations, Pelican calculated that Barr executed 2,000 inmates over a three-year period. Barr was transferred from Hamburg prison to Minden by one of Pelican's colleagues, Captain Walter Freud, who was also serving in No 2 War Crimes Investigation Unit. Barr's confession was typed and awaited his signature. It was eventually sworn by Walter Freud, who had escorted Barr to Minden.[18]

Fred Pelican, himself a survivor of Dachau before the war, was also sent to investigate the mysterious disappearance of a number of RAF pilots who were shot down over Germany. One case, involving the death of a pilot on Christmas Eve 1943, took Pelican to Neuss on the Rhine.[19] He proceeded to interview the most senior police officer at the police headquarters and was shown a report about the incident. The report indicated that the captured airman was being escorted to police HQ when a car carrying local

Nazi leader Hans Esser and his two henchmen pulled up. The airman was bundled into the car, taken to HQ and never seen again. At the end of the war Hans Esser went into hiding. Now Pelican was on his trail for war crimes. He instructed two CID officers to find the policeman who had originally arrested the pilot. Having located him, Pelican interrogated him and was led to interview a lady who lived opposite the HQ. In the meantime, the CID officers located Esser's two henchmen.

The lady that Pelican interviewed had witnessed a fair amount of what happened that fateful day, and had heard shots from the building. The following day, Pelican interrogated one of the henchmen, then shortly afterwards the other one. Within forty-eight hours Pelican had in front of him two sworn statements. His ongoing investigation into Esser's location took him to the main POW camp at Recklinghausen, where top Nazis were being held by the British. Esser was not found in the camp, but Pelican conducted an interview of the highest ranking Nazi there – the Gauleiter for the Rhineland. The gauleiter knew Hans Esser but denied knowledge of his whereabouts. Pelican comments: 'all the time I questioned him, he was completely baffled by who I could possibly be and how it came about that I possessed such intimate knowledge of German and the Nazi party structure.'[20] Having little success with the gauleiter, Pelican then went off to interview his wife, who proceeded to give away Esser's location. Pelican sent the two CID officers to stake out the secluded place where Esser was living, masking as members of the local council. They returned with the information Pelican needed. Esser was living in one of a cluster of isolated houses in a small clearing in a forest between Düsseldorf and Hilden. Pelican describes his subsequent arrest of Esser in the middle of the night:

> At precisely 4.00 a.m. the first blow fell. One of the hefty officers lifted the piece of wood and smashed the window, glass flying everywhere. While the woman inside started to scream, I managed to scramble inside, my leather gloves shoving aside the glass, and switch on the light. I ordered the man to raise both arms. The lights in the neighbourhood went on everywhere, I heard people shouting to call the *Polizie*. By that time both officers had got inside the house. I ordered one of them to take the man, whom I assumed to be Esser, to the jeep, not allowing him to dress, just in his *Nachthemd* [nightshirt] and slippers … The neighbours rushed out of their houses to arrest the robbers. Noticing me in uniform, they soon changed their minds, especially

as I took a threatening attitude. Myself and one CID officer searched the house from top to bottom, but found no sign of stolen Party funds anywhere. I told the wife she was at liberty to see me at police HQ in Neuss and could bring some clothing for her husband. The operation was completed in less than half an hour. We walked back to the jeep where Esser was held by the officer, still clad in nightshirt with a coat loosely over his person. Getting back to my office, I kept Esser at police HQ.[21]

The following day Pelican prepared the paperwork and questions for interrogating Esser. Esser admitted to having been the Ortsgruppenführer of Neuss and evading automatic arrest which would have landed him in the British internment camp at Recklinghausen. The issue of the murdered pilot seemed to have slipped his memory. Pelican recalls: 'He became so turgid and arrogant that momentarily I was speechless. He showed not the slightest sign of perturbation.' During the ensuing interrogation Pelican admits to assaulting Esser standing in front of him, in the same way Esser had assaulted the pilot before his death. The pilot turned out to be a Canadian whose dead body, Esser claimed, was lying in the basement of HQ. Esser had dragged it into a sack, pulled it into the boot of a car and driven to the river where he proceeded to throw it over the bridge. Pelican decided to test Esser's story and took him back to the site:

When we reached the exact spot, I halted. I marked it on the map which became an exhibit to be added to my file. At the same time I convinced myself what he told me made sense. As I looked over the bridge, he stood well away, his head bowed. 'Come here Esser,' I said. 'I want you to reflect on what you did to that young Canadian pilot. You threw him like a dog into the fast-flowing river. Whatever you may have in mind, I can assure you that you are going to hang, now I want to see whether you are man enough to jump into the river.' Of course I would not have allowed him to do so, I would have restrained him physically, I was much stronger and more powerful than him. I was astounded when he fell on his knees, crying and begging me not to push him into the water. The cowardice he displayed disgusted me immensely. It proved to me once again that Nazis were not the heroes they made themselves out to be. Where was the super-race that was to last a thousand years? I took the coward back to prison.[22]

★★★

As fate would have it, Freddie Benson (Fritz Berger) was assigned by the British forces as war crimes investigator and interrogator of the man who had murdered his father on Kristallnacht. His father, Richard Berger, was a construction engineer and president of the small Austrian Jewish community of Innsbruck. The perpetrator who killed his father was Obersturmbannführer Gerhard Lausegger. Whilst serving in the British forces on denazification work at the end of the war, Freddie Benson managed to secure Lausegger's arrest. Benson subsequently interrogated him and obtained a full confession. The interrogations took place over two consecutive days on 1 and 2 June 1946. A summary report of the interrogations written by Benson has survived:

> Prisoner was interrogated about his activities since March 1938. Detailed reports concerning his moves since that date have been handed over to the Austrian Police in Innsbruck. Prisoner was asked to give a detailed account of his whereabouts and Nazi activities in November 1938 as information from other prisoners stated, that prisoner had taken part in Nazi-activities committed against the Jews in November 1938. During six hours of intense and continuous interrogation prisoner maintained that not only had he himself not taken any part in such atrocities, but he did not even know anything about them, neither had he heard about any such incidents. The Interrogating Officer mentioned to prisoner that all these atrocities had been committed by SS personnel. To this point prisoner reacted very strangely by stating that although he had held the rank of SS Obersturmführer since March '38 he showed no interest anymore in anything connected with SS in Innsbruck. Prisoner was kept under continuous heavy pressure and eventually broke completely, giving all the details of how he himself with another two of his SS comrades had murdered Oberbaurat Ing Richard Berger during the night November 9th, 1938.[23]

Gerhard Lausegger was eventually held in custody in Innsbruck, but unfortunately, during the ensuing year, escaped from prison. Not satisfied that his father's killer was on the run again, Freddie Benson wrote from London to the intelligence officer in South Tyrol on 7 July 1947:

> Dear sir, I am in constant contact with the Austrian Police headquarters in Innsbruck regarding this case Gerhard Lausegger. Kriminalinspektor Sokser is the Officer dealing with this case. Lausegger who was imprisoned at

Wolfsberg, Carynthia, Austria, and who was interrogated by myself, admitted after many hours of hard pressure the murder of Ing. Richard Berger who was my father. I then handed him over to the respective authorities and was promised he would be taken to Innsbruck for trial. After many months the Innsbruck civilian police succeeded in obtaining a permit for Lausegger's transfer to Innsbruck. Then he escaped at the main station at Villach on 6th March 1947 ... I should be very grateful if you could pass this information on to the respective FSS Sections and should I be able to be of any help in your search.[24]

In spite of efforts to trace Gerhard Lausegger, he was never found or brought to justice.

★★★

Walter Freud was set on the trail of suspected Danish Nazi war criminal Christian Gustaf Jepsen. In April 1945 Walter was parachuted into the Styria region of Austria with the SOE in a dangerous blind drop at night. His survival behind enemy lines is told in full in *Freuds' War*. A few weeks after his return to England he was posted to Germany with the War Crimes Investigation Unit and assigned to the case of Jepsen. The British authorities wanted Jepsen extradited for trial under a British court. In January 1946 Walter travelled to Denmark to search for Jepsen. It took nearly four months. Jepsen was finally arrested in April 1946. A copy of the report written immediately after his arrest survives amongst the family papers of the late Walter Freud. It is dated 26 April 1946 and translated from Danish reads:[25]

Group Captain A.G. Somerhaugh, Judge Attorney-General Branch, War Crimes Section, H.Q., B.A.O.R. and Captain A.W. Freud, War Crimes Investigation Unit, H.Q., B.A.O.R., presented themselves on 23rd of this month in Assistant Secretary Schoen's office to discuss the case concerning the surrender of Christian Gustaf Jepsen. They confirmed the earlier received information that Jepsen is charged with cruelty and murder of concentration camp prisoners in Germany and they cited that Jepsen had admitted to 6 murders, whereas he undoubtedly is guilty of a much larger amount. With reference to the others accused in this case, all being German nationals, it was from the British viewpoint important Jepsen was handed over for judgment under the British military court, which was to hear the case. If it was not possible to hand him to the court to be prosecuted it is to be expected that the others accused will put the responsibility on him, and that Jepsen on the other hand, if his case later comes to judgment in front of a Danish court, will try to push the responsibility on to his German co-accused. The Assistant Secretary Schoen explained the view of the Ministry of Justice and stressed that it would be seen as quite extraordinary to surrender a Danish citizen for legal proceedings outside Denmark. The charge against Jepsen was of such a nature that he would undoubtedly be sentenced to death in this country, and there would therefore be no doubt the Danish would make sure that justice was carried out. The Assistant Secretary questioned whether the case could not be brought to justice if Jepsen only attended as a witness because he would be under no obligation to give his account on matters that could incriminate him.

Group Captain Somerhaugh declared that the British side was prepared to give a guarantee to ensure that any breach of the Danish prescriptive principle would be minimised. Accordingly one was prepared to let a Danish officer have a seat in the Court Martial, and one would if so wished, not execute the punishment, without the Danish authorities had had chance to consider the judgement. Group Captain Somerhaugh also referred to the fact that the war crimes of which Jepsen was accused were of such a nature that the limitations in the rules of extradition ought not to be enforced. The bringing to justice of war criminals should be put on the same footing as the fight against piracy, concerning which there was a recognized principle, that the punishment was an international matter. Assistant Secretary Schoen stated that the position, which so far had been assumed from the Danish side, depended on the resolution by the Ministry of Justice, before any departure from the agreement of fundamentals. Following discussion with Departmental Secretary Vetli in the Ministry of Justice the two English officers were referred to the officials in the Ministry to make their views known. The officers pointed out that the case was not urgent and they could wait one or two weeks for an answer from the Danes. The further discussions could be conducted with the local British military mission.

A year later, Gustaf Jepsen was convicted of war crimes. On 26 June 1947 he was hanged at Hameln Prison along with a number of other Nazi war criminals executed that day. Walter's search for Jepsen in Denmark during 1946 also had an unexpected twist. It was there in the spring of 1946 that he met his future wife, a Danish girl by the name of Annette Krarup. They married in 1947.

★★★

Jack Knight's work with war criminals took him all over Germany and Austria.[26] He was assigned to War Crimes Group South-East Europe and served first with the judge advocate general. He comments: 'I could speak German but I was put in the Japanese section. We were interviewing British POWs who had returned from Japan. This we did for three and a half months. I had had enough of this – I was very young at the time and had nightmares as a result of the interviewing work.' In early 1946 Knight was sent back to the War Office in London and informed that Major Hunt, a prosecutor in Wuppertal, Germany, needed a typist. Knight was sent to Wuppertal where the unit had set up a court in the local zoo. The unit was involved in the interrogation of the most senior SS officers who had been in France, as Knight explains: 'During the war seven or eight members of the British SAS had been captured and executed by SS officers. These SS officers were now being investigated as war criminals. Major Hunt was determined to track down the perpetrators. He knew that I spoke fluent German, so he assigned me to the interrogation of the German POWs and witnesses.' From there Knight was then posted to Italy for nine months, where the unit was investigating the Ardeatine Cave Massacre outside Rome. Nazi SS officer Erich Priebke was eventually tried for war crimes for his part in the killing of 335 civilians. Knight comments: 'We traced the war criminals in Germany and arrested them, handing them over to the Italians. From there I was posted to Carinthia in Austria, based at Ferlach near the Yugoslav border. In my new role I travelled all over Germany and Austria in the four Allied Zones with authority to interrogate anyone under the rank of Colonel for assistance with war crimes.' At the end of 1946, early 1947, Knight was asked to go to Dachau concentration camp to interrogate Nazi war criminal Otto Skorzeny, who was then a POW of the Americans. Skorzeny was wanted for questioning by the British because he had been appointed by Hitler as leader of the plot to assassinate Churchill, Stalin and Roosevelt at the Tehran Conference in 1943. The plot failed and those involved were eventually captured. Skorzeny was also wanted by the Americans for war crimes in the Ardennes. The Americans refused Jack Knight permission to interrogate him. A few months later Skorzeny escaped to Spain, but in 1947 the US acquitted him of war crimes. He became a businessman and died in 1974. Jack Knight carried on his work in the British forces until demobbed, being involved in parallel small trials.

★★★

Garry Rogers (Gunter Baumgart) joined the Control Commission in Germany and was transferred to the city of Cologne, which had suffered heavy Allied bombing during the war. Very little was left standing and the famous cathedral had been severely damaged in the bombing raids. Rogers was stationed 5 miles outside the city in a large German army barracks which became a POW camp. Several thousand German prisoners were encamped in large concrete blocks and an office was set up for the interpreters. 'Life was very pleasant,' comments Rogers, 'and as a Sergeant I was entitled to many privileges and escaped the monotonous duties of the Other Ranks.' Then he received orders to report to a new unit, the 4th CIC (Civilian Internment Camp), which was a branch of the Intelligence Corps dealing with interned war criminals and known Nazis. His destination was Recklinghausen, Westphalia, near the centre of the Ruhr Gebiet, the industrial and coal-mining centre of West Germany. 'Not a pretty town by any stretch of the imagination,' he says, 'but we weren't there for the scenery.' The camp was situated outside the town and consisted of Nissen huts with high perimeter fences and guard towers. The camp was then divided into smaller camps which served different purposes. The top security compound was for known war criminals who were suspected of having committed acts of atrocity. These included guards from concentration camps. Another compound was allocated for members of the SS and SA; another for industrialists and minor politicians. Rogers describes the work there:

> We had long lists of suspects, but they were just names, and most of the German soldiers had lost or destroyed their documents. We had some trials in the camp but these were mainly for misbehaviour by the inmates, thefts, fights or arguments. My job was to interrogate prisoners and hope to get information from them. Rather an arduous task. Why would anyone admit guilt? We were not in the Gestapo or the KGB and our methods to extract information were strictly controlled. We were not allowed to handle any suspect physically, although the temptation was often great. British 'fair play' had to come above everything else. One fellow sergeant who gave a prisoner a clip behind the ear was demoted and transferred quickly. It was a question of picking on the weakest link and with promises and threats to obtain evidence against fellow inmates. We managed to get some convictions.[27]

Coming into direct contact with perpetrators was never going to be easy for ex-German Jewish refugees returning on war crimes work for the Allies, as Rogers recalls:

> Feelings were very mixed. The Germans we met were very different from the arrogant people I left behind only six years earlier. They were a pitiful sight in the midst of the ruins, foraging for food and not daring to look anyone in the eye. The Nazis and Officer types were easier to handle. They were the enemy, and it was not difficult to hate them. The British Army was always determined to stick to the rules and the Geneva Convention, and any physical expression of hate was not tolerated. Maybe we were naïve at first and believed everyone who said, 'I was never a Nazi, I did not know about any atrocities'. Gradually it became normal to have some communication with the people we met. For decades afterwards I hid my feelings and experiences in Germany as a boy. It may have been this subconscious loss of memory which allowed me to be like the rest of the conquering forces. Most of the history of that time had not yet come to light until many years later. It is clear now that not just a few, but tens, maybe hundreds of thousands were actively involved in the extermination of six million Jews in Europe. At the time we were looking for just the top echelon of the Nazi Party; the SS, the concentration camp guards and commanders and the special *Einsatz Gruppen* [murder squads]. My job was to find these and bring them to justice. I hope I did my job well and was instrumental in finding and sentencing many war criminals. Many thousands were never found and have lived out their lives in comfort, untroubled by their consciences. I have great regrets that I did not devote my life to weeding out these cancers of society.

Working with German POWs at the end of the war taught ex-refugees like Garry Rogers an important lesson. The personal interaction brought a change of perspective for him:

> When I realised that not everyone in the camp was a Nazi, I got to know some prisoners better. This is a curiosity which most people, and particularly my Jewish friends, could not understand. I could not hate an entire population, having met some perfectly normal people. By entering Germany as a soldier, and being able to get to know people on a personal level, it was possible to sort out my feelings at the time.

Revenge must have been tempting on a number of occasions. However, the majority behaved with decency, determined not to lower themselves to the level of brutality that they had experienced under Nazism. Walter Eberstadt, who served in the Oxfordshire & Bucks Light Infantry, comments:

> I tried not to abuse my power. We had innumerable discussions, often late into the night, about the past and future. I tried not to impose my opinions, let alone bully, because of the authority vested in me by a British officer's uniform, because Britain had won the war, because my parents had been kicked out of Germany, my grandparents had died at Belsen, because Germany had been responsible for two world wars, for killing six million Jews. By setting myself strict standards, I hoped it would become self-evident to those with whom I was in contact that Jews were not what they had been made out to be by Hitler. I wanted to earn respect by what I did, not because I wore a uniform and we had won and they had lost. Personal example provides the only effective form of leadership.[28]

It is true that some Nazi war criminals evaded capture at the end of the war. Some successfully fled to Spain, South America and Cuba. In the coming decades the search for them continued with Nazi-hunters like Simon Wiesenthal, who dedicated a lifetime to hunting them down and bringing them to justice, with varying degrees of success. Ultimately the Allied forces could not get to Adolf Hitler, Heinrich Himmler and Joseph Goebbels, who evaded justice through committing suicide. Apart from them, the highest echelons of Nazi leadership were brought to trial and found guilty of war crimes. The German-speaking refugees who served in the British army see this as a victory and endorse the denazification process as a success, albeit limited in some aspects. It is a huge irony and twist of fate that those whom the Nazis would have annihilated had they stayed in Germany, ended up capturing the perpetrators of war crimes whilst serving in the British forces. So many of these veterans had lost their families at the hands of the Nazi regime but returned as victors involved in some aspect of war crimes investigations. These veterans worked as soldiers in the British army but did not receive British nationality until after their demob in 1946–47, or as late as 1950. The task of interviewing and denazifying lesser Nazis is covered in a later chapter.

Notes

1. Odessa stands for Organisation Der Ehemaligen SS Angehorgen.

2. Interview with the author.

3. Interview with the author.

4. Ian Dear, *Ten Commando*, p. 186.

5. IWM, ref: 05/14/1.

6. Quoted from Höss' sworn statement.

7. Based on interviews with the author in 2008 & 2009.

8. Based on interviews with the author in 2005.

9. Anita Lasker-Wallfisch, *Inherit the Truth*, pp. 131–5.

10. Mark Lynton, *Accidental Journey*, pp. 182–3.

11. Ibid., pp. 184–5.

12. Ibid., pp. 185–6.

13. Ibid., p. 181.

14. For background to the rescue of Danish Jews, see Ellen Levine, *Darkness Over Denmark* and Emmy Werner, *A Conspiracy of Decency*. This period has been fictionalised by J.H. Schryer in the novel *Moonlight Over Denmark*.

15. Lynton, op. cit., pp. 228–9.

16. Anthony Kemp, *The Secret Hunters*, p. 83.

17. Fred Pelican, *From Dachau to Dunkirk*, pp. 162–70.

18. Ibid., p. 170.

19. Ibid., pp. 135–50.

20. Ibid., p. 139.

21. Ibid., p. 140ff.

22. Ibid., p. 148.

23. Papers lent to the author.

24. Ibid.

25. I am grateful to Ulla Harvey for translating this document from Danish into English.

26. Based on interview with the author.

27. Garry Rogers, *Interesting Times*, p. 168.

28. Walter Eberstadt, *Whence We Came, Where We Went*, p. 340.

Three

WAR CRIMES INVESTIGATIONS

Whilst teams were searching for named Nazi war criminals, parallel units were gathering evidence for the war crimes trials which the Allied forces knew had to be part of any successful justice and denazification programme. Ahead lay months of careful gathering of information and evidence against known and suspected war criminals, as well as German companies like Tesch & Stabenow that supplied Zyklon B gas to the concentration camps. The German-speaking refugees in the British forces were essential to this work in the period leading up to and during the trials. Their fluency in German meant that they were invaluable for interviewing eye-witnesses, interrogating suspected war criminals or their families, or translating German documents that had been impounded from industrial plants or government property. Later, some of them carried out translation work and interpretative duties at the war crimes trials. In this respect the German-speakers were an indispensable asset to British Military Government in Germany and Austria at that time.

The War Crimes Investigation Unit for the British sector in Germany was based at the British Army of the Rhine HQ at Bad Oeynhausen. From there work was allocated to various German-speaking refugees in the army. One major investigation concerned the Neuengamme concentration camp outside Hamburg. On 2 May 1945 British troops arrived at Neuengamme to find the camp virtually empty. A few days earlier the inmates had been evacuated. Nine thousand of them were believed to have been boarded onto three ships. Two of them, the *Cap Arcona* and *Thielbek*, were bombed in the bay of Lübeck in a British attack which had not expected the ships to be carrying concentration camp survivors. Neuengamme was not intended as a death camp, but thousands certainly died there. It had a crematorium and punishment cells. Of 106,000 prisoners, only half survived. Amongst them were Dutch and French resistance fighters, homosexuals, Jehovah's Witnesses, 500 gypsies and 13,000 Jews. Medical experiments were carried out on children, and other inmates worked in harsh conditions in nearby factories. By the time British soldiers arrived, the SS guards had fled and gone into hiding. Whilst a search was undertaken to find them, along with their camp commandant Max Pauli, work began in earnest to document the war crimes that had been committed there. Pauli and ten guards were eventually caught and imprisoned in Hamburg. In March 1946 a British court sentenced them to death. Dennis Goodman (Hermann Gutmann), in the uniform of the 8th King's Royal Irish Hussars, was posted to Neuengamme in mid-September 1945 and allocated to the Review and Interrogation Staff there. By the time he arrived, the camp was being run as No 6 Civilian Internment Camp for Displaced Persons, surrendering German army personnel and forced labourers. The initial concern was not that individual activities might have been criminal, but whether they were a danger to the security of the British forces. Goodman explains the task that faced him:

> We were a small unit of around seven linguistically qualified personnel plus administrative staff under the command of Major Bateman and then Captain van Peborgh of the Intelligence Corps, quartered in Bergedorf with offices in a building near the entrance of the camp. Most individuals arrested in the Hamburg area fell into arrestable categories: members of the SS, senior officials of the Nazi apparatus and government, Justices, court officials, senior Army and Naval officers (U-boat commanders) and members of the Hamburg *Abwehr* (Nazi intelligence). They were brought to Neuengamme where they completed an initial questionnaire and then it was our task to interrogate and assess them. We had to write-up a report on each of them. It was extremely hard work because we were always too few to cope with the number of people brought to the camp. Many of our evenings were spent discussing individual cases. It was also depressing to learn how it was possible for Nazism to dominate to such an extent as to eliminate civic courage amongst the vast majority, suppress opposition and abolish the rule of law as understood in a civilized world. It didn't take me long to realise that every German must have known what was happening but turned their heads because of fear or apathy.[1]

During Goodman's time at Neuengamme, the suspected Nazi war criminal Rudolf von Alvensleben was arrested and brought into the camp. It was rumoured that von Alvensleben had had close connections to Himmler. He was shown immediately into Goodman's office and interrogated several times:

> I knew only what was filled in on his questionnaire and it is possible that I had seen his name on a listing of suspected war criminals. He was a self-possessed man but with an ingratiating mien which conveyed to me a feeling that his rank and area of service combined with personality required thorough investigation, and my assessment stated that he was a potential danger to security and likely to attempt an escape. I impressed on the officer-in-charge of the camp guards that the man should be held in the high security compound. This was disregarded. I went on leave and on return reported back at Hamburg Intelligence Headquarters to be greeted by the words: 'von Alvensleben has escaped'. Everyone knew how concerned I had been about the man who, it transpired, was not only a General of the SS Police but also a close associate of Himmler and responsible for the murder of many Jews, Russians and Poles. My subsequent investigation at the camp found that he had left in an ambulance in substitution for another 'ill' patient. I had heard of the existence of well-planned escape routes with safe houses and border crossings and was very keen to track him down, but at this point I had to hand over to Bad Oeynhausen. It always irked me and when in my subsequent career I spent time in Buenos Aires in 1949, I was befriended by my dentist. He also worked at the University Dental Clinic at which many Germans were being treated. I had told him the von Alvensleben story and some told me that he was living in the province under an assumed name. It was common knowledge that Argentina's President Peron had offered asylum and made use of a number of Nazi war criminals. Although von Alvensleben was sentenced to death *in absentia* by a German Court, he died in Argentina in 1970. He was never brought to justice.

Another refugee who carried out work relating to Neuengamme was Vienna-born Walter Freud, mentioned in the previous chapter. Although Freud visited Neuengamme as part of his war crimes investigations, he was based in Hamburg. He was assigned to No 2 War Crimes Team which consisted of Lieutenant Colonel Norman Ashton Hill, Major Ronald Bentham Green, Captain Alan Nightingale, Captain Richard O'Neill-Major, Captain

John Bramwell, Captain Peter Nixon, Captain Harry Cartmell, Captain Brian Bone, Captain Frederick Lee and Staff Sergeant Fred Pelican, also a refugee in the British army.[2] Part of Walter Freud's brief was to interrogate Leopold Falkensammer, a former commander of Altengamme camp, a sub-camp of Neuengamme. Amongst Freud's papers in the private family archive is an eighty to ninety-page typed manuscript in English entitled *The British Officer Told Me to Write My Story*. It is a full account written by Leopold Falkensammer of the war crimes that occurred at Altengamme. In it Falkensammer confesses to committing some of the atrocities, including co-operating with horrific medical experiments on POWs there. In July 1946, whilst Falkensammer was in custody in Fuhlsbüttel Prison, Hamburg, Freud persuaded him to write an account of everything he could remember. The report begins:

> The British Officer has given me plenty of paper and a few pencils. He even told the guard to sharpen my pencils as I am not allowed a knife. Pencil sharpeners are not available here. It is winter now and my little cell is cold. I wish I knew how my wife was. The poor girl, she hasn't had much fun; but it was all her own fault, we could have been so very happy. The British Officer said that if I wrote a truthful account of my life I would be allowed to receive letters from my wife. I have no illusions about my eventual fate, so I shall write what I conceive to be the whole truth.[3]

In the spring of 1942, Falkensammer had been ordered to report to Altengamme near Hamburg. Unbeknown to him, Altengamme was to serve as the place where Zyklon B gas would be tested to gain knowledge of the optimal levels needed in a sealed room to achieve a quick death. Once perfected, the process would be extended to death camps in the east:

> I was excited about my new job about which I knew nothing. I travelled to Hamburg full of curious anticipation. At Altengamme I was allocated my billet and I was then briefed by the camp commander in roughly the following words: *We at Altengamme have been given a great responsibility by the top leadership. It concerns the final solution of the Jewish problem. Immediately before the war, about one million Jews lived in Germany, including Austria and the Protectorate. We got rid of a lot of them by emigration. Since the war, we have gained another six million Jews, and there is now no further possibility of emigration. The Jews are our sworn enemies, and we must make quite sure that they cannot harm us ... We at*

Altengamme have been selected to develop a method of 'special treatment', and your job will be its technical supervision. As soon as we have perfected such a method on a pilot scale, it will be transferred to the east for large scale application. Our job, including yours, will be to ensure that the 'special treatment' developed here will work satisfactorily. Naturally, this is a state secret.

My knowledge of chemistry and evaluation made me an eminently suitable candidate for the job, and no valid excuse occurred to me to refuse it. I made up my mind to treat my new job as if I had been asked to look for ways and means of eliminating cockroaches and to keep all personal feelings at bay.

Altengamme was chosen because it was close to Hamburg, where the firm Tesch & Stabenow were based; a company which could supply the camp with Zyklon B gas for the gas chambers. Falkensammer confesses that he was not happy with his new post once he realised what was involved. Like many Germans at the end of the war, he claimed he had no choice and was obeying orders:

I would like to assure the British Officer that I was not pleased with this assignment. Killing hundreds of people, even Jews and Russians, was not my idea of a pleasant job. But what could I do? If I had raised any objection, I would at once have been branded a Jew lover and I had already been warned what that meant. In wartime one has to tackle unpleasant jobs, and mine was, in comparison with fighting on the Eastern Front, a safe one. I was in no physical danger. The barracks I lived and worked in were heated. I slept in a comfortable bed and the food was good and sufficient. If I had shown any reluctance to carry out the allocated duties, I would either have become an inmate myself or sent to the Eastern Front.

Falkensammer provided a detailed explanation of how the Zyklon B gas was tested in Altengamme ready for wider use in the concentration camps:

I had to calculate the space required for the fumigation. Allowing three square feet per person, i.e. an area of twenty inches by twenty inches, a room seventeen feet square would hold one hundred persons. I base my calculation on these data. I had a building erected with the above inside dimensions. I used concrete blocks for the building material, as wood might not have been strong enough. It was difficult to make the structure airtight, which was essential to avoid the escape of poisonous gas. The design of an effective door seal was a particularly difficult problem. Except for the metal door, the room had only two other fixtures. One was an electric fire for heating the room to the required 26°C. The other was a short length of stove pipe, passing through the ceiling, with a tight lid on the upper, outside end. One hundred Russian POWs, most of them wounded or disabled, were assembled. Fit ones were too valuable for this use. The room was preheated, and the POWs were told to go into the room for delousing. The door was then bolted from the outside. One of my assistants, equipped with a respirator, climbed onto the roof and dropped a measure quantity of Zyklon B powder into the room through the stove pipe. We could hear a lot of commotion from the inside. When this had subsided, after a measured time interval, another lot of prisoners were told to open the door and remove the bodies. These were later cremated, but this was outside my responsibility. After three or four tries, I had all the data which were needed. It included the optimum quantity of Zyklon B required, the size of the heater and the time taken to assure 100 per cent success. The most difficult problem was the avoidance of gas leakage. I had to experiment with a number of gaskets. Luckily I was an expert on rubber which enabled me to select the best gasket made from the most suitable type of rubber ...

If the British Officer should think that guarding concentration camps is a pleasant or simple job, I would like to disillusion him. It is a terrible job. One naturally despised the prisoners as being obstacles in the way of Germany's aspirations. On the other hand, one could not but regret that the prisoners had been misguided enough to get into the position they were in. There was also a feeling of disgust that the prisoners' behaviour necessitated our harsh treatment. We reduced this problem by handing over the internal administration of the camps to nominated prisoners called Kapos. These were given slightly better rations and accommodation, and in return they organised for the prison population. Towards the end of the war, we had very little direct contact with the inmates. It was all left to the Kapos. Some of the cruelties and atrocities of which I have been accused were actually committed by the Kapos.

Later in his statement, Falkensammer revealed the nature of the horrendous medical experimentation at Altengamme. This shocked Walter Freud to the core and he asked to be transferred off the case. For the rest of his life Freud spoke very little about this period with his family, only admitting that what he had discovered in the camp was too much for him to take. A chance discovery of the report during the writing of *Freuds' War* revealed the true extent of the evidence that Freud confronted. The extract below from Falkensammer's report is graphic and horrific:

The British Officer will recall that in the spring of 1942 we had been allocated a number of Russian POWs, about 500, for the Zyklon B experiments. By careful design of the experiments, only four hundred of them were actually used. In the meantime, half of the rest had died of natural causes, so we had another fifty 'to spare'. They were miserable specimens but by increasing their diet slightly and by somewhat reducing their work load, most of them recovered quite well. In my opinion, they were fit enough to be the subjects for a medical research project which I considered of great importance. I contacted a well-known Hamburg surgeon, and honorary SS officer, to whom I outlined my ideas. He was at the top of his profession and could count many senior and well-known party members among his patients. My ideas were enthusiastically received and he was very grateful to me to be given such a unique opportunity. He and I together designed an experiment, which, had it worked, would have been of very great benefit to our wounded soldiers.

We picked out ten of the healthiest POWs; five of them with penises of normal length, and another five with very long penises. They were hospitalised in our camp hospital, and to each I allocated 2 prisoners as nurses, who had to look after the patients day and night. This proved to be a very wise precaution. When the POWs inadvertently learned of the nature of the proposed experiments, a few tried, and one or two succeeded, in taking their own lives. The usual way of committing suicide was by running towards the high-tension wire-fence. If they managed to reach it, they were electrocuted; if not, they would be shot by our watchful guards. Finally, the prisoners had to be shackled with handcuffs to their beds. We could not afford to lose prisoners once the experiment had started. When the first lot of five prisoners were in a good state of general health, the surgeon amputated their penises, leaving only a one inch stump on each testee. Naturally, this was done under a full anaesthetic and proper operating theatre conditions. There was no cruelty involved. The stumps were left to heal under antiseptic conditions, which took about six weeks. One of the more difficult and unforeseen problems which we had to overcome was the negative attitude of the prisoners towards our experiments. One would have thought they would be proud to be allowed to serve humanity, but these Russians were too uncultured to appreciate the honour! When they realised that their [penis] had been cut off, some of them, restrained from committing suicide by any other means, went on hunger strike and refused to eat. We told their nurses that if they could not make their charges eat, they too would have their private parts cut off. Somehow or other, and we did not inquire too closely how, the nurses overcame the prisoners' reluctance to take in food. The second part of our experiment then commenced. The surgeon amputated the long penises from the second lot of prisoners. Long penises had been chosen because the extra length made it easier for the surgeon to operate. He had literally more in hand. As each penis was cut off, the surgeon transplanted it on one of the amputated stumps of the first lot. In other words, if a soldier had lost his penis due to war injuries, or other causes, this technique would have enabled his surgeon to replace it from a suitable donor. Our experiment simulated actuality reasonably well. A wounded soldier would have his first operation, the necessary amputation, in a field hospital. He would then be transported to a base hospital where facilities for replacement surgery were available; this would normally take some weeks. There a suitable donor, say a criminal waiting for execution, would be placed in a bed beside him in the operating theatre, and the amputation and transplant would take place with minimum delay.

Much has been documented about medical experiments in Auschwitz, but those carried out at Altengamme, I believe, are largely unknown. When the guards fled at the end of the war, so too did Falkensammer. A warrant went out for his arrest. Falkensammer was still in Hamburg but decided he had to disappear from Germany for a time and return when it was safe to do so. He decided on Sweden as the place for temporary asylum. He disguised his appearance: grew a moustache and beard and dyed his hair a darker colour and wore glasses. He boarded a ship at Lübeck for Sweden but the ship's captain began asking him questions about his Austrian nationality. It is not clear whether Falkensammer reached Sweden even for a short time. All that is known is that when the ship returned to Lübeck, a jeep with British soldiers was waiting to arrest him. Falkensammer was taken to Fuhlsbüttel Prison. To the very end he resolutely blamed the Jews for his downfall, as seen in the closing paragraphs of his written report. Falkensammer was found guilty of war crimes against humanity and sentenced to death. In September 1946 he was executed by hanging at Fuhlsbüttel Prison.

As part of the extensive investigations of war crimes relating to Altengamme, Walter Freud with another ex-refugee, Fred Pelican, carried out interrogations of staff at the Hamburg-based company Tesch & Stabenow.[4] It was originally a firm of fumigators for ships bringing grain to

Europe from America. After each trip the ships had to be fumigated for rats and mice. For that procedure, Zyklon B was supplied by Tesch & Stabenow. As Falkensammer's confession showed, during the war the Nazis singled out the company to provide Zyklon B for Hitler's Final Solution. At the height of the extermination of the Jews, the firm supplied 2 tons a month for the concentration camps. Having fluent knowledge of German, Freud carried out a number of interrogations of the staff at the company. He wrote about those investigations:

> The man in charge [at Tesch & Stabenow] said: 'Yes of course. I supplied so much Zyklon B to the concentration camps. But I had no idea it was used for humans.' He couldn't deny it because we found all the receipts, but [he said] they were for the clothes of the prisoners, they were full of mice. He was a dreadful person, not only from my point of view but also his own employees, and they all came and they said the following: 'There was a meeting between Dr Tesch and the SS, where he was told what the gas was for. His technicians advised the SS on how to do it because it is a dangerous powder, and you had to have the technique of introducing it into the chambers and so on.' It was Dr Tesch's staff who advised the SS on how to do it, so there was no excuse and he was hanged. He was one of the very first German technicians who were actually hanged and not excused or let free after a few years. He was an absolute die-hard Nazi, an honorary SS man, and his books were only Nazi books. It's interesting for instance that when Hamburg was so badly bombed, Himmler wrote a letter to the Mayor of Hamburg saying: 'please help Tesch to get up on his feet again.' Only Stabenow was given that privileged treatment.[5]

This was clearly one of the most significant cases that Freud ever worked on. The investigation affected him deeply. He wrote extensively about the case in his unpublished memoir *An Austrian Grandfather*. During his work he interrogated the medical orderly who was responsible for pouring the powder into prison cells in an experiment. Freud's comments are worth quoting here in full:

> The fumigant used was Prussic acid absorbed on a chalk-like substance and the resultant powder had the trade-name 'Zyklon B' made by I.G. Farben. In the absorbed state it was relatively harmless when cold and could be handled with a minimum of precautions. When heated to about 40°C (104°F) the

Prussic acid would be liberated from the chalk, become active and would quickly kill any mammal breathing it in. In January 1942, at the time of the first reverses of the German army outside Moscow, there took place in the Berlin suburb of Wannsee a high-level conference to discuss the 'Final Solution' [of the Jewish Problem]. This meeting decided to try gassing as an effective and cheap way of exterminating the Jews. In order to obtain the 'scientific' data, a pilot experiment was subsequently conducted at the concentration camp of Neuengamme outside Hamburg, conveniently located for the firm of Tesch and Stabenow, using Russian prisoners of war as guinea pigs. A number of prison cells inside the camp were fitted with electric heaters, the Russian POWs were locked inside, and varying amounts of Zyklon B powder were introduced through the ceilings of the individual cells. The heaters were then switched on and as soon as the temperature in the cells had reached a certain level, the Prussic acid gas was liberated and took effect. This experiment established the optimum amounts of Zyklon B, the time factor and other operating data required for later and large-scale use in the extermination camps.

I am certain of the above facts, because after the war I interrogated the SS medical orderly who was at the sharp end of that experiment; i.e. he was the chap who had to climb onto the roof of the cells in order to drop the powder into them. He was of simple farming background, but not stupid. When he signed his deposition, given quite voluntarily, he said to me: 'I am now signing my own death warrant'. While I am not quite sure of his eventual fate, I believe he was right. I am however quite sure of the fate of three senior employees of the firm of Tesch and Stabenow. Mr Tesch, his accountant and the technical representative were brought to trial in Hamburg. Their defence was that 'yes', they supplied Zyklon B to the SS but as far as they knew at the time it was used only to fumigate the clothes of their Russian prisoners of war of which there were many. However, we found witnesses who confirmed that Tesch had been informed by the SS to what use his powder was going to be put and that he had voluntarily agreed to supply it for the purpose of killing.[6]

Having questioned one of the staff from Tesch & Stabenow, Captain Freud and Fred Pelican discovered that Bruno Tesch had gone partly into hiding. But not only was he still operating his business – now newly named Chemical Industries – but he was also supplying the necessary material for the fumigation of shipping for the British military forces in Germany.

Freud telephoned HQ and explained the situation. It was decided that Tesch had to be arrested. At 10 a.m. that day Freud and Pelican went to the district where Dr Tesch's offices were situated and proceeded to arrest him. Pelican recalls:

> Without knocking, Captain Freud entered, myself right behind him. 'Get up!' Captain Freud shouted. 'Raise your arms!' I went straight over to him [Tesch], carrying out a quick search for a weapon. 'Are you Bruno Tesch?' Captain Freud enquired. '*Jahwohl* [yes],' he replied in a clear voice. Freud – 'Keep him there, Staff Sergeant, while I go and have a look next door.' The general office next door proved to be a rather busy place, fifteen or twenty girls working full out. Captain Freud ordered the staff to leave and return the following morning. Great nervousness and upheaval prevailed. He locked the offices and we grabbed Tesch and sent him straight to prison in Altona with instructions for him to be interrogated.

Freud and Pelican returned to Tesch's office to search the premises but found no incriminating documents of his wartime activities. That would be reserved for Pelican's search of Tesch's home later on. Little did Freud and Pelican realise that the arrest of Tesch would cause utter consternation amongst the British authorities, who still needed the firm to supply material to fumigate their ships. As it happened, Freud's unit cleared one of the employees to carry on the business whilst Tesch remained firmly behind bars. Both Freud and Pelican admit in their memoirs that the Tesch & Stabenow case was the most important that they dealt with in their work.

In the spring of 1947 Bruno Tesch and his accountant Karl Weinbacher were tried before a British army war crimes tribunal in Hamburg lasting seven days.[7] One of the witnesses who gave evidence was Perry Broad, who had been employed as a typist in the office at Auschwitz concentration camp from 1942 until early 1945. Little did Broad know then that he too would be tried as a war criminal nearly twenty years later, at the Auschwitz Trial in Frankfurt in 1964.[8] Both Tesch and Weinbacher were found guilty of war crimes and condemned to death. On 26 April 1947 Field Marshal Montgomery signed their death warrants and the men were hanged in Hameln Prison. The technical representative, against whom prior knowledge could not be proved, was acquitted. For Walter Freud, this particular investigation had a direct family link which he poignantly reflected upon after the war:

How does the above story of the supplier of poison-gas to the concentration camps relate to Grandfather? He had four sisters in Vienna, all over 70 years of age and either spinsters or widows. These four old ladies were left behind in Vienna with sufficient funds for the remainder of their lives. But these lives were brutally cut short by their transportation, to various extermination camps, and by the application of the same Zyklon B gas whose suppliers I, their grand-nephew, helped to prosecute. I am sure Grandfather would have approved.[9]

After the war, the exact fate of Sigmund Freud's sisters became known. Two of them, 82-year-old Marie and 80-year-old Pauline, were murdered in Treblinka concentration camp in 1942. The other sister, 84-year-old Rosa, perished in the gas chambers of Auschwitz, and the youngest sister, Adolfine, died of starvation in Theresienstadt. The leading industrial company I.G. Farben, which had manufactured Zyklon B, was the subject of war crimes investigations. At the end of the war the company was liquidated due to the severity of its crimes. Its directors were tried at the 'subsequent Nuremberg Trials'. Of the twenty-four defendants, thirteen were found guilty of war crimes and given prison sentences.

Walter Freud's work also took him to investigate another leading German industrialist company – Krupp's – which was thought to have helped the Nazis at the highest level and supplied munitions for Germany's war machine. Freud himself found no evidence to convict Gustav Krupp, the head of the firm, and concluded that most of the documentation had already been destroyed. However, a number of other investigations were carried out on the wartime activities of the firm, including its use of foreign civilians and POWs for forced labour. Krupp had built a large fuse factory at Auschwitz where Jews were worked to exhaustion and then sent to their deaths in the gas chambers. A detachment of 3 Troop was assigned to the denazification of German industries – interrogation work that covered the Krupp factory. Amongst the detachment was Sergeant Waller and Max Dickson (Max Dobriner). Dickson, who served in the Pioneer Corps then 3 Troop of No 10 Inter-Allied Commando, attached to 41 Royal Marine Commando, was initially engaged in the demobilisation of the German army. He recalls: 'One day, one of our Jewish boys was interrogating a Gestapo man who had sent his parents to their deaths. We had to restrain him physically.' Dickson was posted to 98 Field Security and sent to an outpost at Beckum, south of Osnabrück, in Westphalia. It was from here that he visited the Krupp factory. He recalls:

We had meetings once a week and were given a list of people to interrogate and write up a report. Our group covered the districts of Beckum,
Tecklenburg and Münsterland. We had to flush out some of the Nazi war
criminals. It was all top secret. Four of us went to Krupps factory in Essen. We
had to go through all their papers. It was a huge factory which had employed
over 50,000 workers. The company was responsible for making guns, tanks,
ammunitions and heavy armament. Krupp employed a lot of foreign labour
and it was our task to investigate crimes committed against the people who
had worked for him. By the time we visited, they were making pots and pans
and machines for other factories. I was disgusted by the working conditions
for the employees.

After thorough investigations, Gustav Krupp was listed as a major war criminal at Nuremberg, but he was found too ill to stand trial after he suffered
a stroke.[10] He was never tried for war crimes. Attention turned to his son
Alfried Krupp, who, on 31 July 1948, faced charges at a Nuremberg military
tribunal. Alfried Krupp stood in a courtroom before Judge Anderson and
Judge Daly to hear the guilty verdict:

> That this growth and expansion on the part of the Krupp firm was due in
> large measure to the favoured position it held with Hitler there can be no
> doubt. The close relationship between Krupp on the one hand and the Reich
> government, particularly the Army and Navy Command, on the other hand,
> amounted to a veritable alliance. The wartime activities of the Krupp concern
> were based in part upon spoliation of other countries and on exploitation
> and maltreatment of large masses of forced foreign labour.[11]

Judge Daly then proceeded to read out his sentence: 'On the counts of the
indictment on which you have been convicted, the tribunal sentences you
to imprisonment for twelve years and orders forfeiture of all your property,
both real and personal.'

***

In the autumn of 1945, Fred Warner (Manfred Werner, b. Hamburg), who
had been parachuted behind enemy lines into Austria on a SOE mission,
was given instructions to join the War Crimes Investigation Unit in
Germany.[12] He had no desire to return to Germany, but an order was an
order. He had also received confirmation that his parents and young sister

had perished in Auschwitz. He felt this was his opportunity to catch some of the perpetrators who had a hand in his family's deaths. He joined one of the investigation teams first in Bünde, near Bad Oeynhausen, and then Hamburg, to arrest and interrogate suspected Nazi war criminals. If they had not yet been arrested, he was to find and interview witnesses to prepare the case for the Legal Section. In his unpublished memoirs, he gives an example: 'Another officer and I had to arrest the owner and the foreman of a quarry near Bad Eilsen. Inmates from the nearby Lahde-Weser concentration camp, who were forced to carry out extremely heavy work there in terrible conditions, had been ill-treated and a number had died there.'

During war crimes business, Warner spent time with Field Security in Heide, Schleswig-Holstein, on the day that Rudolf Höss was arrested by members of that unit. He accompanied some of the unit to an assembly point for members of the Wehrmacht, 'in order to discharge as many as possible and send them home. Schleswig-Holstein was the main concentration area in the British zone of Germany for German armed personnel. As there were so many candidates and the final interrogations given them seemed rather short, I offered to help. This was gladly accepted and I can now claim to have been instrumental in the demilitarization of Germany.'[13] Warner served as War Crimes Liaison Officer for short periods with 8 Corps in Plön, 30 Corps in Lüneburg and also the British Infantry Brigade in West Berlin. Some of his work took him to Denmark to interview witnesses. One of his responsibilities was occasionally to look after witnesses for the war crimes trials. One such witness was Sylvia Salvesen, the wife of the Norwegian king's personal physician. Sylvia Salvesen had been sent to Ravensbrück concentration camp by the Nazis and she was now needed as a witness for the prosecution. Another key witness from the camp whom Warner came into contact with was French SOE fighter Odette Churchill, whose testimony was to be so crucial at the trial. She was interviewed extensively by ex-Viennese lawyer in the British army Stephen Stewart (Stephen Strauss); there is more about his work in the next chapter.

Warner was often called up to transport prisoners:

We also had to take suspects from 'Tomato' prison to other prisons and from interrogation centres to Hamburg, where they had to give evidence at trials. In the case of the Höhere SS and Polizeiführer von Bassewitz-Behr (a senior Security Official), whom I had to take to West Berlin, the British War Crimes Liaison Officer handed him over to the Russians. Prior to his posting to

Hamburg he had been stationed in Russia where he had been responsible for mass shootings. On another occasion, my boss Joe Leniewski and I took the head of the Bremen Gestapo, Dr Schweder, to Hamburg where he was to give evidence at a War Crimes Trial.

During Warner's time with 30 Corps at Lüneburg, he was ordered to interview a German ex-naval rating to get information to be used in the case against Admiral Raeder, who was being tried in Nuremberg with the other top Nazi leaders. The German was being held at the time in prison in Schleswig-Holstein for a minor criminal offence. Warner was to bring his statement immediately to the British prosecution staff at Nuremberg. While down in the American zone of Germany, he was also given another brief:

> a short interrogation of one of the SS officers responsible for the most murders committed by the SS outside the concentration and extermination camps. He was Obergruppenführer Otto Ohlendorf, the head of the Einsatz Gruppen [Action Groups] who arrested and shot thousands of Russian commissars and Jews in Russia. He had already been tried by the Americans and was awaiting his sentence in jail in Nuremberg. All that was wanted was the answer to one question, which could have helped one of his fellow SS officers on trial by the British. When I asked him what he did at the Reichs-Sicherheits Haupt Amt [RSHA], the main security headquarters in Berlin, where he was a leading figure, he had the cheek to say that he looked out of the window all day long admiring the trees and flowers in the garden below. That was the end of the interrogation. Ohlendorf was sentenced to death by hanging.[14]

Whilst in the American zone, Warner attended the Nuremberg Trials for a day as an observer. He reflected on the experience:

> I had seen some of these evil men before I left Germany, and Hess in Wales during the war. They looked a motley lot and, with the exception of Goering and Schacht, they appeared fairly downcast. Goering seemed to enjoy the proceedings. I was in uniform and sat in the Visitors' Gallery next to Air Commodore Fielding, the Head of the King's Flight. During the break, he asked me rather incredulously if I really could understand German so well that I could listen to the original language. I told him that I could, but wondered if he believed me or thought that I was showing off.[15]

In early 1947, Warner was promoted to leader of the Investigation Team, during which time he handled many important cases and saw some of the most brutal Nazi figures brought to justice. This included investigations into the Fuhlsbüttel Gestapo Prison in Hamburg. The team arrested around sixty prison staff, constituting most of the prison's personnel. The staff was eventually brought to trial in Hamburg in two separate groups. Warner recalls how three figures stood out for him as particularly brutal at the prison: the prison Commandant Sturmbannführer (Colonel SS) Tessmann; the prison doctor; and one of the warders, Paul Reppin, who thought nothing of kicking pregnant women in the stomach. A blow from Reppin and the victim would collapse to the ground immediately. A number of the staff at the prison, including Commandant Tessmann, were condemned to death by hanging; others received prison sentences, and some were acquitted. Warner comments: 'War Crimes officers were supposed to attend a hanging. This was meant to make us realise the importance, responsibility and the consequences attached to our job. Luckily I was always busy when hangings took place and therefore missed out on this unpleasant experience.'[16]

Warner's work occasionally overlapped with investigations of the atrocities at the Neuengamme concentration camp. He was finally demobilised in August 1948, and as such was amongst the last of the enemy aliens to be discharged from the forces. In November 1948 Warner returned to Germany in a civilian capacity, working in the Intelligence Division of the Control Commission for Germany.

★★★

Flight Sergeant Wieselmann was given the task of investigating the murder of fifty RAF pilots in Stalag Luft 3 at Sagan in Poland, the famous camp of the 'great escapees'. Fred Simms (Alfred Georg Simonson, b. Berlin) served in the Royal Artillery in Italy and Greece. When hostilities came to an end he was assigned to war crimes investigations in Austria. Simms' unit moved into the Styrian region of Austria over the Präbichl Pass and into Eisenerz. The mountains in the region were known for their rich source of iron ore. It was processed in iron and steel works at Leoben, a few miles from Eisenerz. The mining company was the centre of employment in the area. Simms recalls:

> The director was a rabid Nazi and he was dismissed when the war ended. One of his son-in-laws was a high-powered SS officer. Officially recorded as

77

missing at the end of the war, he was wanted as a named war criminal. But his wife worked at first as interpreter to the British Town Mayor until it was pointed out that she was unsuitable for such a sensitive position. The little town lies in a deep valley, surrounded by steep wooded slopes. Although only perhaps a mile from the main road, a little army could hide there without anyone in the valley knowing about it. That is why the SS general's wife was so dangerous, she could easily support him if he was hiding there and as interpreter get to know everything. My job as interpreter was not very demanding at that point. If one of the quartermasters needed any local supplies, I went with him to requisition them.

The winter brought an unexpected change for Simms and his colleagues. In early December snowfall on the Präbichl Pass, some 1,000ft above Eisenerz, meant it was firm enough for skiing. Simms explains the importance of this to the army: 'The army urgently needed troops capable of mountain and snow warfare, and all units had to start skiing training as soon as possible. Ours was indeed the first with enough snow to do so. We had a couple of excellent local skiers, former soldiers, as instructors, but who spoke no English. I was therefore in the first squad under instruction.' When Simms returned to Eisenerz, he was immediately told about an important development in the town. Vague rumours had already surfaced about something terrible having happened not long before the end of the war, but no one in the area would talk. On the other side of the valley there had been a labour camp which consisted mainly of Russian forced labour. The labour force had been ordered to build a road to bypass the steep Präbichl. Atrocities were alleged to have occurred in the camp. That was not all that came to light, as Simms explains:

> The attention of our authorities was drawn to a site deep in the forest, a couple of miles or so from Eisenerz. This had evidently been dug not more than a year ago. Trials soon revealed it as a burial ground with corpses just thrown into a big hole. The mayor and other citizens were ordered to dig it up, which they did under some protest. This was soon silenced when the full truth was revealed. The mass grave contained some 180 corpses, fully dressed, with their pitiful belongings. Documents showed them to be Hungarian Jews, mostly from Budapest. I had to transcribe some of the papers that were still legible. Quite a lot was in German. I can still recall the papers in a wallet belonging to a Budapest dentist, Weiss. The full story took a little time to piece together.

By the middle of 1944, the Nazis took over effective control of Hungary and the fate of the Hungarian Jews was sealed. Wallenberg, a Swedish diplomat, worked wonders providing many of them with travel documents to safety, but the vast majority was not so lucky. In the autumn, 100,000 of them were assembled in Budapest and made to march to the concentration camp Mauthausen in Austria. This huge column was accompanied by SS guards and local home guard units reinforced them on the march through each area. The column included women and children, the old and sick, so naturally many fell behind during the march, only to be shot by the guards. When months later, this column reached its destination – the concentration camp Mauthausen – there were only 111 people left of the 100,000 that had started. When the column reached the Eisenerz area, the local home guard had a field day. They used the Jews for target practice. They killed so many that even the permanent SS guard were appalled and ordered them to stop. An estimate of at least 180 murders was committed on that day. The captain of the Eisenerz home guard was by all accounts the main culprit, as he had encouraged and led the massacre. We could not catch him as he committed suicide and, whilst I was there, the evidence to convene a war crime court had not been completed.

In another valley, some 30 miles away, there had been a small prisoner-of-war camp with about 200 British POWs. They complained of maltreatment by the commandant and the local doctor. On that occasion a war crimes court was convened early in 1946. I was asked to be an interpreter at the proceedings. Here again, the obviously guilty commandant committed suicide in prison, leaving his doddering old second-in-command to take the rap. The local doctor and his assistant (his daughter) were also indicted. The chief interpreter was an Israeli whose knowledge of German and English was not as good as mine. However, he was an excellent interpreter, familiar with all the technicalities of a court of law. I found the experience most interesting, as every remark in one language had to be turned into the other, sentence by sentence. The President of the Court preferred to take the minutes of the proceedings in long-hand, since this would greatly reduce the time for the verdict of the Court to be confirmed. This meant that the proceedings took a bit longer. The whole trial lasted about a week. I got so used to my role, that I translated quite automatically.[17]

★★★

S.H. Gruber (b. Vienna) was also posted to Austria and transferred from the 6th Airborne Division to War Crimes Group SE Europe, Kirschentheuer near Klagenfurt. During the war he had served in both the Royal Electrical and Mechanical Engineers and then the 6th Airborne Division. In the autumn of 1946 he had been posted to a German POW camp at Monymusk near Aberdeen in Scotland. His role there was as camp interpreter. His main duties consisted of interviewing and classifying prisoners. The categories of classification were: WHITE – to repatriate as soon as possible; GREY – to repatriate later; and BLACK – to repatriate when safe to do so. In the spring of 1947, Gruber was transferred to the War Crimes Group SE Europe in Austria as investigator, interpreter and general assistant to the Judge Advocates General Branch. He explains his work there:

Our group was responsible for crimes committed during the war in Italy and Austria. It was housed in a so-called 'Lebensborn Mutterheim', an establishment where Himmler tried to breed the master race by selecting suitable Aryan types to beget children, creating an elite. My own involvements were with the cases concerning the Loibl Pass concentration camp, a branch of the infamous establishment at Mauthausen. The prisoners were made to drive a tunnel through the Karawanken, a chain of the southern Alps separating Austria from Slovenia, a strategic connection. The second major case was the massacre at the Ardeatine Caves near Rome in retaliation for an attack by Italian partisans. With me in Klagenfurt were Captain Kennedy MC MM, ex-Foreign Legion, Pioneer Corps and Special Services; and other ex-refugees Sergeant Forrester, an ex-German, and Charly Braun, originally from Vienna.

In the case of the Loibl Pass camp the commandant had already been arrested, an SS man called Winkler. We also dealt with the cases of SS General Rösener and Gauleiter Rainer. The task was to collect statements from former inmates by so-called search teams. They usually comprised of one officer investigating, one Senior NCO interpreter and a driver with jeep, or two Senior NCOs plus driver and jeep. This work necessitated travelling to Germany and France which in those days was quite a venture, even for military personnel. Crossing frontiers was only allowed in special cases. It enabled me to see the devastation caused by the war, especially in Germany in towns like Düsseldorf and Berlin. I thought they got what they asked for. I worked for almost a week to translate a speech by one of the prosecutors, a barrister from the Inns of Court on what is meant in English law by 'innocent unless proved guilty beyond reasonable doubt'. Especially the 'beyond reasonable doubt' bit was difficult. However we obtained a verdict. The Allied Military

Court, a British Colonel, two British and two French Officers issued death sentences and the executions were carried out in Graz.

For the case of the Ardeatine Cave Massacre it fell upon my team to establish the whereabouts of certain units at the critical time in order to find out who might have been involved. The commanding general of one of the divisions had been arrested in order to be interviewed and I was the interpreter. I collected him from the local jail. A smallish man in a long greatcoat that had once been a uniform, more a harmless mouse than a commandant. The interview took place in the local town hall. A huge table covered by a large scale map of the relevant area had been placed in the centre of the room. There was also a selection of coloured flags to be used as markers. After the usual preliminaries I asked the man in the greatcoat to mark the dispositions of his troops on the map. For a while he looked down on the map. Then he drew himself up, took off his coat and selected a flag. 'My headquarters', he said and suddenly every inch a general. One could almost hear him issuing orders, proving to us what a good general he had been. It left a lasting impression on me. Nothing much came out of it. The case however produced verdicts and one of the sentenced officers was the last war criminal to be released from an Italian jail in the 1960s and returned to Austria.[18]

Another ex-refugee who worked in War Crimes Group SE Europe was Jack Knight. His work tracking war criminals was outlined in the previous chapter.

The War Crimes Investigation Units in Germany and Austria had some measure of success, but it was always going to be an impossible task to gather sufficient evidence against some of the Nazi war criminals. Inevitably, some of them lived out their lives in peace in other countries, never facing justice. Fred Pelican comments in his autobiography:

I was appalled to hear of the closing down of my unit in 1948. In plain terms it amounted to the renouncing of justice. This decision, no doubt, must have come from the highest political quarters. Who were the men who literally gave *carte blanche* to those who had escaped our clutches? Commendably, forty years after the end of the war, an all-party parliamentary war crimes group was formed. While it has no executive powers, its dedication in seeking justice must be highly commended. I am fully aware of the great difficulty any government would encounter bringing alleged war criminals to justice.[19]

The War Crimes Investigation Units in Germany and Austria had their work cut out. Were they successful? Gruber argues:

> As long as the prosecution of war crimes rested with the military of the allies, justice was more or less done. When for both practical and more so for political reasons, the Cold War was on, the fronts had changed, the trials were handed over to the German and Austrian authorities, expediency took precedence over justice, but that is another story.[20]

Notes

1. Based on interviews with the author.
2. Documents in Freud family papers; also Fred Pelican, *From Dachau to Dunkirk*, pp. 109–11, 112–24.
3. Leopold Falkensammer, *The British Officer Told Me to Write My Story*, p. 1. Copy lent to the author.
4. Unpublished papers in the Freud archive at the IWM and Freud family papers; also Pelican, *From Dachau to Dunkirk*, pp. 171–92.
5. Video interview with Walter Freud by Bea Lewkowicz, the Jewish Museum, London.
6. Walter Freud, *An Austrian Grandfather*.
7. PRO, ref: WO235/83.
8. See extensive references to Perry Broad in Herman Rothman, *Hitler's Will*.
9. Freud, *An Austrian Grandfather*, chapter 1, pp. 4–5.
10. He died on 16 January 1950.
11. William Manchester, *The Arms of Krupp*, p. 657.
12. Fred Warner, *Personal Account of SOE Period*, unpublished memoirs.
13. Ibid., p. 103.
14. Ibid., p. 99.
15. Ibid., pp. 100–2.
16. Ibid., p. 107.
17. Extensive correspondence with the author.
18. Based on extensive correspondence with the author.
19. Pelican, p. 197.
20. Interview and correspondence with the author.

Four

WAR CRIMES TRIALS
AND COURTS

On Tuesday 20 November 1945 the Nuremberg Trials opened. It was history in the making as an International Tribunal was sitting for the first time for new crimes which had never before been tried in such a court. The men and women defendants were being charged on four accounts: crimes against peace, war crimes, crimes against humanity and conspiracy to commit other crimes. In the dock sat the top echelon of the Nazi regime: Hermann Göring, Rudolf Höss, Joachim von Ribbentrop, Ernst Kaltenbrunner, Alfred Rosenberg, Hans Frank, Julius Streicher, Erich Raeder, Hjalmar Schacht, Franz von Papen, Wilhelm Frick, Fritz Sauckel, Robert Ley, Arthur Seyss-Inquart, Albert Speer, Wilhelm Keitel, Karl Dönitz, Alfred Jodl and Constantin von Neurath. As some of the perpetrators of the atrocities were gradually brought to trial, the enemy aliens in the British forces were called upon to carry out translation work. Every town and city court needed interpreters and this is where the German-speaking refugees in the forces came to the fore. Their work often overlapped with the war crimes investigations and sometimes brought them in close proximity to the highest ranking Nazi war criminals. Captain Forest (originally from Vienna) and Captain Palmer acted as court translators with Captain W. Frank and Sergeant Hachenberg as the main interpreters at Nuremberg. Dr Hans Hachenberg (b. Mannheim, 1897), a lawyer who had survived Dachau and served in 249 Company Pioneer Corps, became an interpreter at the Trials after the war. Roger Bryan (Roger Britzmann, b. Berlin) also became a translator in court. Having come to England prior to the outbreak of war, he was interned in 1940 and sent to Australia. On release he then served in the Pioneer Corps. In 1946 he was assigned to the Neuengamme concentration camp, outside Hamburg, to document war crimes and interrogate soldiers and Nazi officials. Shortly afterwards he transferred to the Nuremberg Trials, of which he wrote: 'I translated German terms and phrases for British prosecutors in the courtroom. To see the whole rogues' gallery of defendants, not more than 20 feet in front of me, was overwhelming. Goering, with a derisive grin most of the time, Streicher, Rudolf Hess and other Nazi criminals. Hess was either a great actor or mentally disturbed.'[1]

After the Trials, Roger Bryan worked for the British Film and Documentation Unit of the RAF. The work could be unexpectedly traumatic. Sometimes it brought men like him into direct contact with the horrendous crimes perpetrated in the Holocaust. Bryan wrote of his work with the film unit: 'We had samples of tattooed human skin that had been made into lamp shades and gloves. Even more devastating was the collection of photographs taken by German soldiers. The most haunting one showed a trench the prisoners had dug before being shot at the edge of it. One of the victims looked like my mother. I had trouble sleeping for nights.'[2]

In December 1945 Bill Oakfield (b. Werner Oppenheim) arrived at the Nuremberg Trials to undertake duties as a translator: 'I was plunged into the most harrowing experience of my life. I had just found out from a friend of my mother's, who survived Theresienstadt, that my parents had been transported to Auschwitz in September 1944 and not been heard of since.'[3] In the courtroom he faced Göring, Kaltenbrunner, Streicher and the others. His lasting impression of that period was the day he heard the president of the court pronounce the death sentence over most of the accused. At the end of October 1946 he was demobbed: 'The train steamed out of the station just as the blood-sun was setting over the accursed city of Nuremberg. At last I was able to look forward to a normal life after the most terrible seven years of the 20th century.'[4]

★★★

The Trials at Nuremberg were not the only war crimes trials to be opened in the autumn of 1945. The Allies had caught a number of named and suspected war criminals who were awaiting trial. British teams had been conducting war crimes investigations and preparing evidence for the Belsen Trial – for war crimes committed at Belsen concentration camp, which British forces had liberated on 15 April that year. Josef Kramer, the Commandant of Belsen, was being held in a fortress in eastern Belgium, awaiting trial. Ex-refugee Tony Hare (Anton Haas, b. Moravia) was in charge of his welfare. Hare recalls:

> Kramer was a tall and exceptionally strong man, over 6 feet, reportedly a doctor of medicine, which enabled him to think up the various medical experiments and cruelties which took place. My job consisted mainly of talking to him every morning, seeing that he was properly looked after with a toothbrush and similar toilet articles. It was his only possibility to talk to someone in his own language. At the time when I first saw him he had been imprisoned there for several days and had just had time to think, to become aware of the situation and realise some of the deeds he had done. Increasingly every morning, he complained of 'brainstorms' which kept him from sleeping. He cried like a child when these moments of clarity came ... I saw very clearly that this man had already been judged and condemned before he even stood before a human court. In a way that I could not explain at all at the time, it gave me the feeling that there was a higher justice.[5]

Also being held at the fortress was Heinrich Himmler's brother. Hare found that this man had opposing views to that of his brother. In conversations with him, Hare saw a completely different man – one of moderation with an alternative outlook to Heinrich Himmler, who had reached the level of Reichsführer SS.

On 17 September 1945, the Belsen Trial opened at Lüneburg. A team of prosecutors sat at a military war crimes tribunal where they heard evidence against Commandant Josef Kramer and forty-four guards of the Belsen concentration camp. The judge advocate was C.L. Stirling, Esq., CBE, KC, and the counsel for the prosecution consisted of Colonel T.M. Backhouse, MBE, TD; Major H.G. Murton-Neale; Captain S.M. Stewart; and Lieutenant Colonel L.J. Genn. One prosecutor was Viennese-born lawyer Stephen Malcolm Stewart (Stephen Strauss). During 1945–47 he was to play a key role in the prosecution teams at a number of war crimes trials. Prior to the war, the Nazis had considered him a left-wing lawyer. Consequently his life was at risk. He fled Austria, was smuggled into Poland and came to Britain, where he was eventually drafted into the Pioneer Corps. In 1940 he was appointed a liaison officer with the Free French Forces and the Belgian army. In 1945, in the rank of major, he was assigned to the judge advocate general's office of the 21st Army. In September 1945 Stewart was appointed assistant prosecutor in the tribunal convened in Lüneburg, for the trial of those involved in the Belsen atrocities. In his opening prosecution statement in Lüneburg he addressed the issue that the Allies were accused of exacting revenge as the victors. He firmly outlined that nothing could be further from the truth and such assertions were not only dangerous, but also wrong in law. He went on to establish why the defendants were being prosecuted for war crimes and the nature of their guilt:

Captain Stewart, sworn, examined by Colonel Backhouse said – I am Captain on the legal section of the Judge Advocate General's branch, Headquarters, British Army of the Rhine, and produce an analysis made from 1875 death certificates referring to persons who died at Belsen Camp. These are ordinary death certificates made by the German authorities at the camp. I made the analysis in three ways: first, according to cause of death; second, by nationalities of the deceased; third, according to periods of time covered by each of the series of certificates. Regarding causes of death, I found that 22 people had died of old age, 46 from exhaustion, 31 from Pneumonia, 199 from tuberculosis, 1297 from weakness and 280 from other causes. With regard to 264 Hungarians, 258 Poles, 139 Stateless, 113 Belgians, 70 Italians, 29 Albanians, 25 Croatians, 20 Yugoslavs, 15 English and 190 other nationalities. On 22 May 1945, I went to the citadel at Diest and read out, in view with Major Pollard, when I had acted as interpreter. This statement he signed. No pressure was made whatsoever on Josef Kramer, either to make or to sign that statement.

Captain Stewart then read to the court the statement by Josef Kramer, Exhibit No 12.

Anita Lasker-Wallfisch, who as a survivor of Belsen had been helped by an ex-Berliner in the British forces, Captain Howard Alexander, mentioned in Chapter 2, became a key witness at the Belsen Trial. She writes:

I was called as a witness. The trial struck me as a huge race. I came face to face with British justice, under which you are innocent unless proven guilty for the first time. This is no doubt a commendable principle, but it is difficult to apply or even adapt to the sort of crimes that were being dealt with in Lüneburg. I saw them there all lined up: Kramer (the Belsen Camp Commander), Klein (a doctor), Grese, the lot, and with them, admittedly at the end of the line, some of the Kapos who had distinguished themselves by their bestial behaviour towards their fellow prisoners. My command of the English language was reasonably good by then and I was able to dispense with an interpreter. First, I had to identify the prisoners. That was easy enough. (I wonder what went through Kramer's head when I identified him?)

Then came the absurd aspect of the proceedings. For example, there were questions like: '… did you ever see any of these people kill anybody?' If you answered 'yes', the next question would be: 'which day of the week was this, and what time exactly?' Naturally you had to answer 'I don't know'. You were under oath but in the camp you had neither a watch nor a calendar, nor would you have been the slightest bit interested whether it was Monday or Tuesday. That you simply could not answer such a question was enough to make you feel you were not telling the truth. It was hard for me to reconcile myself to the fact that these criminals actually had a counsel for their defence, just as in a normal British law court.[6]

The court closed on 17 November 1945. At the end of the trial, lasting eight weeks, twelve of the defendants received the death sentence. At the top of the list were Josef Kramer, Irma Grese, SS Dr Fritz Klein, Elisabeth Völkenrath and Franz Hössler. Less than a month later, on 13 December 1945, the twelve were all hanged on the same day in Hameln Prison. Nineteen others received various lengths of prison sentences, whilst the others were acquitted and released.

In 1946 Stephen Stewart, mentioned above, was responsible for preparing the evidence against fourteen members of staff of the Neuengamme concentration camp and presided as principal prosecutor at their trial in Hamburg. Then as chief prosecutor, he headed the legal team which investigated and prosecuted those responsible for torture and the deaths of tens of thousands of women in the Ravensbrück concentration camp. Its capacity was supposed to hold 6,000 inmates. At the time of its liberation in April 1945 it held 36,000. Stewart was instrumental in gathering eye-witness testimonies from the survivors of the camp. One of the key witnesses was SOE resistance heroine Odette Churchill, who had suffered horrific torture in Ravensbrück. Stewart's evidence read out at the war crimes trials was often the first time such atrocities were heard in public. The result shocked the world.

***

Clive Teddern (Kurt Tebrich) found himself back in Hamburg, the city of his birth, on war crimes trials. In his unpublished memoirs he gives a vivid account of what it was like to return to the city devastated by Allied bombing:

It is strange to be living once more in the city of my childhood. I remember the Sunday morning routine when my parents and I, reluctantly, walked round the Alster Lake. We passed these villas without much thought of their occupants. What happened to them? Many of the buildings on the other side have disappeared, others re-open memories. The swans still look the same. On the skyline, I recognise once more the church steeples whose names I had to learn at school. There are fewer and some show extensive damage. It is strange to hear the flat twang of Hamburg dialect, to see childhood familiar places. The industrial suburbs; the docks have been flattened; the area where I played, lived and dreamed, died in the firestorm of '43. The commercial area, the main shopping and entertainment centre remained comparatively unscathed. The part where the Jewish community lived is still intact. It was only the Jewish people who were destroyed.[7]

He reported to whom he describes as 'a non-military looking Sergeant Major with a very strong central European accent'. 'Welcome to the War Crime Trial Centre', he told Teddern. The following morning Teddern walked up the steps of the war crimes trial centre and recalls:

This building too holds memories: it used to be the Assembly Hall where the 'German Jewish Youth' organisation held its annual performance of songs and sketches before we were banned by the Nazis. Now the rather ugly hall and some of the adjoining areas have been converted into a Court Room. The large complex also houses offices and detention cells. I look into one court where a number of concentration camp guards wait to be sent to the gallows, including the infamous, tearful Irmgard Grese. 'I am innocent. I was only obeying orders! I had no choice!'

The case I was involved in is called the 'Terror Flyers Case'. The trial concerned an order issued by General Keitel to the effect that Allied airmen shot down over Germany were not to be protected against attacks by the populace. They were labelled 'Terror Flyers' and as such denied the protection of the Geneva Convention. Quite a number of them were torn to pieces after air raids while their guards looked on. The accused is the General in charge of all Home Command Luftwaffe formations (those based on German soil), General-Oberst Stumpff. In the dock he looks like someone's kindly grandfather. Captain Sanders explains the legal structure which is completely different to the many charges of a conventional court: 'In War Crimes there are only three charges: Crimes against Peace, War Crimes and Crimes against Humanity. All carry the death penalty.'[8]

Stumpff was accused of endorsing the Keitel Order by passing it to units under his command. He denied this. Teddern remembers the trial clearly:

There is clear evidence that the Keitel Order was put into effect on many occasions but he has an excellent defence team. They produced a number of Luftwaffe officers who were brought in from internment camps. Right arrogant swine they were. Typical blond Aryan examples of Teutonic manhood. Naturally they swore blind that they had never seen that order. But were there no others? We also have his secretary. It is quite clear that she has seen that order but apparently her loyalty has been established horizontally. She is not very bright but stubbornly loyal; queries the translations whenever she is caught out in a porkie. There is one witness, a real hero – an insignificant little man with glasses and really puny. He was administrating officer at a Luftwaffe base. As a practising Catholic, when he came across the Keitel Order, he could not justify it with his deeply felt religious convictions and instead of passing it on to the base commander, he 'lost' it. He was found out and was only saved from the firing squad when the Americans overran the base. The trial dragged on for eight weeks, witnesses are re-called. Lord Justice Stirling, who presides over the court, gives a brilliant summing up but after long deliberations Stumpff is acquitted. Of course he is not set free but goes back to an internment camp. We all know that he is guilty but it cannot be proved. The day after the acquittal, two Canadian RCAF officers turn up with written statements by former Canadian POWs. If that evidence had been available a few days earlier, Stumpff would have hanged!

A British Military Court convened in Essen on 18–19 December and 21/22 December 1945 for the trial of two Germans and a number of civilians in the killing of three British airmen. Hauptmann Heyer, a captain in the German army, and Private Koenen were alleged to have been instrumental in the shooting of the three RAF pilots. Three German civilians, Johann Braschoss, Karl Kaufer and Hugo Boddenberg, were also implicated in their deaths. All were found guilty by the British court. Private Koenen, Karl Kaufer and Hugo Boddenberg received jail sentences. Hauptmann Heyer and Johann Braschoss received death sentences. On 8 March 1946 they were both hanged. Later that year, in October 1946, another court convened in Essen for the trial of twenty-two Germans accused of shooting British RAF pilots. Peter Eden (Werner Engel, b. Breslau) was in attendance as an interpreter.[9] Before the trial, Eden had been stationed in Düsseldorf with Field Security (the Intelligence Corps), in charge of security at the Stahof, HQ of British Military Government. He also spent time in Cologne, from where he and an officer from Scotland Yard visited a number of prisons under their jurisdiction. This included Klingelputz in Cologne, a prison holding 2,000 civilian prisoners; the high security prison Zuchthaus in Siegburg, again for civilian prisoners; and Bonn Prison. Eden can vividly recall the war crimes trial at Essen that autumn of 1946:

> The twenty-two accused sat in a boxed area with a lawyer each for their defence seated in front of them. They were surrounded by armed military police. It was quite a scene. The presiding judge was O'Neill. The twenty-two were accused of taking the airmen to a cemetery and shooting them. Two airmen feigned death and survived. They were picked up by our unit. We produced them at the trial as witnesses. All the accused were sentenced by the court.[10]

It was during Eden's next posting to Munsterlager, a huge holding camp for German POWs, that his unit was assigned to arrest and interrogate war criminals. In February 1947 they brought one of the guards of the *Totenkopf* – Death's Head SS squad from Belsen concentration camp. Eden remembers:

> There were seven of us in my section, nicknamed 'the Avengers'. In March 1947 we arrested the likes of Margaret Vollrath, an SS guard at Ravensbrück. She was hanged after a verdict of guilty before a British war crimes trial. We had a list of over 30,000 names of wanted people, all categorized. It was called CROWCASS – pretty much like a telephone directory. We spent most of our time interrogating people, especially German soldiers. They had all disposed of their papers and identification. The first priority was to remove their shirts and see whether they had an SS blood group tattoo on their arm. If so, there was no doubt about them – they were under immediate arrest and transferred to another British unit. If not, we spent a substantial amount of time interrogating them to find out where they had served in the war, which unit, which commander. Of course, they all denied everything and said they hadn't been Nazis. We often suspected otherwise and continued interrogations until we pieced together their story. We had been taught to remember where every German regiment fought in the war,

the names of every commanding officer and second-in-command, and all insignia of German soldiers.

It was a busy time at Munsterlager. From one day to the next, Eden did not know what was in store for him and his unit. At Christmas 1946 they were suddenly sent on a combined operation with the Americans called Operation Snatch: 'The German Werewolves [die-hard Nazis] were still operating as an underground movement and had threatened to spread bacteria. The Allied powers decided to hunt the groups down. That night we arrested 600 people who were then transferred for special investigation.'

Peter Eden was eventually demobbed in May 1947.

★★★

A number of other enemy aliens were employed in vital work in the courts: George Bennett (Artur Bratu, b. Offenbach) became prosecutor in the court in Dormstadt; and Herbert Anderson (Helmut Fuerst, b. Vienna), who had been with the SOE, served as chief interpreter at the trial of fifteen members of the management board of Volkswagen. Michael Merton (Ludwig Georg Blumenfeld, b. Berlin), firstly in the Pioneer Corps and then 3 Troop of No 10 Inter-Allied Commando, became prosecutor in the Military Court in Düsseldorf and then Intelligence Service in Kiel. David Michael Compton (Hans Gunther Hoffman, b. Hamburg) was accepted for parachute training and served with the 21st Independent Parachute Company.[11] He saw action during Operation Manna, a parachute drop near Athens, then Operation Kelso for the occupation of the Greek island of Salonika, and service in Italy. At the end of the war Compton volunteered for interpreter duties and was accepted. He was posted to the 820 Detachment of Control Commission for Germany, Allied Military Government in Lübeck, where he acted as the chief interpreter at the Military Court: 'It was a very interesting period as we dealt with any breach of regulations or laws by the civilian population from being in possession of goods of Allied origin (perhaps cigarettes or chocolate which we had bartered with them ourselves!!) to theft, rape and murder committed mainly by some of the thousands of Displaced Persons in the area.'

Ex-Berliner Herman Rothman (b. Hermann Rothmann), who was amongst those who translated parts of Hitler's will, detailed in the next chapter, found himself as a witness in the Auschwitz Trial in Frankfurt in 1964–65. Eighteen years earlier he had been working in the same office as some German POWs, one of whom was Perry Broad. Broad had at one time been administrator at Auschwitz and had been arrested by the British on suspicion of war crimes but released again. Whilst he had been working in Rothman's office, he had been encouraged by Rothman to write down as much as he could about his life. This constituted Perry Broad's diaries. Six copies of the diaries were made, but only one seemed to have survived in Rothman's attic. In the early 1960s Broad was re-arrested. In 1964 he stood before the court on charges of war crimes. The only surviving copy of his diaries was sent to the War Office and used in the trial. It was to prove crucial evidence for the prosecutors. Rothman wrote about the trial and Perry Broad in his autobiography:

> I entered the hall and took my place on the raised dais. It became clear to me why this particular venue had been chosen. To the left were seated nearly all the defendants, together with their respective counsels and their advisers and assistants; and to the right sat the prosecuting counsel with their entourage. There were a great number of interested parties, as well as the worldwide press occupying the rear of the hall. In the gallery sat the public. The first one or two rows were reserved for VIPs. I was sworn in and the questioning began in German.
>
> When I had finished my evidence, the chairman of the court interrupted the proceedings to welcome in the sixty-nine-year-old international Jewish leader and world chairman of the Zionist Federation, Nahum Goldman, accompanied by his entourage. They took their seats in the front row of the public gallery. My father revered this man and to my family and me he was a legendary figure. Understandably, the judge paid him this honour. The chairman then continued and announced that the diary of Perry Broad would be read aloud to the court; the reading to be shared with two of his colleagues. There was a short break and the judges reconvened.
>
> After a short explanation about the background of Broad's diary, he commenced reading aloud to an absolutely silent court. The delivery of Perry Broad's diary made a completely unexpected impact amongst the public and officials in this makeshift courtroom. It impressed me greatly that the chief justice started the reading, two judges continued after him, and then he finished the last part. The descriptions read out produced diverse reactions from the audience. There were cries of horror and anguish. People screamed out and several fainted. I realised that when I had first read this report some eighteen years before, there was a multitude of horrors being continuously

reported on the radio and in the press, and this report was just one of many hundreds. The atrocities had become almost part of daily life. I myself had visited Bergen-Belsen shortly after its liberation. Now, eighteen years later, when people thought they had heard everything and laid it to rest, it was suddenly all churned up again in greater force. Examined during the trial under oath, I confirmed that Perry Broad had written the diary by himself and that it roughly covered what Broad had told me in person.[12]

Perry Broad was found guilty of war crimes and sentenced to four years imprisonment.

Working at the war crimes trials was never going to be easy for the enemy aliens. It brought them physically close to the perpetrators of the most horrendous crimes against humanity and, in many cases, those who had sent their own family members to their deaths. However, although it did not bring back their families murdered in the Holocaust, it gave satisfaction to see these men and women brought to justice. Although the major trials had been closed by the end of 1946, smaller trials would continue in the coming decades.

Notes

1. Quoted from obituary in *The North Devon Journal*, 28 August 2008, p. 16.
2. Ibid.
3. Quoted from Alan Gill, *Interrupted Journeys*, p. 202.
4. Ibid.
5. Tony Hare, *Spanning the Century*, pp. 121–2.
6. Anita Lasker-Wallfisch, *Inherit the Truth*, p. 124.
7. Clive Teddern, *Boy with a Suitcase*, unpublished memoirs, copy given to the author, p. 95.
8. Ibid., p. 96.
9. Eden had been interned on the *Dunera* in Australia for a year, and returned to England to join the Pioneer Corps. Then eventually he landed at Algiers with the 1st Army and worked with the explosives corps of the Royal Engineers. After North Africa, he served in Palestine until 1945.
10. Interviews with the author in 2004 and 2009.
11. David Compton, *Life Story of a Friendly Enemy Alien Paratrooper Pathfinder*.
12. Herman Rothman, *Hitler's Will*, pp. 154–5.

Five

INTERPRETERS, INTERROGATORS AND TRANSLATORS

Work as interpreters, interrogators and translators varied for the enemy aliens in the British army from civil or domestic court work to war crimes trials and all aspects of military and civic government. This work often overlapped with war crimes investigations and sometimes brought them into close proximity to the highest ranking Nazi war criminals. Their roles as interpreters provided an important part of post-war administration. Every unit functioning in post-war Germany and Austria needed its share of German-speakers. Major Reitlinger, who had been drafted into the SOE, became interpreter to the British High Commissioner and commander-in-chief of the British forces in Austria. Henry Mortimer (Heinrich Mosenthal) of the First Tank Regiment, whilst stationed at Itzehoe, acted as interpreter to the Military Court at Rendsburg, near Kiel Canal in Schleswig-Holstein. Because of his legal knowledge, he quickly rose to the position of court administrator. Work as court interpreter and examination of war criminals was also the brief of Alfred Summerfield (Sommerfeld, b. East Prussia) who was attached to the Coldstream Guards, stationed at the HQ of No 1 Army Corps. Peter Wayne (Dieter Wolff, b. Berlin) became chief interpreter at the war crimes tribunal in Minden post-1945 in North Rhine Westphalia.

As interrogators, the enemy aliens had a strong sense of integrity to act above their Nazi persecutors, through the responsibility invested in them by the British army uniform. Often they adapted their own highly effective means of interrogation, based on their previous experience of how the

German mentality operated. In his autobiography *Accidental Journey*, Mark Lynton, who conducted interrogations for a short time with his unit in Berlin, Hamburg and Kiel, offers some observations on techniques:[1]

– Silence is a great interrogation tool. Look at your man and say nothing; let him start talking. If he stops, keep quiet, let him start again. It does not always work and before getting into a trappist séance, you had better say something but give it a try.

– Always give the impression that you already know most of what he is telling you; do not ever look or act surprised.

– The more startling the information you get, the less you should react immediately. Just let it go by, let him talk of something else, come back to it later, and on a 'just by the way' basis.

– Take your time, set your own pace, do not have outside interruptions (unless they suit you, in which case, stage them).

– Always ask open-ended, oblique, 'laundry list' questions; do not tip your hand as to what you are looking for. 'Are you a war criminal?' will not elicit a very informative response.

– Keep control of your interrogation pattern; make up your mind whether and when you want to cajole or bully, be empathetic, or be remote, and when and whether you want to switch moods. Do not lose your thread or your temper (unless it suits your pattern).

– Almost all interrogations are 'jigsaws'; he will not tell the whole story in sequence, and sometimes he really only knows parts of it. Try and get a grasp of the general outline as soon as you can and note the missing parts. Keep on fishing for them as the interrogation progresses.

– Above all, listen! Listen to what is being said, how it is being said, what is not being said.

Gary Leon (Gerhard Leon, b. Berlin), who worked for a branch of MI5, was posted to Kempton Park Racecourse outside London, where there was a prisoner-of-war Interrogation Section (Home).[2] Here the unit was expecting the arrival of German POWs: 'We had to take away their identity papers because they contained the units to which the soldiers belonged. It was all rather a muddle since neither the officers nor we knew exactly what to look for once we had the papers. However, after a day or two we were properly briefed each morning, with directions from the War Office, so that we became a very efficient unit.'

After Kempton Park, Leon was posted to a house in Kensington Palace Gardens, where the unit had offices, interrogation rooms and secure facilities to hold prisoners. Leon comments:

Mine was an interesting and responsible job. One incident of many has remained in my recollection. We were trying to get some information from a group of German prisoners concerning their precise orders before they were captured. They remained totally uncooperative, until one of them broke his silence and started giving us some details. Next morning he was found hanging in his cell, murdered by his comrades. At the subsequent Old Bailey trial my CO, a certain Col. Scotland, gave evidence. That afternoon, the *Evening Standard* ran a story, repeated the following morning in the *Daily Express*, under the banner headline 'Master Spy Oberst Schottland'. It was stated that my commanding officer was in fact a spy with access to Hitler's General Staff. The allegation was, of course, unfounded.

Getting information out of prisoners was not always easy. It could take painstaking hours of patience and questioning. Leon recalls:

I was interrogating a rather difficult prisoner. He was a German sergeant, who had participated in the shooting of about a dozen British soldiers whom his unit had captured in battle. I was trying to get him to admit this crime. He would not talk. I asked him if he was married and told that he had a wife and a little daughter. I asked where they were and he told me. I then put it to him that the Russians were about to take that town, if indeed they were not already in it, and a word from me to the Soviet Embassy next door would make sure that he would never see his wife and child again. He broke down and told me enough for the case to be brought to trial after the war in Hamburg. Unfortunately for me he was able to plead undue influence, in that his confession had been extracted from him by threats on my part. He mentioned the location of the Russian Embassy as being 'next door'. I was very disappointed to have slipped up in this instance, to have let him get away with his criminal breach of the Geneva Convention.[3]

Henry Stenhàm (Heinz Sternheim, b. Hamburg) transferred from the Pioneer Corps to the Intelligence Section of the Interpreters Corps, stationed in Berleburg, Westphalia. From regimental HQ he was sent out to POW camps to conduct interrogations: 'The POWs I encountered were

1 Invasion troops enter Berlin. The lead tank of the Royal Armoured Corps is being driven by ex-refugee Willy Field. *Courtesy of Willy Field*

2 The Victory Parade, Berlin, 21 July 1945. *Courtesy of Willy Field*

3　Charlottenburg district of Berlin, May 1945. *Courtesy of John Langford*

5 Surrender of POWs on the German border. *Courtesy of John Langford*

6 Surrender of POWs, 2 May 1945. Ex-refugee John Langford is the British soldier in the foreground. *Courtesy of John Langford*

Opposite 4 The German Parliament, Berlin. *Courtesy of Willy Field*

7 Bombed ruins of Hitler's Chancery, Berlin, May 1945. *Courtesy of Willy Field*

8 Inside Hitler's bunker, Berlin. *Courtesy of David Brett*

9 Outside the courthouse of the Belsen Trial, September 1945. *Courtesy of David Brett*

10 Hans Alexander who was in the team that arrested Rudolf Höss and Oswald Pohl. *Courtesy of Hans Alexander*

11 Rudolf Höss, the notorious Commandant of Auschwitz. *Courtesy of Gerry Moore*

12 The site of the Potsdam Conference, July 1945. *Courtesy of John Langford*

13 Prime Minister Winston Churchill's study at Potsdam. *Courtesy of John Langford*

14 John Langford, Churchill's bodyguard at Potsdam. *Courtesy of John Langford*

15 Potsdam, July
1945. *Courtesy of John
Langford*

16 Potsdam, July
1945. *Courtesy of John
Langford*

17 John Langford at
a party where they
lifted the floorboards
in search of Himmler.
*Courtesy of John
Langford*

18 Geoffrey Perry delivers the first Allied broadcast from Radio Hamburg with the microphone last used by William Joyce two days earlier. *Courtesy of Geoffrey Perry*

19 Reconstruction of the shooting of William Joyce (aka Lord Haw-Haw). *Courtesy of Geoffrey Perry*

20 William Joyce moments after his arrest by Geoffrey Perry. *Courtesy of Geoffrey Perry*

21 William Joyce being taken away by British soldiers after being shot and arrested by Geoffrey Perry. *Courtesy of Geoffrey Perry*

22 War Crimes Tribunal, Essen, 1946.
Courtesy of Peter Eden

23 Peter Eden. *Courtesy of Peter Eden*

24 Herman Rothman in the office at Fallingbostel where he translated Goebbels' addendum to Hitler's will. *Courtesy of Herman Rothman*

25 No 3 Counter-Intelligence Section at Fallingbostel, 1945. Standing at the back, from left to right: Henry Roberts and Ralph Parker. In front row: Herman Rothman between two members of staff. *Courtesy of Herman Rothman*

27 The White House, Wilton Park, used by the CSDIC. *Courtesy of Fritz Lustig*

28 The permanent staff of 300 POW camp, Wilton Park, at the end of the war. All are German POWs, except Lt Eric Bourne (in beret in second row, seated), Lt Col. St Clare Grondona and Capt Ritchie. *Courtesy of Eric Bourne*

Opposite 26 Staff of No 2 Distribution Centre of Combined Services Detailed Interrogation Centre (CSDIC) in front of Latimer House. Most are German refugees serving in the British Forces. *Courtesy of Fritz Lustig*

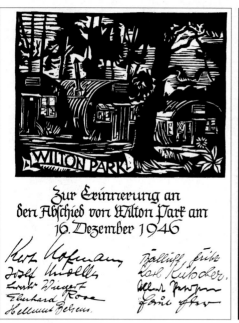

29 & 30 Lino drawings by German POWs, given to Eric Bourne at 300 POW camp, Wilton Park. *Courtesy of Eric Bourne*

31 Christmas card given to Eric Bourne by one of the German POWs at Wilton Park. *Courtesy of Eric Bourne*

Top 32 German POW camp at Laindon, Essex. Peter Sinclair is standing by artifacts made by the German POWs in the camp. *Courtesy of Peter Sinclair*

Above 33 Staff of German POW camp at Laindon. All are German POWs, except Peter Sinclair who is seated third from the left. *Courtesy of Peter Sinclair*

34 Peter Sinclair of the Royal Fusiliers. *Courtesy of Peter Sinclair*

35 The Farm Hall listening team. From left to right: Brodie, Heilbron, Rittner, Ganz, unknown, unknown, Pulay, Lehmann. *Courtesy of Peter Ganz*

36 Hans Engel of the Royal Army Medical Corps who carried out relief work with the survivors of Belsen and Sandbostel camps. *Courtesy of Dr Hans Engel*

37 Rudy Karrell, transferred to D Detachment, No 2 T Force Unit in Hamburg in charge of civil labour at the Hotel Reichshof, which housed the German atomic bomb scientists. *Courtesy of Rudy Karrell*

tired of the war and ready for peace,' he says. Stenham also visited various munitions factories to check they had ceased producing arms and converted their business to civilian use. 'I visited factories, for example, where aluminium planes were manufactured. They had changed to the production of aluminium cooking pots instead.' Every day, Stenham was required to attend morning church services to monitor what was being said. 'Germans at that time were not allowed to meet in groups of more than about ten. These church services attracted 200–300 people. They didn't know that this British soldier could understand all they were saying. One of the sermons, I recall, was at the time of Hiroshima. The priest said that the Allies were lucky that the Germans didn't get the atomic bomb first because the war would have ended in a different way. That sermon always stuck with me in later years.'[4]

The work of the enemy aliens at the end of the war was to have some unexpected surprises, as the following story demonstrates. A group of five German-speaking refugees were posted to Fallingbostel, a village south-east of Bremen. They were assigned to No 3 Counter-Intelligence Corps of the British army under Captain Rollo Reid. Fallingbostel camp, known as Stalag 11B, was finally liberated by British forces in mid-April 1945. It became an internment camp run by British forces for holding German POWs. The five German-speakers were Herman Rothman, Henry Howard Marcel Roberts (Hans Hermann Herzfeld, b. Peine), Ralph Parker, Peter Blake (formerly Blau) and Ernest Alastair Gordon MacGarrety. It was here that, in November 1945, they were part of an extraordinary find that would take them close to the last days of Adolf Hitler. Rothman writes:

> Given our strict adherence to routine, it came as a huge shock when the telephone rang at 5 a.m. one autumn morning. We were all naturally fast asleep. I thought it was part of my dream, but the telephone continued to ring. Then I realised it was no dream but something of importance. I picked it up and heard Rollo Reid say, 'Please come to the office immediately. I will explain then.' To say it sounded strange would be an understatement. My mind was racing as I quickly dressed, had a coffee and dashed to the office. We all assembled before Reid … Reid immediately ordered one of us to lock the door. Everything appeared to be odd. What could be so important for all of us to be summoned to one room and the door locked?[5]

A German by the name of Heinz Lorenz was captured on the border and brought into Fallingbostel POW camp. In the camp Lance Bombardier

Rowe, who was experienced in the tailoring business before the war, had grown suspicious of the shoulder pads of Lorenz's jacket and asked for the seams to be opened. The discovery was extraordinary and unexpected. Sewn into the lining of the jacket was the last original will and testament of Adolf Hitler, plus Goebbels' addendum to Hitler's will. Captain Reid had immediately called for his team of five German-speakers. Herman Rothman recalls what happened next:

> Rollo Reid proceeded to distribute the parchments amongst us. He asked whether we could identify what we held in our hands. This was the first time I had seen such large impressive typed characters. Unanimously we burst out saying, 'This is Hitler's Will. Not a copy but the *original*.'
>
> The pages changed hands; we carefully read and scrutinised the papers and confirmed earlier findings. Captain Reid then began to organise the translation amongst us. The documents of Hitler's private Will and his political Will were given to my colleagues. Goebbels' addendum to Hitler's Political Will was given to me. We retired to our offices, one man per office and were ordered to lock the door. We were not to be disturbed until we had finished our translation. This was serious, top-secret business. Once alone I felt totally isolated. There was no one to talk to and no one to consult. My office, sparsely furnished with a desk, several chairs and filing cabinets, without home comforts, produced a surreal feeling. Realising the urgency of the translation, nevertheless, I felt momentarily handicapped by my Germanic obsession for detail which caused a break in my work. I read the addendum several times to understand what Goebbels wished to convey. My first reaction on reading it endorsed my opinion of the man – blindly loyal, a lover of words and opinionated. Goebbels camouflaged reality, equating his power base with that of Hitler. Goering and Himmler in contrast had seen the collapse of the regime as a political opportunity to rise again by discarding Hitler but not abandoning Nazi ideology.
>
> I translated the addendum which consisted of long sentences – the specific hallmark of Goebbels; he rigidly kept to this. The opening words of the addendum were: 'In this delirium of betrayal …' When the translation was finally filed with the official government papers, my original translation of the phrase 'in this delirium of betrayal' was changed to 'in this delirium of treason'.[6]

Excited by the discovery, the team under Rollo Reid went straight to the top and informed Lieutenant-General Brian Horrocks, commander of

30 Corps District. This caused some consternation with their immediate superior Colonel Proudlock, because Proudlock had been short-circuited in the chain of command. The men were apparently due a medal for their discovery but, as Herman Rothman suggests, it seems that their failure to follow procedure led to their being denied it. The day after the discovery one member of the team, Henry Roberts, received a personal letter from Lieutenant-General Horrocks. The letter is dated 16 November 1945:

> It has been brought to my notice that on 15 November 1945 you were shown some documents which had been found by No. 1729991 L/Bdr. Rowe. On inspection of these documents you at once realised their value and took the necessary steps to bring them to the notice of the proper authorities. I wish to congratulate you on your perspicacity and initiative: by your prompt action these most valuable documents, which might easily have been overlooked, are now in safe keeping.[7]

But for Roberts' quick action the documents may never have come to light. A copy of Hitler's personal and political wills with Goebbels' addendum exists in the Imperial War Museum, London. The top-secret British intelligence report, compiled after the interrogation of Heinz Lorenz, has now been declassified at The National Archive and confirms the above events:

> Hitler's will has been discovered. It was found on Heinz Lorenz, INB journalist who had been attached to Hitler's staff since 1936. Before the war Lorenz attended a number of important conferences between Hitler and foreign statesmen and recorded the proceedings in shorthand. During the war he was attached to the Führer's headquarters and took down news received from foreign broadcasts and passed it direct to the Führer's Staff. In this capacity he was working at the bunker in the Reichchancellery from 18th April '45 onwards, his receiving set acting as the only link between the outside world and the Führer's bunker (he was unable to transmit messages). It was he who broke to Hitler the news of Mussolini's death and also of Himmler's negotiations with Count Bernadotte. He [Lorenz] was arrested in the British Zone, where he was living under an alias, taken to an internment camp and there searched. Sewn into the shoulder padding of his coat were found the following documents: Hitler's Personal Will, Hitler's Personal Testament, An Appendix by Goebbels to Hitler's Political Testament. He has been interrogated in detail on how he came into possession of these documents and he

has given a story of the last days in Hitler's bunker which agrees practically in every detail with that already given to the Press on 1st November. As he was so frequently in the bunker he was in contact with Hitler's adjutants and members of his staff and was able to obtain a very good idea of what was going on. He says that it was the news of Himmler's negotiations which made Hitler finally decide to marry Eva Braun and commit suicide. At 0400 hrs, on 29th April, Hitler made his wills, which were witnessed by Bormann, Goebbels, Gen. Krebs (Chief of the General Staff), Gen. Burgdorf and Col. von Below (Luftwaffe Adjutant at Führer HQ). Between 0900 and 1000 hrs on the same morning, Lorenz was summoned by Bormann who gave him Hitler's personal and political wills. He was then given Goebbels' declaration by Goebbels himself. He was instructed to leave Berlin at once in civilian clothes and convey the wills to [Admiral] Doenitz if possible, or failing him, the nearest German High Command ... Lorenz's story has been checked against all available evidence and appears to be entirely reliable. The signatures on the documents have been compared with other signatures of Hitler, Bormann and Goebbels and pronounced by an expert to be genuine. They have also been shown to Otto Dietrich, Hitler's Press Chief, and were immediately recognised by him. The wills bear out the evidence we have from other sources that Hitler intended to commit suicide and have his body burnt together with that of Eva Braun. He definitely states this intention in his personal will, in which he leaves all his possessions to the Party (or the State if the Party no longer exists), except for his paintings which are to be used for the foundation of a picture gallery at Linz, and any personal mementos which his family or his former Secretaries might wish to keep.[8]

Notorious business tycoon Robert Maxwell (Abraham Lajbi Hoch, b. Czech village of Slatinské Doly), who had been awarded the Military Cross by Montgomery, came into contact with another figure who was carrying a third copy of Hitler's will – Willi Johannmeier.[9] On 7 January 1946 Maxwell wrote home to his wife Betty, a French heiress and daughter of a wealthy silk mill owner: 'Willi Johannmeier who had the third copy of Adolf's testament was here with us but I am not allowed to discuss this subject any further.' Johannmeier was en route to deliver a copy of the will to Field Marshal Schoerne when he was picked up by the British. It fell to Maxwell to interrogate him at Iserlohn, but Johannmeier refused to part with the will unless Maxwell guaranteed his freedom. Maxwell was not in a position to do this. It was at this point that Hugh Trevor-Roper flew over from England to investigate the last days of Hitler. He interviewed Johannmeier and per-suaded him to hand over the will. Johannmeier was not taken into custody like Heinz Lorenz and Wilhelm Zander, the bearers of the other two copies of the will. At the time, Maxwell was well respected by his colleagues and the other ex-refugees stationed in the region. His other top-secret work at Iserlohn involved detaining Nazi war criminal and industrialist Friedrich Flick. Maxwell went out to arrest Flick and found him at his castle near Düsseldorf in bed with a 16-year-old girl. Maxwell's biographer, Joe Haines, writes of the incident: 'It was the rule that those leading Nazis arrested for suspected war crimes had to be thoroughly searched for the possession of cyanide pills. Given his nakedness, there was only one possible place where Herr Flick might have been hiding the means to suicide, but he refused to bend over until Maxwell slapped him with his officer's stick.'

No cyanide pills were found on Flick. He stood trial at Nuremberg with the other top Nazi leaders and was found guilty of using slave labour and co-operating with the SS, but not guilty of crimes against humanity. As such, Flick received a sentence of seven years' imprisonment. Maxwell also interrogated Lieutenant-Colonel Herman Gishes, the chief of German Counter-Espionage in northern France and the Low Countries, an area where it has been suspected there were double-betrayals in the deaths of British SOE agents. Gishes was eventually taken to London but no evi-dence of war crimes was found against him. During his time at Iserlohn, Maxwell also interrogated the German scientists.

★★★

The work of the enemy aliens was varied and interesting. Colin Anson (Claus Leopold Octavio Ascher, b. Berlin), mentioned in Chapter 1, fled Germany for England in February 1939. His father had died in Dachau as a political prisoner in October 1937. During the war Anson trained as part of 3 Troop, No 10 Inter-Allied Commando. With No 40 Royal Marine Commando he was involved in the invasion of Sicily and Italy, and also raids into the Yugoslav islands and Albania. At the end of the war he asked to be posted to Frankfurt with the British forces so that he might find his mother who, he discovered, had survived the war in Germany.[10] His request was granted and he was attached to the Control Commission for Germany, stationed with Field Intelligence Agency Technical [FIAT] at the British enclave at Höchst, near Frankfurt. Here his fluency in German was to be used in an aspect of the denazification process. His work with FIAT

concerned the background of German scientific and industrial factories.
He recalls:

> Frankfurt was in the American occupation zone but FIAT, based outside of
> Höchst in the original IG Farben headquarters and the village of Sindringen,
> was in effect a British enclave. All kinds of personnel were attached to FIAT
> for various duties under the charge of Colonel Davson. Most of them, both
> men and women, had been in the forces. I was assigned to Colonel Davson
> as his personal assistant. It was an extremely interesting time because we
> translated all kinds of documentation, mostly to do with industry, science,
> medical progress, and some military matters. Half of my time was spent
> translating these documents, the other half spent travelling all over Germany,
> having contact with German scientists or industrialists. I spent time working
> with interesting professionals from Britain who were at the peak of their
> careers and had come to Germany to exchange notes with their counterparts:
> doctors, visiting German generals in the Medical Corps, as well as liaising
> with surgeons and industrial scientists. I acted as translator for them. We made
> contact with their German counterparts, with whom they had had no com-
> munication during the six years of war. I prided myself on getting to the stage
> where I got ignored, so that people began talking to each other, not realising
> that there was an interpreter (me) in between. I visited underground facto-
> ries in Bavaria, met high-grade medical people in the company of a medical
> brigadier that I was interpreter for. It was a very rewarding time.[11]

Whilst posted temporarily to Berlin, Anson was given the task of translating
top-secret military documents in Albert Speer's Ministry of Weapons and
Equipment. For his work at Speer's Ministry, Anson was allocated two bilin-
gual secretaries to help get through the volume of documents:

> I rattled off chunks of documentation, translating for the secretaries to type
> up. We got through a lot of dictation work in the morning; then in the after-
> noon I dictated to the other secretary, whilst the other one transcribed the
> morning's work. It proved to be fascinating work because of the contents
> of the documents, much dealing with the development of new German
> weaponry. One was a sub-machine gun which could fire round the corner
> with a little mirror (periscope) and a curved barrel with increased bore going
> around so the bullet could get around a corner at close range. This would
> be very useful in street fighting to stay undercover whilst shooting around a

corner. Also, the casting techniques for high grade steel gun barrels. The cen-trifugal casting techniques were used for artillery gun barrels. Different grades of steel would even-out different expansion co-efficients and absorb heat, and the innermost layer would be a high-grade chrome steel for wear resistance. These were just examples of many interesting and resourceful ingenuities. But the most interesting aspect was the departmental in-fighting where, for instance, the production facilities of the ammunition to suit the StG 44, the sub-machine gun/assault rifle which had the curved-barrel version, were diverted by someone outranking those who were demanding increased pro-duction. The generals were screaming for more assault rifles to provide the increased volume of fire desperately needed on the Eastern Front. Some of the documents I translated revealed this in-fighting and difference of opinion between different sections of the German military.[12]

Albert Speer stood trial as a war criminal at Nuremberg, along with other leaders of the Nazi government, including Göring, Höss and Frank. Speer was found guilty and sentenced to imprisonment.

★★★

Another 3 Trooper, Harry Drew (Harry Nomburg, b. Coburg), was attached to 12 Commando, 6 Commando and then 3 Commando for operations, including the D-Day landings, and, wounded in action, became an inter-preter at the end of the war in Hamburg, Schleswig-Holstein and Berlin. John Envers (Hanns Engel, b. Breslau), who had also landed in Normandy on D-Day, but with 4 Commando Brigade and was wounded in action, was posted to Field Security near Lübeck interrogating prominent Nazis. He then transferred to Egypt for the re-education of German POWs there. Gerald Nichols (Heinz Hermann Nell) of 3 Troop, attached to 6 Commando for the Normandy landings, then to No 41 Royal Marine Commando and wounded in action, was stationed at the end of the war with 447 Field Service Section on the hunt for Nazi war criminals. Geoffrey Stuart (Gerd Werner Stein), who had seen front-line fighting in France and Belgium with the 8th King's Royal Irish Hussars and wounded in action, was at the end of the war appointed personal interpreter to Brigadier Bordass and promoted to the rank of sergeant. Once this work was completed, he was posted to Control Commission and was involved with the denazification process in Brunswick. His primary duty was to ascertain whether any of the local people had committed war crimes. 'These people needed official

clearance,' he comments, 'to enable them to work in the new Germany.'[13]
Richard Burnett (Richard Behrendt, b. Berlin) became an interpreter with
the coal commissioner in Wetter/Ruhr. Peter Johnson (Wolfgang Joseps,
b. Berlin), interned in Australia, and then with the Pioneer Corps had landed
at Arromanches on D-Day, was posted at the end of the war to Hildesheim
as an interpreter.

At almost the age of 100, Werner Philipp (b. Cologne, 1910) can still
clearly remember events of the war. Having emigrated via France and
served initially in the French Labour Corps, he fled to England and later
served in the Pioneer Corps. He was employed for some of the war teaching
French to British officers and was selected to be part of the administration of AMGOT (Allied Military Government) once France was liberated.
Shortly after D-Day, he was posted to Lingfield POW camp in England
to interrogate officers, and then to Toft Hall Camp (No 190 POW camp)
to interrogate hundreds of prisoners of war, mainly to obtain information
about V1 rocket shooting ramps. In February 1945 he was incorporated into
the 52 RHU, No 2 Sub-Unit stationed in Bruges, Belgium: 'I was on guard
the night the Nazi army surrendered and had tears in my eyes listening to
the BBC information.'[14] In July 1945 Philipp returned to Cologne – the
city of his birth:

> We were confronted with the oppressive silence of destroyed towns – the
> inhabitants had fled or had been killed. The only noise was the steps of very
> few people mounting and descending on a path over the debris of the build-
> ings of the Hohenstrasse, once the main commercial street. For the civilians
> I passed, I was a soldier of the victorious army marching on what remained
> of the destroyed town, like a Roman soldier roaming the ruins of Carthage.
> And humbly they wanted to give way. Yet I did not consider myself a victor
> but a survivor of a war without victors and only defeats: between Stalingrad
> and Brest, Narvik and Cassino, hundreds of towns destroyed like Cologne,
> tens of millions of deaths, Jews murdered in extermination camps, soldiers
> killed during the battles and civilians killed during air raids. My haughtiness
> of the victor when I questioned German prisoners of war in June 1944 had
> disappeared. At that time, I was still very far from knowing the dimension of
> the crimes Hitler's Germany had committed.

In August 1945 Philipp became an interpreter at the British Military HQ
in Berlin, occupying a small section which had not been destroyed. They

were billeted in requisitioned flats. Philipp was given an unusual job by the occupying authorities:

> My job was to guide journalists and to show them interesting sites: Hitler's bombed chancery and his bunker; and the railway stations full of refugees waiting to be taken to the Allied occupied part of Germany and the different zones of Berlin. I had to find some interesting items to be reported in their newspapers. They also wanted interviews with Germans. This was easy. I stopped a man or a woman in the street. But of course nobody had ever been on Hitler's side. Everybody totally ignored that Jews had been deported and killed. Some journalists thought themselves more clever than everybody else and, for example, asked Admiral Raeder's wife where her husband was hiding, thinking she would answer them. She was the only interviewed person still defending Hitler. She told us that what Hitler had done was necessary and it was a pity that he failed in the end.[15]

★★★

Ken Ambrose (Kurt Abrahamsohn, b. Stettin) was one of the few Germans who joined the RAF. In the spring of 1945 Ambrose was assigned as Interpreter German Technical in the rank of sergeant, and posted to a small group of officers in British Bombing Research Mission (BBRM) who were going to Germany to assess RAF bomb damage. He comments:

> Our headquarters were in a little chateau outside Paris. The war was nearly over, but not quite. We were instructed that if we went anywhere near the Rhine, we had to wear tin hats because the Germans were still shooting from the other side. We were billeted on the outskirts of Cologne which had been bombed to pieces. Our work was interesting. We visited the local Bürgermeister or directors of hospitals, anywhere where we could gather information on our bombing raids. The officers interrogated them and I acted as interpreter. We visited bombed sites to see what had happened in human terms, damage to buildings, etc.[16]

As the Allied forces advanced into Germany, the unit moved to Hanover and was stationed just west of the city at Bad Nenndorf. The unit was renamed British Bombing Survey Unit. In Bad Nenndorf, Ambrose worked as a translator in the unit and travelled occasionally back to London. Most of his time was soon taken up with finding and helping Jewish survivors at the Displaced Persons camp in Deggendorf, not far from the Czech border in southern Bavaria. In a letter dated 16 September 1945, he expressed his feelings on returning to a defeated Germany: 'We are, it is true, in a state of "no war", but if you saw what I see around me every day and then read the *Economist* as well, you would hardly call it peace. It is for the peoples of Europe, but especially the Germans, a state of very grim war-existence without the shooting, and there is not safe ground anywhere in sight on which to build a new life.'[17]

In December 1945 Ambrose was posted back to HQ in London where he translated documents seized from the German authorities, sometimes of a highly technical, scientific nature. He was also engaged in translating documentation relating to V2 rockets. He worked there until his demobilisation in 1947. Saacha Manierka, who joined the RAF, also served with Ken Ambrose in the British Bombing Survey Unit in Paris, and then as a technical translator in Bad Nenndorf.

Another ex-refugee who served in the RAF was Lord Claus Moser (b. Berlin). Positions in the RAF were strictly limited for those of German nationality, so Moser became an instrument repairer Class I, repairing and checking instruments in the planes before they left on their sorties. In early 1945 Moser was posted to Bomber Command Headquarters at High Wycombe, where he became part of a research team. He was charged with assessing how much damage the RAF had done in the bombing raids over Germany. As different parts of Germany came under Allied control, he was sent on trips to those areas to analyse the destruction. His fluency in German was useful for the Allies, who assigned him to interrogate heads of German businesses and factories to ascertain whether the official RAF reports of damage were, in fact, accurate. Acting as interpreter was for Moser the only point at which he felt his German background accorded him any importance in the RAF. The European Headquarters of this operation was located in Versailles and visits to Germany were planned from there. It was during one of these visits that Moser was involved in a serious car accident. He survived but was sent back to England to the famous East Grinstead Hospital, led by the great plastic surgeon, Sir Archibald McIndoe:

> McIndoe was treating severely injured pilots, amongst others, all of whom were dreadfully injured, often with burnt hands and burnt parts of the face. On the first day, Sir Archibald came to see me and said, 'We start operating tomorrow. But there is one rule – you must watch some of my operations

to see what an art it is and to realise that most patients here are in a terribly worse state than you.' So, I found myself in a largely RAF community with aircrew and soldiers, often particularly good-looking, now disfigured by their appalling injuries. During the nine months that I was there, I really learned about human survival. I gained an understanding of the human spirit and what people can do to help each other to survive, however physically damaged.[18]

After a number of operations at East Grinstead Hospital, Moser was posted to Bomber Command Education Service at High Wycombe, and promoted to the rank of sergeant. There he taught RAF personnel about politics and economics until his demobilisation in 1946.

★★★

The wartime duties with the RAF of ex-Berliner John Hereford (Joachim Herzog), the son of a lawyer, were top secret. At the age of only 18 he joined the RAF unit with the highest fatality rate. He flew with 101 Squadron in bombers over Germany as a wireless operator, disrupting the Luftwaffe's night fighter operations by jamming their control frequencies. Hereford was one of a small group of aircrew known as 'spec ops' (special operators). Of this group, a number were Jews, some of them from Germany. They flew as the eighth member of a bomber crew, occupying a screened-off, lonely and unheated position in the rear of the aircraft where they used specialised and highly secret radio equipment. Hereford first flew on Stirlings and Flying Fortresses with 214 Squadron in the bomber support role. In addition to jamming the enemy radio frequencies, 'window', small strips of metal foil, was dropped to jam the German early-warning radar. After ten operations over Germany, and in support of the Allied landings in Normandy, Hereford then transferred to 101 Squadron operating in the Lancaster. He flew a further twenty-one missions involving intense night bombing operations over Germany. The highest number of casualties of any RAF squadron was sustained by 101 Squadron, and it was not until the war was over that it was learned the Germans had perfected a technique to home in on the Lancaster's transmissions. The Jewish 'spec ops' flew in the full knowledge of the high casualty rate, and the fate of some who were shot down remains unknown.

At the end of the war, Hereford's work was equally interesting, if less dangerous. He was sent to Germany with the Air Disarmament Wing and spent many months at the Hermann Göring Research Institute for Aeronautics near Braunschweig. He acted as an interpreter and analyst for Operation Surgeon, the collection of monographs and debriefings from German scientists about their research. This work was followed by the selection and transference to Britain of any equipment thought to be valuable. Hereford also monitored German telephone calls and was intrigued by the number of messages that ended with '*acht und achtzig*'. When he matched up the numbers (88) to the letters of the alphabet he realised that the senders were signing off 'HH' – Heil Hitler. His discovery led to the arrest of a number of senior Nazis who might otherwise have escaped. During his time at the institute, Hereford fell in love and married a leading ballerina: the blonde, blue-eyed Ursula Vaupel who had danced for, and been introduced to, Hitler in Berlin.

★★★

Like many German-speakers in the British army, Leo Horn (Leo Schwarz, b. Berlin) was required to report to the Interpreters Pool in Brussels at the end of the war. He had lived through front-line fighting after D-Day with 5th Battalion, the Wiltshire Regiment of 129th Infantry Brigade. From Brussels he was posted to the office of the Ordnance Corps in Iserlohn, east of Düsseldorf, Westphalia:

> I became interpreter to the Colonel in charge of all the supplies. We could take over anything; factories and equipment. We were interested in a large pipe factory which we had just requisitioned. Engineers arrived from England to dismantle it and transport it back to England for its technology. With the war over, I received an order to see the Major in his office one day. He said, 'I've got a special job for you. It's hush hush. Go and requisition as many skis as you can for the British Army.' I was given lorries and jeeps with drivers. Skis were made in factories in Bavaria, then in the American zone. I drove into Wuppertal in the British zone where there was a sports shop and asked the German owner to accompany me to Bavaria in the American zone to requisition skis. Our group went to the first factory and impounded whatever skis they had. We went to the next factory, and the next. Nothing. They had been forewarned. Eventually we went to the Bürgermeister and explained that the British army wanted skis and they would be given a special form signed by DDOS [Deputy Director of Ordinance Services] and myself promising payment for them. We returned to the factories and sure enough there were plenty of skis for us. What did the British army want with so many skis?

Churchill had intended to invade Russia because the Russians were going into Austria and the Balkan States. He gave the order for the British army to receive skiing instructions in anticipation of invasion. I was given ski training in France and we were issued with the best quality skis and boots.[19]

Leo was demobilised in December 1948 in the rank of sergeant. After the war he discovered the shocking truth that fifteen members of his father's family and four of his mother's had perished in the death camps. He has no regrets about his role in the British forces: 'I felt good that I had joined a fighting unit, particularly when I knew what had happened to my parents and family in the Holocaust.'

Notes

1. Mark Lynton, *Accidental Journey*, pp. 209–10.
2. His life story is told in his autobiography, *The Way it Was*.
3. Leon, *The Way it Was*, p. 59.
4. Interview with the author.
5. Herman Rothman, *Hitler's Will*, p. 98.
6. Ibid., pp. 104–5.
7. Copy of letter lent to the author by the family of the late Henry Roberts.
8. The National Archives, ref: WO 208/3779 (The Last Will and Testament of Adolf Hitler) and WO 208/3781 (Investigations into the Last Days and Death of Adolf Hitler).
9. For a fuller account of his life, see Joe Haines, *Maxwell*; T. Bower, *Maxwell: the Final Verdict* and Elisabeth Maxwell, *A Mind of My Own*. In compiling this profile, I am exceedingly grateful to Dr Elisabeth Maxwell for providing material from the family archives.
10. Conditions were difficult for her, as told in Helen Fry, *German Schoolboy, British Commando*.
11. Fry, *German Schoolboy, British Commando*, pp. 147–8.
12. Ibid., pp. 152–3.
13. Interviews with the author. For a fuller profile of Geoffrey Stuart, see Helen Fry, *The King's Most Loyal Enemy Aliens*.
14. Correspondence with the author.
15. Interview with the author.
16. Interview at the Sound Archive, IWM, ref: 22682.
17. Ken Ambrose, *The Suitcase in the Garage*, p. 365.
18. Based on interview with the author.
19. Based on interview with the author.

Six

MILITARY GOVERNMENT

Military Government was established in Germany and Austria by the four Allied powers – Britain, France, USA and USSR, each responsible for their respective zones. As personnel were gradually demobbed, the duties carried out by the British Army of the Rhine (BAOR) were replaced by the Allied Control Commission (ACC). The roles within each necessitated the experience of the German-speaking refugees. They came into their own in this respect. Of those enemy aliens who were posted back to Germany and Austria on denazification work, most spent at least two weeks beforehand at the Interpreters Corps in Brussels. There they underwent a short period of training ahead of their new duties. When they were posted to Germany and Austria, these duties ranged widely in connection to Military Government.

Every level of German society was subject to the denazification process, including industry, the judiciary, civic government and public sector employment like education, health and transport. Ordinary Germans had to be passed through the process to hold public office. The enemy aliens were often assigned to work in this area. So, for example, Sergeant Rawdon (b. Vienna) became interpreter for the Military Police unit that led British troops into Berlin. Francis Carsten (Franz Carsten, b. Berlin) served in the Political Warfare Executive at the War Office, where he compiled a handbook for use by Military Government in Germany. Ernest Brown (Ernst Braun) served in Military Government at Mönchengladbach and Löhne, halfway between Bielefeld and Minden. Alfred Spier was in British Military Government in Lippstadt, Münster and Bielefeld. Michael Thomas (Ulrich Hollander, b. Berlin) became liaison officer for Konrad Adenauer, the Bürgermeister of Cologne. Leo Dorffmann, who had been in the Pioneer

Corps and sent after D–Day to Bayeux working on supply lines for fighting units, was transferred after May 1945 to Military Government in Solingen in the Rhineland. His interpreter role led to him also carrying out translation work in local court cases. Walter Beck (b. Vienna), who had been in the Austrian army during the First World War, found himself in the British army's Pioneer Corps in the Second World War. At its end he was sent to Germany as an interpreter with 298 Military Government in Schleswig, halfway between Rendsburg and Flensburg. Alfred Arnott (Alfred Arnsdorf, b. East Prussia), an internee on the *Dunera*, then in the Pioneer Corps, transferred to the Interpreters Corps in Military Government at Althorn near Ottenburg, looking after Displaced Persons. His twin brother, Max Arnott (Max Arnsdorf), served with Field Security at Nienburg near Hanover. Also looking after Displaced Persons was Walter Foster (Walter Frost, b. Vienna). He had been first in the Pioneer Corps, then REME. At the end of the war he was stationed in Westphalia with the ACC, overseeing Displaced Persons from Stutthof concentration camp in Poland, near the Vistula estuary. Reginald Pringle (Paul Rosenzweig), a survivor of Dachau, was stationed with a security unit at Bad Oeynhausen and Minden. His brief was to search houses and flats for Nazi sympathisers and Nazi literature. Walter Fast was stationed with Military Government in Münster for the interrogation of war criminals and the inspection of jails in Westphalia. He became deputy chief of the legal department at Münster. Interpreter Robert Kennard (b. Vienna) was attached to a railway company of the Royal Engineers. Whilst in Magdeburg, he was the only British forces person who could speak German fluently, so was given the job of stationmaster. Eventually he became responsible for the control of all trains and passenger movement crossing the British zone.

Those with a legal background were given central roles within Military Government for the translation of new laws in both Germany and Austria. Amongst them was Major Norvill (Kurt Nagler), an Austrian lawyer who served in the Pioneer Corps and then the Royal Armoured Corps. He first became an officer in Military Government at Lübeck and then was posted to Vienna for work in the British-Austrian Legation Unit (BALU). He was appointed by another ex-refugee Major Lasky (Laszky), a well-known lawyer in pre-Nazi Austria. The other German-speakers in the unit were Eric Sanders (Ignaz Schwarz, b. Vienna),[1] George Bryant (Georg Bräuer) and Theo Neumann – all formerly of the SOE – Captain Rhodes and Captain Keynes. Major Dr Friedrich Schnek and Captain Blair (Blau) worked in the Graz branch of the British Legal Division. Eric Sanders, although not having a legal background, was accepted to work in BALU and told by Major Lasky: 'although you are not legally trained I am sure you will be suitable.' BALU vetted all legislation and new laws of the Austrian parliament and influenced the appointment of Austrian judges, checking them out for a possible Nazi past. Since the Anschluss of March 1938, Austria had been integrated into Germany (the Ostmark) and governed by German Nazi law. One of the key processes in the denazification of Austria as a newly 'liberated' country was to reinstate a democratic Austrian legal system. This was not a matter of merely passing pre-1938 statutes. Each new law had to be approved in special sessions by the four occupying powers (British, Russian, American and French), known as the 'four elements'. Before ramification, extensive and precise translations of the texts and drafts were to be submitted for approval to the Allied Legal Council of the 'four elements'. Eric Sanders explains:

> Vienna was also divided into four zones. As the Russian-occupied zone of Austria extended beyond Vienna, travelling from Vienna to the British zone, for example, meant passing through the Russian zone before entering the British one. The point of crossing from one zone to the other was like going from one country to another. Visa-like documentation was necessary and luggage was checked by the Russians. Trains were sometimes held up for hours. The inner district of Vienna was under the aegis of all the four elements who took weekly turns to be in charge. A military jeep with military policemen of the four nationalities was regularly seen cruising through the 'Inner City', each week flying a different flag. The office of the British Legal Division was situated in the district in which I had lived before the war. The head of the Division was Lord Schuster.[2]

The fluent English and German-speakers were recruited into the British section, BALU, to translate the laws into English. Translations were important and could take many hours. Eric Sanders recalls:

> A completely new code of laws had to be enacted by the Austrian parliament. Before this could be done, every major law had to be passed by the Legal Council of the four elements. The process required for each draft of a new law to be translated into the four languages. It may seem odd but the Americans and the British each did their own translations. Our offices were

on the ground floor of the Division's house. When we had finished translating sections of the law, we would all meet at Lasky's flat in Vienna and read the translation word for word, sentence by sentence, until Lasky felt certain that there were no mistakes. Lasky would then take the translated laws to the next regular session of the four Elements, where it was discussed and a final text eventually approved. BALU had a typing pool where the completed translations were typed and Gestetner duplicated. We all took part sometimes in collating the many pages of an act and stapling them. The work was very routine but I enjoyed it. There was a wonderful camaraderie between us.[3]

No such separate unit as BALU existed in Germany. However, Military Government made use of those enemy aliens with a legal mind: Lieutenant-Colonel Farnborough became legal adviser to HQ; Major Romberg liaised with German judiciary; Lieutenant-Colonel Wilhelm Cohn was a judge at Hanover; Dr Ernest Cohen became British first legal assistant to the ACC, later deputy judge advocate in the British Army of the Rhine (BAOR); Captain Michael Merton (Blumenfeld) was appointed public prosecutor at the Military Court in Düsseldorf; and Captain Renow supervised the trials of war criminals.

★★★

Little did John Langford (Erwin Lehmann b. East Prussia) realise when he enlisted in the Pioneer Corps, that he would eventually become bodyguard to two British prime ministers. Having served with the 6th Airborne Division during action, he was seconded to its intelligence section. Langford received a telegram instructing him to report to HQ First Allied Airborne Corps at Moor Park in Hertfordshire. From there he was sent on a secret mission, flying from Croydon to an airfield near Hanover. He and Captain Hill were the first British personnel to cross the demarcation line into the Russian zone, in preparation for making Potsdam the headquarters of the forthcoming Potsdam Conference, due to take place in July 1945. Langford was part of the 317 (Parachute) Para Field Security Section under Captain Ede. In July 1945 he attended the Potsdam Conference as one of Prime Minister Winston Churchill's bodyguards. He guarded Churchill for three weeks:

This was possibly the highlight of my army career because we were living in a beautiful villa at Potsdam originally belonging to Prof. Dr. Urbig, and it was quite an honour for me as a German refugee to be given the post of security bodyguard to our Prime Minister. I attended various functions and meetings between the heads of the four governments: Eisenhower, Churchill, Stalin, the French head of Government.

John Langford was not the only ex-German refugee working on military and guard duties at the Potsdam Conference. With him were Sergeant Shaw, Henry Leyton and Edward Norton (Edward Franz Noether). The latter, originally from Heidelberg, had carried out intelligence work for 8th Corps General Staff Intelligence and acted as an army ski instructor. For the Potsdam Conference he became head of the Security Office located at Babelsberg, a suburb. During the final week of the conference, John Langford acted as bodyguard to the new British prime minister, Clement Attlee, after the general election defeat when Churchill became leader of the opposition: 'One morning, the doors opened. We were not used to seeing Churchill so early because he worked from his room in the mornings. We were surprised when in walked Clement Atlee. He was hardly known to any of us at that point. We knew he must be the new Prime Minister, so we saluted him. He said, "Don't bother boys. You'll be seeing more of me now."'[4]

Langford was amongst the security guards in a photograph taken of the three leaders, Stalin, Churchill and Truman, on the steps of the conference villa. After four glorious weeks at the Potsdam Conference, Langford was transferred to Berlin HQ of British Military Government, together with another Field Security officer, a staff sergeant and ten sergeants. They were stationed in the private residence of the German Reich Bank Minister, Dr Schacht, and acted for the Charlottenburg and Tiergarten areas of Berlin. During the final eighteen months of his army career, Langford was based at the famous Spandau Prison, involved in the interrogation of many Germans returning from Russia and the east:

I personally was in charge of Field Security at Spandau Prison where I interrogated repatriated East German civilians and German soldiers released from Russian prisoner-of-war camps. It was through the interrogations that I learned about conditions in the East, which is where I had originally come from. No German admitted to being a Nazi, so we had to judge whether to give them their freedom or continue to have them under observation by security. We also had instruction to find hidden Nazis. We were looking for the Nazi Martin Bormann, head of Hitler's Chancellery, who had had considerable power, signing various edicts through the war. At one dinner party, we lifted the floorboards because rumour had it he was hiding under the floorboards of the house. I also carried out interpretative duties.[5]

Langford remained in the British army until January 1947. Because of his personal assignment to two British prime ministers at Potsdam, and in recognition of his work, he believes that he was the first alien soldier to be naturalised as a British citizen whilst still in uniform.

★★★

Fred Gillard (Friedrich Goldenberg, b. Vienna) was attached to the Intelligence Section of the First Buckinghamshire Battalion, whose HQ was in Hasselt, not far from Nijmegen in Holland.[6] Eventually he was posted to Meppen, a site which had been the long-range weapon test ground for the German industrialist Krupp. Gillard organised the transport of heavy equipment, visited factories and carried out translation work: 'The infrastructure of the country was damaged so that every time it rained, there were power cuts. We therefore had to travel around to repair the damage to cables. Days passed when we were ferrying German electricity workers to restore electric supplies or being called to stop looting of potato fields (it is amazing what the sight of a Sten gun can do to stop it).' Then there was an unexpected find for Gillard's small team:

A German scientist was apprehended and we were told that some very important documents were buried in the woods nearby. It was alleged the afore-mentioned person knew the location. We reached the place in question where soldiers were digging. We found a box which looked like an outsize coffin. The box was opened. The contents were covered by a flag. Not the normal one. It had a swastika in the middle surrounded by a serrated wheel. The box and contents were sent to London for examination. Then I was given seven days' leave in London. It was whilst in London that I read in the newspapers … that documents relating to rocket-assisted shells were uncovered. I have not the slightest doubt they were the ones which we unearthed in Meppen. By the time of returning after my seven days leave I had quite a job to find our HQ which had moved to Kamen in Westphalia. My job was to do interpreting for visiting scientists from Britain, Canada, Australia and USA which proved very interesting. I also had the task of arranging the dismantling and shipping of equipment confiscated for examination and assessment. I visited many firms, such as IG Farben, Mannesmann and Krupp. I had a technical dictionary at my disposal. Only on one occasion did my work take me to a court to translate.[7]

After that Gillard was based for a time in Essen-Heysingen, in the former Gestapo HQ, carrying out translation work.

★★★

Peter Henley (Otto Lichtenstein, b. Mayen near Koblenz) was also in the Intelligence Section of the First Buckinghamshire Battalion, a light infantry regiment. Decades later he cannot remember whether Fred Gillard was part of his particular section; however, their work overlapped significantly. Henley entered Germany with T Force of the First Bucks:

> We were always ahead of the main army because when we entered Germany it was our task to take over the three utilities water, gas and electricity. We were instructed to head for a certain town where the army was due later that day. The absolute priority for us was to make sure the Germans did not sabotage these vital structures. That would delay reconstruction of the country post-war. There was enough damage from the wartime bombing, so we didn't want to deal with restoring basic resources due to German sabotage. Ours was therefore a key role at that point. Once we entered the designated town, we had to find the locations of the three utility works, then ask to see whoever was in charge – usually a Nazi. That person was immediately dismissed and replaced by one of the workforce whom we thought was trustworthy. This was a basic but fundamental part of the denazification process.[8]

In the Ruhr region and Essen, Henley's team found the gas infrastructure not working, but the electricity and water were fine. Once they had secured a works from sabotage, by entrusting it to capable workers, the next stage was handed over to Military Government and Henley's team moved on to the next town. When they reached Kamen in the Ruhr there had just been an explosion in a mine with substantial loss of life. 'We handled the rescue operation,' recalls Henley. After this, Henley and his unit were given a list of wanted men and instructed to search for them in the POW camps. Little did he know exactly who he was searching for, as he explains:

At the time there was a race to find important Germans, although I was unaware precisely who they were. The Russians, British and Americans were all on the hunt for them. In the end, they each found some of them on their list. With my team, I found three of them. We had their pre-war addresses, visited and made enquiries. Usually relatives were still at those addresses and told us where they were. This is where my knowledge of German came in useful. A British officer and I then visited where these scientists were – I was the interpreter. Once we had confirmation of their location, we informed Military Government who took over. We were not responsible for moving them to a secret location. Back then, the names on our list didn't mean anything to me. It only meant something to higher intelligence services.

Another task given to Henley's search team was to find Adrema printing machines, used in most offices and factories in Germany. 'We impounded about 80 of them,' he says. 'The machines were loaded onto lorries and transported to England – no idea why they were sent to England. It wasn't our place to ask questions. Our work became routine and we just got on with it.' Henley was demobbed in June 1946.

***

George Clare (Georg Klaar, b. Vienna) had a varied brief with his post-war work. He found himself posted to British Military Government HQ in Berlin under Major Banfield.[9] Clare's job was to accompany the major on his inspections. Besides that, he worked in the office translating German documents. Movement for ordinary Germans was restricted by the four occupying powers. One of Clare's responsibilities was to issue travel permits to indigenous Germans who wanted to travel to another part of Germany. In that capacity he came into contact with the widow of General von Stülpnagel. Her late husband had collaborated in a failed revolt against Hitler in Paris in July 1944 and was consequently executed as a traitor. His widow wanted a pass to travel to another part of Germany and told George Clare that she wanted no special privileges, but to be treated like other Germans. During the course of his work, Clare also acted as an interrogator and was engaged in recording the minutes at the meetings of the Four Power Committee, a sub-committee of the Allied (*Kommandatura*) Cultural Affairs Committee, advising on denazification. The committee supervised the *Spruchkammer* – the German denazification panel for cultural affairs.

It was Clare's job to oversee the German staff of thirty-two and issue their ration cards, travel permits and meal passes.

Another ex-Vienneser, Ian Harris (Hans Hajos, b. Vienna), who had trained as part of 3 Troop, saw front-line action with 46 Royal Marine Commando, then 45 RM Commando. He was wounded twice, first in France at Dozulé after crossing the River Dives, and second at the River Weser, in which he lost an eye. After a period of convalescence he was assigned to duties in Germany. It was now 1945. Harris was stationed at Brunswick where he was offered the post of chief ski instructor at the BAOR Centre in Winterberg, in charge of fifty German skiing instructors. Harris worked on various duties as an interpreter for two years. After his demobilisation, he was offered employment as administrative assistant to the former commanding officer of French Troop, 10 Commando, who knew him from his commando days. Harris worked as his assistant in an agency engaged in collecting valuables, assets, machinery, paintings and gold from the Germans and distributing them amongst the sixteen victorious nations. This included aiding the chief of mission in post-war Berlin and Brussels:

> It was a very good job and highly paid but it ruined me for normal civilian life! I was driving Field Marshal Goering's convertible light blue Mercedes around Berlin; and from Berlin to the British Zone and through the Russian Zone. It was a job of a lifetime until I had an accident in it and wrote it off. It was a heavy vehicle but it just floated across the ice into a lorry on the autobahn![10]

Corporal Harris was one of the few enemy aliens to be decorated with the Military Medal for his part in the war. His citation was written by Lieutenant-Colonel Blake and signed by Field Marshal Montgomery, who at that time was in charge of 21st Army Group.

★★★

At the end of the war Clement Freud (b. Vienna, 1924), a grandson of Sigmund Freud, was assigned to a number of different duties in the British occupation zone in Germany. It was a colourful time. For a while he was stationed in Bad Oeynhausen in charge of an employment exchange which used German POWs to serve in the British Officers' Mess. He was then briefly attached to Field Marshal Montgomery's staff as 'a sort of catering adviser. My job was to ensure that Montgomery was never given anything messed about or "frenchified" to eat; he was especially suspicious of salad dressing.'¹¹ In the winter of 1945 the entire Sergeants' Mess in Bielefeld contracted a sexually transmitted disease from the same barmaid. For a period, Freud found himself VD officer. He recalled that he was:

> instructed how to give penicillin injections, slap the man on the bum, stick in the needle where you slapped and he is slightly anaesthetised, pump in the penicillin and give the puncture point a wipe with cotton wool dipped in Dettol. I received one complaint during my short tenure of office. A soldier came to me confidentially to complain that he had gonorrhea and for his daily visits to the hospital had to share transportation with men who had syphilis. I called him a snob and told him to sod off.¹²

The main part of Clement Freud's post-war work was locating minor war criminals whose names appeared on a list issued by the International Military Tribunal in Nuremberg. This work included interrogation of suspects, some interpretation work, and collecting witnesses and escorting them to the Trials. In October 1947 he was demobbed in the rank of lieutenant and returned to England. In civilian life he became a much respected journalist, television personality, broadcaster and Liberal MP. Stephan Freud, eldest brother of Clement, also enlisted in the British forces. In 1944 he was stationed in Italy with a self-propelled Field Regiment with the Royal Artillery. At the end of the war he was posted to the German Personnel Research Bureau, running examinations for important German civilians to ascertain whether they were suitable to work in the newly democratic state of Germany. He was demobbed as a captain in 1946.

***

Rudy Karrell (Rudi Katz, b. Berlin) enlisted in the British forces from internment in Australia, firstly into the Pioneer Corps. From August 1946 to January 1947 he transferred to Military Government, 2 Area Intelligence Office, BAOR stationed at the *Rathaus* in Stade. It was here that he acted as interpreter and was involved in welfare activities where people with problems could come for help and advice; this included rape victims. He was also in charge of cinema arrangements. He comments:

> I took over the Apollo cinema on behalf of military government in Stade to show films from the Army Kinema Corporation. I also arranged for the

exchange of films between the army and RAF for entertainment of the occupying troops. This was an important consideration at the end of the war. One had to maintain morale and give the soldiers entertainment. I organised shows with stars like Frankie Howard and Jack Warner.[13]

From Stade, Karrell was transferred to D Detachment, No 2 T Force Unit in Hamburg, in charge of civil labour at the Hotel Reichshof. It was being exclusively used as a transit place for the German scientists involved in the rocket programme, who were awaiting transfer to America: 'The hotel held German scientists like Werner von Braun. I was in charge of German and British staff at the hotel. That included looking after the rocket scientists. At that stage most of them were happy to go to America and went voluntarily. Some of them had been involved in the V1 and V2 rocket programmes.'

Karrell was demobbed as acting sergeant. He was invited to stay on, which he did for a year, transferring to the Army Kinema Corporation stationed in Gehrden, a district of Hanover. 'It was an interesting post,' he says. 'We had mobile cinema cars which were sent all over the place – wherever there were British troops. My job involved distribution and scheduling of films.' Karrell lost all his family except his brother in the Holocaust. His father was arrested on Kristallnacht and murdered in Sachsenhausen concentration camp a fortnight later. His mother perished in Auschwitz.

★★★

Berlin-born Dr Rudi Herz transferred from the Pioneer Corps to the Royal Engineers. In June 1944 he embarked for service in India where he remained for a year as chief engineer in Bangalore. In October 1945 he was posted back to Germany to work on designing buildings for army quarters and camps for the BAOR. During 1946 he became command works supervisor, No 1 Corps in the area of Osnabrück. An article dated 19 January 1946 in *The Conqueror* reported of Rudi Herz: 'A large NAAFI club will be built at the site of the skeleton of the Bishop's Schloss in Osnabrück. Captain Rudolf Herz, area works officer of the EFI, will be in charge of the construction. Similar clubs are being constructed in Capt Herz's area at Nienburg and Münster. He is putting in overtime by doing much of the interior murals and sculptor work.'[14]

Herz's work continued into 1947 where he was assisting at HQ as works supervisor, NAAFI, West Europe (Germany) and in charge of planning. He was eventually demobbed that year in the rank of captain.

Like Rudi Herz, Eric Fisher (Erich Fischer, b. Vienna) was also posted to India. Fisher transferred from the Royal Army Service Corps to the Royal Electrical and Mechanical Engineers, and served in India for approximately a year as a staff sergeant, seconded to the Indian army. At the end of the war he was eventually posted back to Vienna, the city of his birth. Although trained as a specialist engineer, he was in charge of the administration of the office, dealing with the maintenance of equipment and vehicles. He recalls:

> Occasionally I was required to act as interpreter but not involved in inter-rogation. We were billeted in a splendid villa near the Palace of Schönbrunn which had been requisitioned by the SS. Our Sgt. Major insisted that all the decorations were retained so Nazi murals, portraits and insignia, copies of *Die Sturmer* (the notorious Jew baiting paper) were all on permanent display. I at least managed to get permission to hang Hitler's portrait in the lavatory. As part of the Army Bureau of Current Affairs (ABCA), I was required to organise courses in various subjects for which I had to find tutors. Unable to appoint a suitable candidate for English, I taught the course myself. Whilst in Vienna I tried to find out about the fate of my family, but I failed to get any information about them. It was sometime after my demob that I learnt that my mother and sister were both transported to Minsk and shot on arrival.

Fisher was demobbed on 30 September 1947. He never saw front-line action during the war but, as his discharge documents show, he served as a loyal soldier. He was offered a commission but decided to return to civilian life. He concludes: 'I realise that nothing adventurous occurred to me in the war. My contribution was microscopic but I considered it my duty to show my gratitude to this country which saved my life. I was the only one of my family to survive thanks to Britain giving me refuge.'[15]

★★★

Leslie Brent (Lothar Baruch, b. Köslin, Pomerania) was seconded to the Worcestershire Regiment in Italy, arriving shortly after the end of the war. In 1946 his brigade joined the British Army of the Rhine, stationed on the Lüneburg Heath, north-east of Hanover. 'Our role,' he says, 'was to keep the Russians at bay.' Towards the end of 1946, and now in the rank of captain, Brent's brigade and other units in the area were recruited for Operation Woodpecker:

This was a major project designed to extract timber from the forests of that area, to be sent to Britain to aid the reconstruction programme there. This operation involved tree-logging on a very large scale and shipment of the resulting timber. It was done with the reluctant cooperation of German foresters. It was not indiscriminate. We re-seeded trees at regular intervals. I did not have the slightest compunction about doing this – I had just learnt when visiting war-ravaged Berlin that my family had been 'sent East' to an unknown fate. Decades later I discovered they had been taken to Riga and shot in the woods there immediately after arrival.

Michael Sherwood (Isi Schwarzbard, b. Leipzig) came to England on the Kindertransport and served with REME during the war. In December 1944 he transferred to 908 Military Government and landed in France with that unit. He proceeded with troops forward into Belgium, Holland and finally Germany. By now he had been promoted to the rank of staff sergeant. His unit was stationed in Bersenbrück, responsible for establishing the curfew and overseeing the handing in of weapons by the Germans. A court was set up to deal with violations and offences against the curfew regulations. Sherwood became court translator there. He also carried out interpretative duties between the Bürgermeister and Commandant of Bersenbrück. He comments:

> Bersenbrück was a satellite for Osnabrück. I was involved in interrogating minor local Nazis, one of which was Paula Specker. Most POWs were brought to me for interrogation. I also liaised with the local police, helped set up the Fire Brigade. Having been based in Bersenbrück for a year, I was moved to Osnabrück where again I was dealing with Fire Brigade bids.

From Osnabrück, Sherwood was posted to a police unit in Hanover, where he was required to go out with police patrols during the day or night. He was eventually demobbed in August 1948 and returned to England, where he settled down to civilian life and eventually started a business called Office Installations.

★★★

Ken Ward (Karl Robert Würzburger, b. Frankfurt-am-Main) arrived in England on one of the last Kindertranports in August 1939. Later he landed in Normandy, D-Day+1, with the 1st Royal Tank Regiment (RTR) and was engaged in front-line fighting through France, Belgium and finally the invasion of Germany.[16] He had come through the war without injury, a rare situation for tank personnel involved in combat on the front line. Having survived the loss of four tanks, he still mourns the deaths of his comrades. In September 1945 he was transferred from RTR to 245 Company Military Police to act as interpreter. He was amongst the first British troops to be sent to Berlin:

> The city was in ruins. Knocked out tanks were still littering the streets. In the Kaiserdamm, a main road leading straight up north from the Brandenburg Gate, a German Royal Tiger tank had been dug in up to the hull into the tarmac with its 88mm gun pointing north in the direction from which the Russians had been advancing. It had been knocked out by three shots placed closely together piercing the gun mantelet at its thickest part. I had never seen armour pierced like that by any of our guns and gained great respect for the rough looking, but obviously very effective Russian fighting machines.[17]

Ward was initially stationed in the Berlin Olympic Stadium. All around them, the German population was starving. He comments: 'queues formed at the waste bins and as we scraped our leavings into them, the German civilians, some very old, some very young, scraped out the dustbins and fought over our leavings.' From the stadium, 245 Company Military Police moved their quarters to the Knesebeck Strasse, just off Berlin's fashionable Kufürstendamm. Eventually Ken Ward was promoted to squadron quarter-master sergeant as senior interpreter, attached to the Military Police and then 89th Section of the Special Investigation Branch. In that capacity he dealt with crimes committed by British military personnel and by German civilians against British property.

★★★

David Brett (Dagobert David Bratt, b. Berlin) came to England in 1933 as a political refugee from Nazism for being vice-president of the Socialist Student Organisation. He subsequently enlisted in the Pioneer Corps and served with 219 Company. He landed in France on D-Day+27 with his Pioneer Company, stationed around Bayeux, then eventually went to Brussels where they were guarding a goods station. Once the war was over, Brett was transferred to the Hirings Directorate and Claims Commission, a branch of MI5, at Bremervörde near Bremen in Germany. When inter-viewed, he explained the nature of his work:

My job was to requisition buildings and flats for the British army at Nienburg. We moved the German residents out. I was very gentle in how I explained that these people had to leave their homes, but it was a mixed experience for me and not always an easy one. After I had done my job, sections of the British army moved into the requisitioned buildings. The Allied occupying forces had to have somewhere to live and function to carry out their vital duties.[18]

Educating the local population of Nienburg about the atrocities committed during the Holocaust was an important part of post-war reconstruction and re-education work. Brett organised the screening of films about the concentration camps which the local German people were required to attend. 'Many denied any knowledge of the camps,' he explained. 'So it was a crucial task for us to make sure they were in no doubt about what had happened under Hitler. Of course they also claimed not to have been Nazis, but we knew that most Germans had toed the line.' Once Brett had been demobbed, he returned to England and became a British citizen. He was one of the lucky ones whose parents, sister and grandparents managed to escape Germany before the war.

Another ex-Berliner, Peter Perry (Peter Pinschewer, b. Berlin), transferred from the Pioneer Corps to REME. He received a commission. Perry was posted as a staff captain to the Information Section of the Military Government Staff at Second Army, and shortly afterwards to HQ, 21st Army Group. Ironically for him, his life turned full circle four months later when he was appointed Food and Transport Officer of Charlottenburg, the district of Berlin where he had been born and spent his early childhood. Standing amongst the ruins of the school that he had been forced to leave more than ten years earlier, he writes: 'I stood in the deserted courtyard of the Kaiser-Friedrich-Schule, a Captain in the British army, surveying the empty ruins.' Most of his time was spent in matters relating to the provision and distribution of food to Charlottenburg's population, which at that time numbered just over 200,000 people. The perimeters of the work and rations allocated to the German population had already been agreed by the four Allied powers. Feeding a district was fraught with difficulties because of the continued flow of refugees from East Germany:

Mixed up with this mass migration were freed survivors from the concentration camps and released prisoners of war. I had seen the vanguard of this migration a few months earlier in Westphalia; now I had moved considerably closer to the source in the East and was directly involved with its consequences. We tried to compensate for any shortfalls by importing supplies from the Western Zones into Berlin; but in parts of Western Germany, too, food was dangerously short. The danger of famine in Europe, especially in the event of a severe winter, seemed very real. The Western Allies therefore began to import substantial quantities from their own domestic supplies. In Britain, this resulted for the first time in rationing of bread, which had been freely available at controlled prices throughout the five years of war.[19]

Perry's responsibilities included attending weekly meetings of food conferences with other officers from Military Government. It was here that a range of issues were dealt with and discussed, one of which was the problem of thefts and the black market:

In order to preserve local supplies, we prohibited the purchase of domestic foodstuffs by all soldiers, and the food offices were in turn instructed to forbid the sale of food to allied personnel by German shops. We tried to block a source of temptation by ordering municipal food inspectors not to remove confiscated food themselves, but to have this done by the police, who had to deliver these goods to my *Zentralmagazin*. We arranged for the issue of special ration cards to diabetics. We gave instructions for the expiry dates of ration cards to be prominently displayed in all shops selling rationed goods. Both the food and transport departments were called on to cooperate in specific projects, such as helping with the travel arrangements of Displaced Persons from their camps to their new homes overseas.[20]

In a report dated 12 October 1945, which was submitted by Perry, he stated:

Charlottenburg is particularly exposed to black marketeering in foodstuffs on account of the large number of restaurants, cafes, bars and similar establishments within its perimeter. Restaurants are willing and capable of paying enormous sums for food from any source. But the remainder of the population also consider trading on the Black Market as a normal, and, indeed, essential means of implementing their rations.[21]

In May the following year, Perry received an order from the HQ of British Military Government, entitled 'Object of Military Government, British Sector of Berlin'. It was an attempt to re-examine policy regarding the

Ministry of Food, and asked for feedback and evaluation from the officers' first-hand knowledge. Perry responded with his knowledge of the situation:

> In my section on 'Factors or Information', I expressed the view that 'Nazi ideology still exerts a dominating, often sub-conscious, influence on the majority of the population', and that the Nazis were blamed by a significant number, not so much for having started the war, as for having lost it. In my experience, the co-operation of the present German administration with Military Government was good, and often sincere, but they tended to rely on us for too many minor decisions.

Perry added the following main summary points for HQ:

> – *Political*: The primary object of Military Govt must be the eradication of the mentality which allowed the German people to create, support and tolerate the Nazi regime.
> – *The German Administration*: requires firm, exemplary and sympathetic guidance. It must be taught to work more independently along the lines laid down by Military Govt.
> – *The Food Situation*: Adequate feeding of the population, particularly of the children, is the physical counterpart of re-education. Maximum German food production must be encouraged.
> – *Black Market*: Maximum control is essential.[22]

Perry's work was at the forefront of the practical reconstruction of post-war Berlin. In spite of the difficulties and challenges that he faced, his responsible work was exceptionally rewarding.

★★★

Stephen Dale (Heinz Günther Spanglet, b. Berlin) also returned to Germany with the British forces. A survivor of Sachsenhausen, later an internee in Australia, he enlisted in the Pioneer Corps before transferring to the SOE.[23] During the war he parachuted into the Tramonti region of the Italian Dolomites with three other SOE members: Peter Priestley, Taggart and his batman. The operation was unsuccessful and Dale was taken prisoner. He survived the war in several German POW camps, including Kaisersteinbruch camp (Stalag 17a) and Oflag 79 near Brunswick. He was liberated from Oflag 79 by American forces in April 1945. But that was not the end of Dale's military service. Later that year, in November 1945, he returned to Germany, posted to a port-operating company of the Royal Engineers in Hamburg. He knew the port extremely well and of course spoke fluent German. He then moved with the Royal Engineers to Göttingen, engaged in denazification work at the *Reichsbahn Zentral Amt* (office), the Central German Railway Stores Administration. His particular task was to trawl through thousands of questionnaires and cross-examine employees of the German railways. Anyone suspected of being a Nazi was handed over to Field Security. During his time there, he brought in two high-ranking Nazis; one a brigadier in the SS, the other in administration in the Nazi Party prior to 1933.

★★★

The German police force was subject to the denazification process just as any other public service. That job fell to a branch of Military Government called the Public Safety Branch, which had been set up to assist the military forces in exercising the function of civil government in the restoration of public order. Enemy aliens had their part to play in this respect and were drafted into this unit. In August 1945 Allan White, together with two other members of 3 Troop (Anderson and Walter Burnett), was posted to the Control Commission.[24] White was sent to Hamburg with the Public Safety Branch, where the staff had the authority to control the German civil police and authorise them to take all the necessary measures for maintaining law and order; they had to ensure the German police enforced the German criminal law and assisted the military authorities in the arrest of leading Nazis and suspected war criminals. The Public Safety Branch officers were to prevent and detect revolutionary and political subversive activities, as well as oversee the preservation of life and property in all areas under the control of the local military commander. The occupying forces permitted the German police to continue in their normal police duties, but under tight control and the close supervision of Public Safety Branch officers. Many of these officers were former enemy aliens, like Freddy Gordon working in Hanover (still wearing his red beret) and Allan White in Hamburg (wearing his green beret).

One of the key jobs for men like White was to ensure that policemen who had been active Nazis were removed from their post and replaced by police officers who had a clean past or who had held moderate views. This was a vital part of the democratisation of the police force. Paramilitary police units set up by the Nazi Party were disbanded and their leaders arrested. Regular conferences and consultations took place between Public Safety officers and German senior police officers. Police chiefs were to ensure that regular statistical reports and relevant information was made available to the Public Safety Department to enable them to regulate law and order. One of the most difficult tasks for White was to sanction police action against concentration camp survivors, often Jewish, who had become involved in illegal activities in post-war Hamburg, usually black market activities. Allan White often went out on patrols with the inspector, his counterpart in the German police force. In January 1946 White became a Public Safety Investigator:

> The staff of the Public Safety Branch had to ensure that senior police officers were politically trustworthy, cooperative and reasonably competent. Any German who wanted to work for the Occupation Forces or any branch of the Control Commission had to obtain a Certificate of Good Conduct which stated that 'investigations had failed to disclose any previous arrests or convictions for crimes or moral turpitude'. This really referred to Nazi activities.[25]

Part of the duties of the Public Safety Branch was to ensure that 'designated Nazis' were being arrested at a satisfactory rate and that subversion of any kind (whether neo-Nazi or communist) was successfully combated. White made regular visits to police jails to see that prisoners were not being kept in custody too long, but were sent for trial before a German or Military Court within a reasonable time span. If they were not going to be tried, he ensured that they were released as soon as possible. Close attention had to be paid to the police to monitor for corruption or brutality: 'The fact that today the German police do not have a reputation for undemocratic, corrupt or extreme political behaviour should be a matter of pride for both the former members of the Public Safety Branch of the Control Commission and the German Police themselves.'[26]

★★★

Gideon Behrendt's duties with the Intelligence Section of his unit involved setting up road blocks to check the identity papers of Germans, black market trafficking and the possession of small arms. Similar controls were carried out at railway stations or on incoming trains:

Sometimes we even stopped a train on open track a few miles before it entered the station. All persons had to get out of the train and pass through our control. Controls in railway stations or on open tracks were carried out with the substantial assistance of the German police, who surrounded and cordoned the train off. These procedures usually took several hours and our 'booty' consisted largely of quantities of black market food stuff, cigarettes and alcoholic drinks, imported or home-made. Only seldom was I lucky to discover someone with false identity papers. While these controls kept us busy by day or night, they must have been a pain in the neck for the civilian population. The German policemen, however, may have enjoyed the results since they got a share of some of the spoils.

Twice a week Behrendt sat in his office and received people who had had their homes requisitioned and wanted permission to take certain items from their occupied house. Food was rationed among the civilian population. 'Germans still counted their money in terms of Mark and Pfennig,' comments Behrendt, 'although the accepted currency was mainly cigarettes. The black market price for one single cigarette was 7 Marks in Cologne and a little less in other areas. A bottle of local, home-made liquor or spirit was about 25 Marks.' The black market flourished in all parts of Germany:

There were many Displaced Persons in our occupation zone, as there must have been all over Allied occupied Germany. Most of them were originally from Poland but also from other countries. Some organised themselves into gangs specialising in 'living off the land', dealing in the black market on a large scale, robbery and plundering remote farms. Livestock like cattle, pigs and horses brought high profits and the robbers didn't stop at anything, even killing the farmers or anyone who stood in their way. We were called in to help at all hours of day or night but by the time we arrived on the spot I could only gather evidence and write my report. We never managed to catch any culprit. The farmers just had to lick their wounds. The German Police were still weak and mostly unarmed at the time, while these people were armed and, after what they had gone through during the war, they were ruthless and while we couldn't really condone their activities, we could well understand them.[27]

The above profiles provide just a snapshot of the responsibilities and duties in which the enemy aliens were engaged at the end of the war.

Notes

1. Eric served with BALU in Vienna first as a sergeant and then as a warrant officer II. He finished his military service in the rank of warrant officer I.
2. Correspondence with the author.
3. Interview with the author, 25 August 2006.
4. Based on interviews with the author. Profile also in Helen Fry, *Jews in North Devon during the Second World War*.
5. Unpublished memoirs, copy given to the author.
6. Gillard had been interned in Australia in 1940–41 aboard the *Dunera*. From Australia he enlisted in the Pioneer Corps and returned to England. With his company he eventually landed in Normandy, D-Day+33.
7. Based on interviews with the author in 2008.
8. Interview with the author.
9. For a fuller brief of his post-war work, see George Clare, *Berlin Days*.
10. Correspondence with the author; also the Sound Archive at the IWM, ref: 13389. His wartime service is told in more detail in Helen Fry, *The King's Most Loyal Enemy Aliens*; and also Peter Masters, *Striking Back*.
11. Clement Freud, *Freud Ego*, p. 62f.
12. Ibid., p. 62.
13. Interview with the author.
14. Copy lent to the author by Herz's daughter Sonia Dell.
15. Correspondence with the author.
16. Profile based on Ken Ward's autobiography, *And Then the Music Stopped Playing*, plus interview and correspondence with the author.
17. Ward, *And Then the Music Stopped Playing*, pp. 148–9.
18. Based on interview with the author.
19. Peter Perry, *An Extraordinary Commission*, pp. 101–2.
20. Ibid., p. 110.
21. Ibid., p. 114.
22. Ibid., p. 121.
23. His wartime service is told in privately published memoirs, *Spanglet or By Any Other Name*.
24. Michael Arton, *One Day in York*, copy lent to the author.
25. Ibid., p. 38.
26. Ibid., p. 39.
27. Ibid., pp. 90–1.

Seven

MEDIA AND NEWSPAPERS

An important tool for the Allies in reconstructing Germany was to gain control of the media. This was the mouthpiece of the nation. A key task for the Allies was to take over radio stations and newspaper premises and begin transmitting news to the German public. Those German entertainers who wished to perform publicly had to be vetted. The Information Services Intelligence Control Section in Hamburg, whose brief was to denazify actors, musicians, artists and writers, had a number of enemy aliens working in it. Major Kaye Sely (Kurt Seltz, b. Munich) was the commanding officer. Working for him was George Clare (Georg Klaar, b. Vienna),[1] Sergeant Oliver (German) and Leonard Field (Leo Felix, b. Karlsbad). Leonard Field had been in the Pioneer Corps, Intelligence Corps and Field Security. Eventually he was stationed in Benrath HQ BOAR and became one of the founders of the newspaper *Neue Rhein Zeitung*. Walter Wallich, who had served in the Pioneer Corps and Royal Artillery, was responsible for the *Reichskultkammer* in Berlin, and then controlled broadcasting in the British zone. Peter J. Schnabel (Austrian) of the Pioneer Corps and Cameron Highlanders was posted to Germany as an intelligence officer. In 1946 he became the theatre and music officer of Allied Control Commission Austria.

High on the immediate agenda for British occupying forces was the capture of Radio Hamburg. This was the radio station from where William Joyce, aka Lord Haw-Haw, Britain's most wanted traitor, had broadcast pro-German and fascist propaganda for the duration of the war to the British nation. On the morning of 4 May 1945, a group of T Force stormed the station. Joyce himself had fled the previous day after delivering his final broadcast. Berlin-born Geoffrey Perry (Horst Pinschewer), brother of Peter

Perry mentioned in Chapter 6, was part of T Force whose brief was to take Radio Hamburg:

> We knew where Radio Hamburg was. The broadcasting building sat in one of the main streets, and we had no trouble taking it over with some of the T Force soldiers who made sure the place was safe. Occupying the studios was one thing, but if someone destroyed the transmitter, we would have no station. The problem was we did not know where the transmitter was. It was outside the town, but we did not know where. So while Major Findlay, the engineer, stayed in Hamburg, I headed off to find the transmitter, which I soon discovered was in the Moorfleet suburb in Hamburg. I took with me some T Force soldiers and Radio Hamburg's chief engineer to show us the way. Along the way, he warned me that the transmitter was guarded by 100 German policemen and troops, and we would have a fight on our hands. However, when we arrived, we found that the Germans defending it were either very old – grandfathers – or very young.[2]

At 7 p.m. on 4 May 1945, Radio Hamburg was back on air again under Allied military control. An announcement was made to this effect; Perry recalls that historic moment:

> Then Colonel Lieven handed the microphone over to me. For the next two days, I was the station announcer, and my duties included introducing British and American war reporters who were making broadcasts from Radio Hamburg, both for our local audiences and to be picked up for onward transmission. The irony was that I was broadcasting from the same microphone used only two days earlier by William Joyce.

Joyce had gone into hiding. Although his whereabouts were unknown, it was thought that he was still in Germany. The story was to come full circle at the end of May 1945, as will be explained shortly.

After two days Geoffrey Perry moved to the buildings of the local newspapers which had miraculously escaped Allied bombing. 'News that we were taking over,' comments Perry, 'was received with hostility, especially from a man named Krummer, who was the head of the family who owned the paper, although later we became good friends.' The responsibility on the shoulders of such a young army man was not lost on Perry:

First I had to organise some personnel. I could not produce a newspaper on my own, but equally I could not produce it with Nazis. I had to find staffers who were not Party members and who, by reputation or action, were non-Nazis or certainly not active ones. Krummer was wearing the Party badge, but claimed he was not really a Nazi, so I said: 'Prove it. I need some staff, some people you could not employ on the newspaper.' Within a matter of hours, I had some heads and hands to work on it with me. I also found a journalist and editor named Walther Klahn, a charming man who was quite obviously politically handicapped under the Nazis. The first issue of *Hamburger Nachrichten-Blatt* appeared on 9 May, the day after Germany's unconditional surrender, with a print run of 154,000. It was a large single sheet emblazoned with the headline: 'The War is Over'. And because the newspaper press could do it, every second copy of the paper carried that same headline in red.

The German people were hungry for news, so we also started the larger, twice-weekly *Neue Hamburger Presse*, which for a brief period in June 1945 had a circulation of more than 1.2 million. But then came a shortage of newsprint, and only a week later, sales plummeted to just 100,000. After that the circulation settled at around 400,000 to 500,000, including copies distributed in POW camps.[3]

Whilst Perry was on the newspapers, another ex-refugee, Walter Eberstadt, was brought in to Radio Hamburg. Eberstadt had grown up in Hamburg before the war. He had been wounded serving on the front line in France with the Oxfordshire and Bucks Light Infantry (attached to the Worcestershire Regiment). About Radio Hamburg he writes:

We were 'Radio Hamburg', the military government station. We were on air a few hours each day. Our main job was to relay military government announcements, regulations and some news. We advised our listeners about food rationing, monetary regulations, curfew hours, anything to do with daily living under British military rule. We were the main information link between the British military, German civilians, the disintegrating German army, released prisoners of war, and Displaced Persons from what had been German-occupied Europe. We took our first tentative steps to re-educate the Germans with programmes about their Nazi past. To attract an audience we broadcast lists of missing persons, which reunited many families.[4]

The weight of the responsibilities on his young shoulders was not lost on him either:

> For me, at age twenty-four, to be in on creating the most influential radio programs [sic] in any of the occupation zones was unbelievably interesting and rewarding. I was part of the team laying the foundations for what would become the German equivalent of the BBC. The sensitivities were a constant challenge. It was our mission to 're-educate' the German population. It was our mission to explain and justify the measures of the occupation army and military government, to undertake the first steps of selling the population on democracy.

One of the first priorities was to bring German employees into the staff, people who did not have a record of being Nazis during the Hitler years. Two key German people were appointed: Peter von Zahn and Axel Eggebrecht. It was a challenging time. Eberstadt makes the point that:

> we had to convince those who felt they were 'collaborators', that they were working not for us, the British, but were in on the beginnings of rebuilding a democratic German society, working for themselves, not for the victorious occupying force ... It was hard for Germans who had lived twelve years under dictatorship to believe that Eggebrecht and Zahn were broadcasting of their own free will. If only to establish their credibility, we allowed them considerable latitude to question Allied measures. Our most effective broadcasts were roundtable discussions guided by Eggebrecht, and talks by Zahn and outsiders under the caption: Are we going in the right direction?

By July 1945 the station became state-owned as NWDR (*Nordwestdeutscher Rundfunk*). A satellite station in Cologne eventually became the *Westdeutscher Rundfunk*, as well as one in the British sector of Berlin.

'Our work became rewarding,' wrote Eberstadt. 'Programs were added. Interesting people joined the staff, full-time and part-time. Re-education was intermingled with literature, plays, classical and light music. Pre-1933 plays were put on, books long banned were read. Political parties reappeared on the air.' It was a momentous time for Germany. The nation was also to hear regular broadcasts about German atrocities under the Hitler regime. In the autumn of 1945, broadcaster Axel Eggebrecht was required to cover the Belsen Trial on the radio. The German people heard about the findings of the British Military Court of the crimes committed by the Commandant Josef Kramer and the guards of the concentration camp. 'Night after night he was on the air,' comments Eberstadt, 'earning more opprobrium than approval from the listeners. It was a thankless task. He received hate mail rather than fan mail.'

It was Eberstadt's responsibility to aid Hamburg's first post-war Bürgermeister, Rudolf Petersen, with his broadcasts. Eberstadt recalls the difficulties which Petersen faced in a country that was not used to freedom of speech and free broadcasting:

Petersen had a difficult and delicate task. He had been appointed by the British, not elected by the Germans. The city administration had to be denazi-fied, yet could not be stripped to the point where it no longer functioned. The British let him keep run-of-the-mill fellow travellers (*Mitlaufer*) and thought he did not have his heart in denazification beyond a certain point. He had to persuade the population that their hardships were self-inflicted, the results of the war Germany had started and lost, that food and fuel shortages were not caused by the British. That on the contrary Britain, though herself exhausted by six years of war, was actually a net helper in the British zone. His credibility depended on convincing the population he was doing his best to alleviate the situation, and standing up for them with the occupying power. Early during the occupation there was a huge protest rally in front of the city hall. It was on the verge of getting out of control. The police and the fire brigade were called, but Petersen addressed the protesters from the Rathaus [town hall] balcony and persuaded them to leave quietly. The radio was his main means of communication. For me it was immensely interesting to assist him with his broadcasts. It was within my authority to censor the contents, but it never came to that point.[5]

It was mandatory for the radio station to cover the Nuremberg Trials. This, for Eberstadt, was the high point of his time at NWDR. He travelled with the other German reporter Peter von Zahn to the court:

I spent several days in court, saw the accused, the justices, the helmeted American military police, the prosecutors and the German defence. Journalists, commentators, and cameramen from all over the world had descended upon Nuremberg. The opening sessions and the sentencing, the lengthy pleas by defendants, Goering's suicide and Ribbentrop's disdainful scowls and wry smiles, the you-surely-cannot-mean-me expression and starched white collar attire of Hjalmar Schacht, the stoic inscrutable faces of the admirals and generals in their tunics stripped of all insignia – each and every nuance made front-page news everywhere.

For Zahn and his colleagues Nuremberg was the assignment of a life time, but not an easy one. Full radio and newspaper coverage in all four occupation zones was mandatory, in the Allied world the trial preached to the converted. For Germans, especially those who claimed ignorance, Nuremberg was the centrepiece of the victors' attempt to open German eyes to the Nazi years and stuff their past down reluctant throats. The charge of 'crimes against human-ity' broke new legal ground, but then, so did the crimes. It was futile for the defence to deny what had taken place and to argue that their clients had broken no laws because before the indictment there had been none to break.[6]

The work of ex-refugees like Walter Eberstadt was essential for the recon-struction of post-war Germany. Many of the principles that they instigated provided the foundations for the way German media functions today.

★★★

Back to newspapers, Geoffrey Perry and his unit were officially responsible for all newspapers in the region of Schleswig-Holstein. After Germany's surrender in May 1945, the information control units in the British zone established a total of thirteen newspapers for the German population, some of which were given over to Perry as his responsibility. Once a Canadian newspaperman had arrived in Hamburg to take over the running of the Hamburg newspapers, Perry and his colleague Bertie Lickorish were sent north by Colonel Lieven. Their first stop was Bremen, but 'it had been bombed out completely, reduced to heaps of rubble with barely a single house left intact. Inside the newspaper building, the machines had been smashed so there was nothing left with which to produce a newspaper. We had to move on.' Perry and Lickorish headed for Flensburg, 100 miles north of Hamburg near the Danish frontier, to take over the radio station there. 'In Flensburg,' he recalls, 'we were shocked to find the town teeming with fully armed German officers – this was four days after the war's end. There were only four or five of us, also armed, but we passed ranks of parade-ready German soldiers. They did not look friendly but the last thing we could afford was an incident.' Flensburg at that time was a tiny protected enclave for Admiral Dönitz, who was deputed as Führer after Adolf Hitler's suicide.

Another historic incident was to happen to Perry and his colleague which would bring them face to face with William Joyce:

On 28 May, Bertie Lickorish and I ventured out into the nearby forest to collect some firewood for the cooking stove. There we saw a man walking around on his own looking a bit lost. Lickorish and I did not take any notice of him and busied ourselves picking up bits of firewood and putting them in the truck. The man approached us and asked: 'Would you like me to show you where there is some more firewood?' We said yes. Then Bertie said to me: 'That sounded remarkably like Lord Haw-Haw.' Having engaged the man in conversation, he began talking about deciduous trees. He spoke fluent English and clearly was very knowledgeable, but his voice sounded very much like that of the unmistakable William Joyce. So I said: 'You wouldn't be William Joyce by any chance, would you?' At that, his hand plunged into his pocket.

The war was only just over, and with all the armed Germans in Flensburg, I was very suspicious. Apart from the official army-issue revolver I was carrying, I had in my pocket the Walther police pistol I had confiscated in Hamburg. When Joyce went for his pocket, I pulled it out and fired. I aimed low for his pocket – or rather, his hand – and hit him in his buttocks. He clutched his backside and fell to the ground. As he lay on the ground, I asked him again: 'Are you William Joyce?' He said, 'No, I'm Fritz Hansen.' Suddenly I thought I was in a great deal of trouble. I was in a town I should not be in and had just wounded a German civilian. I imagined he was unarmed and simply reaching for his papers. I had visions of being court-martialled. By this time, Lickorish had approached the scene. While I stood over the wounded man, Lickorish rifled through his pockets and pulled out a German wehrpass, which is like a military passport, in the name of Hansen. He also had one in the name of William Joyce, which came as something of a relief. I tried to apply an army-issue bandage pad, but the bullet had ripped through both cheeks of Joyce's buttocks, creating four holes in all. The field dressing simply had not been designed for such unlikely multiple wounds. As a German in British uniform, the irony of having captured this notorious 'traitor' had not escaped me. It was one of life's coincidences.[7]

William Joyce was found guilty of treason and hanged on 3 January 1946.

Further challenges faced Perry and the team, having acquisitioned the newspapers in a country that had been living under Nazi tyranny with no freedom of speech for twelve years. The enormity of their undertaking could not be underestimated by anyone. Perry recalls:

> The newspapers we published in Germany were produced to strict guide-lines. Copies were flown out daily to London and were read carefully by the Foreign Office. We were required at the time to publish one concentration camp picture every day. And our diktat – and that of every army corps in Germany – was to be scrupulously impartial. We had to go in for straight reporting and not express political opinions ... I spent a great deal of time teaching our German journalists to keep political bias out of the pages, and I deleted any story with comment. News, as far as I was concerned, was sac-rosanct. Comment was allowed of course, but not in the news pages. The Germans eventually said they came to appreciate this.[8]

As the programme of denazification by the Allies came to an end, it was necessary for Military Government to hand over complete control of the media to the Germans and allow a platform for political parties to voice their views:

> We were told to encourage the development of German political life. But as the political parties had no mouthpieces – all the newspapers were produced by us – it was imperative that we did not take sides. I went to great lengths to be scrupulously fair, measuring the column inches each political party received. When we reported on political meetings, I counted the number of lines so that a Communist Party meeting had exactly the same number as a Christian Democrat Party meeting. And I ensured that one political story did not have borders around it, if another did not get exactly the same treatment ... I even compiled detailed statistics, showing how much space was given each party. Obviously, you could not give them exactly the same amount of space on a daily basis, but over a period of two weeks or a month the Communists, the Socialists and the Christian Democrats were treated equally ... When I look back, it is amazing how well we ran these newspapers, considering we were all kids. In 1946 I was only 24. It was quite anomalous for someone my age to run a major news-paper, and I wrote as much in one of the letters my parents saved. But at the time, I do not remember giving it a moment's thought. I loved it and had no problem with it.[9]

A conference to organise the handover of the newspapers took place in Hanover. Applications were shortly received from the German people for licences to publish their own papers:

> We began phasing out our British newspapers and phasing in those that the Germans had published themselves. While control of the German newspapers was being phased out, the Foreign Office felt that we ought to keep one major voice in Germany, one newspaper under our control. So we launched a national newspaper called *Die Welt*, which covered the whole of British-occupied Germany. I was one of a team of six who set it up, along with Colonel Garland, who went on to become Professor of German at Exeter University, England, and my good friend Major Steel McRitchie. It was a *Times*-style newspaper with no party allegiance. The final link in the print media was the news agency, Germany did not have a Reuters or Press Association, so the Foreign Office sent *Daily Express* columnist Sefton Delmer from England.[10] During the war, Delmer had worked for the German service of the BBC. He came to Hamburg, grabbed me from *Die Welt*, and we started the German news agency.

Perry was proud to have been one of the founders of DPD (*Deutscher Presse Dienst*):

> DPD turned out to be one of the most important projects with which I was associated … In the main newsroom, copy from correspondents, teleprinters, monitoring services and other sources was converted into news stories, for final vetting and approval by the British Duty Editor, without whose final approval and signature no stories could be sent to the newspapers. When DPD was formed, our main aim was to hand over to qualified Germans as soon as possible. The main problem with German journalism during Hitler's time was the indiscriminate mixing of fact and comment. In DPD's journalists we aimed to instil a sense of sanctity for fact – and strictly to separate fact from comment. DPD was a great success, and it became one of the most far-reaching and positive influences for good in the British Zone.[11]

Enemy aliens were used throughout the British zone to work at the various newspaper offices. Captain Prince Franz Weikersheim, who originated from southern Germany, headed Sub-Section 3, No 2 Information Control Unit. He became the founder and first chief editor of *Ruhrzeitung*, the leading newspaper in Western Germany. E. Pollitt (Pollitzer, b. Vienna) already had a journalistic background. He transferred from the Pioneer Corps to a propaganda unit and was given the task of broadcasting in German to troops of the Wehrmacht about the true situation in Germany. Later he became the editor of the newspaper *Lubecker Post*. Les Kildare of the Royal Armoured Corps (8th King's Royal Irish Hussars) was taken POW by the Germans during the war. He survived thanks to an English officer there who protected his original Jewish identity. Kildare comments:

> After being liberated from the POW camp, I was given the option either to be demobbed or join the Control Commission of Germany (CCG). Because of my German knowledge I decided to transfer to the CCG, as an interpreter. At first I was with a Medical Section, then I was posted to the Information Control Film Section (ICFS) as a film censor. The purpose of it was to give the Germans some form of clean entertainment after deleting the Nazi propaganda and anti-Allied references. Whilst I was with the ICFS, I made a short film of the section called 'Silly But True'.[12]

Kildare left HQ in Vlotho in September 1946 and returned to England. Eventually he settled in Australia.

★★★

In March 1946, Robert Maxwell, mentioned in Chapter 5, was posted to the Berlin Information Control Unit. In July that year he was appointed Temporary Officer Grade II, Information Services Control Branch. He was in charge of maintaining a free press in the British zone of Berlin and involved in restarting the Springer-Verlag (Press), a leading scientific publishing house. He wrote home to his wife Betty:

> I went out and took eight of my men with me on a security patrol and check-up in my area. I searched quite a few houses and when I had finished I had found three rifles and ammunition and nine German soldiers, four in uniform, the rest in civilian clothes and one Gestapo, not a bad bag. The Germans in the area are dead scared of me and have already nicknamed me the Black Hurricane and there isn't a thing they wouldn't do for me. The Herrenvolk, they make me laugh … I have got to prepare a lecture tonight on how to be a useful citizen because tomorrow morning I am talking about it to the troops … Now that there are no longer any Germans to fight we

have still got to keep the troops occupied and the best way of spending the time before demobilisation is definitely in preparing for their responsibilities in civilian life; I contributed to that end by giving lectures on various subjects and I have also become a teacher for part of the day in that I teach languages for two hours daily. What a change from digging-in and shooting.[13]

After the war, Maxwell went on to create a publishing empire, Pergamon Press, and various business ventures which led to disaster. Having secured a very large fortune, estimated at close to £1 billion, Maxwell entered into a series of disastrous purchases in America, Germany, France, Italy and Israel, at the very time when the world was entering into a recession. He made a number of fatal purchases. By 1990, the scale of his debts and the impossibility of paying the high rates of interest made his downfall inevitable. Yet in 1991 he purchased the American *New York Daily News*. He died on 5 November 1991 in mysterious circumstances, after disappearing from his yacht *Lady Ghislaine*. Even in death, controversy surrounded his financial dealings, and fraudulent transactions on a massive scale were uncovered involving private pension funds. He has been described by one writer as being 'as ruthless and as keen as any self-made businessman of his stature, but there was a flamboyant excess which was already disruptive by the 1960s'.[14] In spite of the disastrous end to his life, Maxwell was a man whose distinguished wartime service earned him a Military Cross due to his lack of regard for personal safety in combat circumstances. He is remembered by some of his army colleagues as a talented man with a colourful and charismatic personality.

Following the war, Geoffrey Perry also established a highly successful publishing business. He created and published a number of profitable magazine titles, among them the women's magazines *Family Circle* and *Living*. After selling his company to Thomsons, he became head of the Thomson Organisation's magazine division. He subsequently bought *Business Traveller* magazine and expanded the title into a group of five magazines, now published in Britain, USA, Germany, the Middle East and the Far East. In December 2008 Perry flew to Berlin as part of a filming schedule for a documentary called *Churchill's German Army*, screened by the National Geographic Channel in 2009. The German media received word of Perry's visit and turned up outside his hotel to interview him. In the interview, the broadcaster of NWDR (*Nord-West Deutscher Rundfunk*) described Perry as 'the father of the German press'.

Notes

1. See George Clare's two books: *Last Waltz in Vienna* and *Berlin Days*.

2. Geoffrey Perry, *When Life Becomes History*, pp. 48–9.

3. Ibid., p. 53.

4. Walter Eberstadt, *Whence We Came, Where We Went*, p. 332.

5. Ibid., pp. 346–7.

6. Ibid., pp. 354–5.

7. Perry, op. cit. pp. 54–5, 57.

8. Ibid., p. 65.

9. Ibid.

10. During the war Sefton Delmer worked for MI6 and headed Milton Bryan, not far from the cipher school at Bletchley Park. Milton Bryan functioned as a propaganda radio station, pretending to transmit as a German station within Germany. It succeeded and operated until Allied forces entered the region of Germany they were purporting to broadcast from.

11. Perry, op. cit., p. 68.

12. Letter to the author.

13. Joe Haines, *Maxwell*, p. 110.

14. *Dictionary of National Biography*, 2004, p. 533.

Eight

POW CAMPS AND RE-EDUCATION

The denazification process did not apply solely to work carried out in Germany and Austria. In Britain there were several German POW camps up and down the country, some holding as many as a thousand or more men. Before repatriation, enemy prisoners were vetted and subjected to a programme of re-education to rid them of any Nazi ideology. This applied to those who were not even categorised as high risk or war criminals. Who better to oversee this necessary work than the enemy aliens in the British forces? Many prisoners denied ever being proper Nazis, but they had toed the party line and as such were subject to the denazification process. The profiles below, including in one case extracts from an unpublished diary of an ex-German refugee working in the POW camp, provide an interesting insight into the work carried out in these camps at the end of the war. To augment the camps, a number of stately homes were requisitioned by the Intelligence Services during and immediately after the war for operations. The aim was to hold important German POWs, listen in to their conversations through bugging devices fitted in their cells and ascertain intelligence information for the British government. Fluent German-speakers in the army were ideal for such work. Over a hundred of them were employed at several places like Wilton Park and Latimer House in Buckinghamshire, and Trent Park in north London, under the auspices of the Combined Services Detailed Interrogation Centre (CSDIC).[1] Ex-refugees like Fritz Lustig were told: 'What you are going to do here is far more important than if you were firing a rifle or driving a tank.' For Lustig it was a relief because: 'we all really wanted to get into a fighting unit. Still, it was far better than digging trenches in the Pioneer Corps. The information we managed to obtain was used to support the Enigma codebreakers at Bletchley Park. Much of the material intercepted by Bletchley couldn't be acted upon because to do so would have alerted the Germans that their codes had been broken. But if there was confirmation from us via a prisoner of war, it enabled the army to make use of it.'[2] It was at Trent Park, located in Cockfosters, that refugees from Nazism eavesdropped on captured German generals.[3] Adam Ganz's father was one of those who listened in on the conversations there:

> From what I read in the transcriptions, there was some extraordinary stuff recorded. The generals talked in some detail about war crimes. Some of them said they didn't understand why the Jews were being killed in the middle of a war when it would be much more sensible to win the war first and deal with the Jews afterwards. Others were repulsed by what was done.[4]

The German generals were well treated at Trent Park, 'a little too much for some people', adds Adam Ganz. 'Churchill complained because the generals were taken on day trips to places like Hampton Court. Occasionally they were taken to lunch at Simpsons in the Strand. The idea was to weaken their morale by demonstrating that German propaganda had exaggerated the damage done to London.' None of the transcripts from Trent Park could be used later at the Nuremberg Trials because the information had not been extracted according to the guidelines of the Geneva Convention. Most of the generals were not tried for war crimes, in spite of their admissions, but were eventually sent back to Germany.

On 3 July 1945, ten men were brought, under conditions of utmost secrecy, to Farm Hall in Cambridgeshire. They were the German scientists who had been working for Hitler on the atomic bomb: Otto Hahn, Max von Laue, Erich Bagge, Walther Gerlach, Kurt Diebner, Werner Heisenberg, Paul Harteck, Karl Wirtz, Carl Friedrich von Weizsacker and Horst Korsching. Amongst them were two Nobel Prize winners, Max von Laue (1914) and Otto Hahn (1944). During the war years a fierce race had been on between the Allies and Germany to be the first to develop the atomic bomb. The Allies had no firm confirmation of how far the German project had advanced. As far as the Allies knew, it was a close call. These top German scientists were arrested primarily by a secret American scientific intelligence unit called the ALSOS mission, operating in Germany. This same unit successfully dismantled the German nuclear equipment – this was their biggest catch.

The scientists had been transferred from Germany via France and Belgium to Farm Hall near Cambridge, where they remained under close surveillance for six months. Here British Intelligence could interview them and covertly listen in to their conversations, under the charge initially of Major T.H. Rittner and then Captain P.L.C. Brodie. MI6 had used Farm Hall as a safe house before the arrival of the scientists. The rooms were fitted out with secret microphones. The conversations of the scientists were monitored by German-speaking refugees in the British forces who had been seconded to intelligence duties. If conversations were significant, the recordings were translated. Classified copies of the reports were then forwarded to officials engaged on the British atomic bomb programme and also to American intelligence. Much to the relief of British and American intelligence services, it soon emerged that the German scientists were way behind their British counterparts. Transcriptions of conversations and interviews form the basis of Jeremy Bernstein's book, *Hitler's Uranium Club: The Secret Recordings at Farm Hall*. Peter Ganz (b. Mainz), survivor of Buchenwald concentration camp even before the war began, was one German speaker who was transferred from Wilton Park near Beaconsfield to Farm Hall. Once the ex-refugees had worked at places like Wilton Park and Trent Park, with a couple of exceptions, they were told they were not permitted to serve abroad because they knew too much.[5] It was at Farm Hall, too, that Peter Ganz listened in to the bugged conversations of the scientists at a time when the bomb was being dropped on Hiroshima on 6 August 1945. The intelligence services wished to know the reaction of the scientists to the news. The previous month the two scientists Diebner and Heisenberg had been overheard saying:

> Diebner: 'I wonder whether there are microphones installed here?'
> Heisenberg: 'Microphones installed? [laughed]. Oh no, they're not as cute as all that. I don't think they know the real Gestapo methods; they're a bit old fashioned in that respect.'

Peter Ganz had huge respect for scientist Otto Hahn in particular. Hahn had been put on suicide watch during his time at Farm Hall because he was greatly upset that his discovery had led to the Nagasaki and Hiroshima bombs. During his internment, Hahn learnt from reading the *Daily Telegraph* that he had been awarded the Nobel Prize for Chemistry, for 'his discovery of the fission of heavy atomic nuclei'. Hahn's whereabouts were unknown to the outside world. Those who held him would not permit him to attend the award ceremony on 10 December 1945. Hahn and the nine other scientists were finally released on 3 January 1946 to return to Germany. Otto Hahn collected his Nobel Prize from King Gustav V of Sweden later that year. After his demob, ex-refugee Peter Ganz, who had listened in to the scientists' conversations, completed his PhD at King's College and eventually became Professor of German at Oxford University.[6]

★★★

The eavesdropping of captive Germans went on during the war at places like Wilton Park and Latimer House. In 1943 around eighty British soldiers (originally refugees from Germany and Austria) had been transferred to the Intelligence Corps from the Pioneer Corps. Their unit was called the Combined Services Detailed Interrogation Centre (CSDIC) because it was a unit where both British intelligence officers and German POWs were from all three services of the army, navy and air force. CSDIC (UK) consisted of three POW camps: one at Latimer House (near Little Chalfont and Latimer in Buckinghamshire), which was officially called No 1 Distribution Centre to disguise its true nature; the second one at Trent Park in London; and the third at Wilton Park, east of Beaconsfield, called No 2 Distribution Centre. One ex-Berliner who was posted first to Latimer House then Wilton Park was Fritz Lustig. He had originally enlisted in the Pioneer Corps and was a member of the Continental Pioneer Corps orchestra at the training centre in Ilfracombe. In 1942 he spent time with Southern Command stationed at Bulford on the Salisbury Plain. From there he was transferred to CSDIC and was required to sign the Official Secrets Act because of the highly confidential nature of the work he was to undertake. He recalls:

> When I arrived at CSDIC, most of our prisoners were either shot-down Luftwaffe pilots or members of U-boat crews who had been rescued when their boat was sunk. There might have been a few army prisoners captured in North Africa, but a major influx of those only started after D-Day. The POWs' cells were bugged. A microphone was concealed in the light fitting, and we had to listen to their conversations in the hope that they would discuss something that might interest our side. There were always two prisoners to a cell, as far as possible from different services or units in order to

encourage them to talk to each other about their experiences. We had to identify which was which by their voices and accents. We operated in teams of about six, each team with a separate room and an officer in charge. We sat at tables which were fitted with record-cutting equipment – this was before electronic tapes were invented – and had a kind of old-fashioned telephone switchboard facing us, where we put plugs into numbered sockets in order to listen to the POWs through our headphones. Each operator usually had to monitor two or three cells, switching from one to the other to see whether something interesting was being discussed. As soon as we heard something which we thought might be valuable, we pushed a switch to start a turn-table revolving, and pulled a small lever to lower the recording-head onto the record. We had to keep a log, noting what our 'charges' were doing or talking about, and indicating at what times and about what subjects we had recorded their conversations. As soon as a record had been cut, somebody else had to take over monitoring, and the operator went to a different room to transcribe what he had just recorded. Not every word that was spoken, of course, but only those bits of the conversation which were important. The transcript was then checked and edited by a more senior operator for any errors, omissions or superfluous material. They were finally translated into English and typed up in both languages in a different section for distribution to various intel-ligence centres and ministries.

We worked in two shifts, early and late. The early shift started at 9 a.m. and ended at 4 p.m. The late shift started at 4 p.m. and finished whenever the pris-oners had stopped talking or went to sleep. All prisoners were interrogated several times, always by officers not working in our monitoring section. We never dealt with any of them face-to-face. Their reaction to interrogation was often particularly fruitful. They would tell their cell-mate what they had. been asked about, what they had managed to conceal from the interrogating officer and how much we (the British) already knew.[7]

The eighty or so enemy aliens working at Wilton Park and Latimer House never came face to face with the POWs. They worked purely behind the scenes listening through the microphone bugs. They recorded not only military intelligence but also any atrocities they may have witnessed. Lustig adds:

those records were kept in an archive, whereas others were scrapped after use; also stories about the German home front, when prisoners related what they had heard or experienced while on leave. Such material was used for 'psycho-logical warfare' purposes: there were several Allied radio stations purporting to be illegal German ones which broadcast stories calculated to undermine the morale of soldiers. After the Allied invasion of the Continent, a steady stream of army prisoners arrived, and we got busy listening to them. The material we obtained was very different from what we had recorded until then, and we felt that what we were doing had suddenly assumed a far greater importance than before.[8]

After May 1945 some staff, including Fritz Lustig, were posted to Bad Nenndorf, a small town near Hanover. A prison camp had been established there. The internees were mainly political prisoners – those suspected of Nazi activities. The camp was called CSDIC WEA (West European Area): 'Our job was exactly the same as in the UK: surreptitious listening-in to the prisoners' conversations. The Camp Commander was Colonel Stevens who came from MI5 and had been in charge of the camp where German spies were interrogated – a very unpleasant man!'[9]

★★★

In the spring of 1946, Eric Bourne (Ulrich Borchard, b. Berlin) was posted as an interpreter officer to No 300 POW camp – Wilton Park. It was a hybrid between a military establishment and a foreign office facility which endeavoured to inculcate some aspects and understanding of democratic processes to selected German prisoners of war. It was reputedly the brain-child of Winston Churchill himself, as a contribution to establishing a successful democracy in post-war Germany. At that time the POW camp was under the command of Lieutenant-Colonel St Clare Grondona. British personnel occupied the mansion called the White House, whilst prisoners were in Nissen huts. Bourne comments: 'security was non-existent so as to emphasize the impression of an educational establishment rather than a place of containment.'[10] Bourne vividly describes the function of Wilton Park at this time:

> The demobilisation of British armed forces was in full swing; consequently the number of available British service personnel was limited. This required the use of prisoners in the running of the camp such that, for example, my own office was administered with Prussian punctiliousness and severity by a Herr Biehle. Prisoners were even required to scan the never-ending

CROWCASS (Central Registry of War Criminals and Security Suspects) reports to reveal any miscreants who might have slipped through the vetting procedures.

The interesting part of Wilton Park was the training centre under the direction of Dr. Heinz Koeppler, himself a German Jewish refugee, staffed by a group of German-speaking university dons and regularly visited and addressed by leading British politicians, academics and intellectuals. All POWs had been graded black, grey or white and the only prisoners considered suitable for training were those in the white category, including many who eventually rose to prominence in the Federal Republic. The curriculum placed considerable emphasis on the study of Germany's development since Bismarck as seen from a non-German point of view. It also contained detailed consideration of British institutions such as the electoral process, the jury system, the accountability of the police and the many other features which had been so conspicuously absent in Nazi Germany. The whole 'enlightenment' process lasted six weeks and concluded with an exam to assess the extent to which prisoners might have absorbed the lessons in which they had participated. As success in this exam usually ensured a speedy release back to Germany, the failure-rate was virtually non-existent.[11]

What turns out to be so interesting about this period is that Wilton Park was unexpectedly transformed into a microcosm of German culture, a culture which had been suppressed, or certainly curtailed, under the Nazi regime. As with the British internment camps of enemy aliens in 1940–41 – on the Isle of Man, in Australia and Canada – miniature universities were established spontaneously and orchestras formed. There was a flourishing of art, music and all academic studies. Much of this has been adequately described elsewhere.[12] Now, in an unexpected turn of events, the enemy aliens working in the German POW camps at the end of the war witnessed a parallel development in terms of intellectual and creative activities. Bourne comments in this respect:

What was perhaps most notable was the cultural flowering which accompanied and, perhaps, even dominated the entire six-week process. Plays were written and produced, drawing and painting were popular pursuits, there was a puppet theatre, music, both orchestral and choral, flourished, a printing machine churned out tracts and cartoons, recitations and poetry readings proliferated, and poetry itself was written by many prisoners recording, often the

German sentimentality, their hopes and aspirations for a new Germany. For many prisoners the escape from military restraint seemed to release a pent-upped and repressed creativity or, perhaps, just a return to near-normality.

Life in the camp with the German POWs was not always straightforward. Bourne spent a good deal of time talking with prisoners in their huts in the evenings. 'What seemed surprising,' he adds, 'was the number of communists who suddenly emerged among the inmates, until one realised that those with homes in east Germany, and about to return there, needed to prepare their alibis in preparation for life in a new totalitarian environment.'

★★★

Eric Sanders, whose post-war work with the British-Austrian Legal Unit (BALU) was explored in Chapter 6, had first been posted to a German camp in Somerset as an interpreter. He found himself at No 665 POW camp at Norton Fitzwarren near Taunton, holding around 200 prisoners, overseen by a company of the Pioneer Corps. The camp leader, Willi Lange, was a German prisoner in charge of the camp inside. He showed Sanders around the camp and, to Sanders' surprise, began to speak freely to him about the other prisoners. Sanders recalls his duties there, which consisted of writing reports and re-educating the prisoners in the art of democracy:

> Captain Wegg-Prosser of the Political Intelligence Department (PID) came to make my acquaintance. He informed me that I had to prepare regular reports about my work and submit them to Major Hemmings, who would forward a copy to the PID. I should also attempt to develop schemes of re-education towards democratic ways of dealing with their future life back home. This was re-enforced by another regular PID visitor, a Flying Officer Strub. They made no suggestions as to how I should do this and, at this point, I had not the slightest idea. Visiting several times in the course of the first few weeks they appeared to approve of my work which was largely routine. I had come to terms with the situation, reasoning that unless I came to know of crimes committed by any of these men I had to treat them as what they were: prisoners of war. Much of my job was administrative, such as passing prisoners' requests concerning their contacts, or lack of them, with their loved ones to the Red Cross office in London and dealing with correspondence, much of it official.
>
> The first unusual job that came my way was to translate a report by one of the POWs who claimed to have invented a process of using ordinary water to

drive engines. I sent his report with drawings to the War Office. In due course two 'boffins' arrived and I acted as interpreter between them and the 'inventor'. They came to the conclusion that he had nothing to offer and was just looking for an easy time in a laboratory, with the British government paying for his experiment. I totally agreed with them. Getting a clear picture of the man when listening to his speech, he struck me as not having more than an elementary knowledge of mechanics.[13]

All prisoners had been interviewed by intelligence officers and graded according to their Nazi sympathies: anti-Nazis or Nazis. Sanders gained the impression that the category was not correct for at least four of the prisoners that he had come to know well. Willi Lange had also claimed that most prisoners did not deserve such low grades as 'not a risk'. Lange was convinced that one of the prisoners was an anti-Nazi. He gained the trust of the four prisoners in question and then asked them about the other prisoners. 'That information,' says Sanders, 'plus personal conversations with many of the men provided me step by step with an overall impression.' In the camp there were still die-hard Nazis who did not believe the war was over for their Fatherland:

> Willi Lange took me around to some twenty older men as examples of real dyed-in-the-wool Nazis. They told me straight out that they believed the war was not over and that all the English newspapers and radio reports to which they had free access were artificially prepared just for the POWs to convince them that the war was over and lost. They were so pathetic I could not build up any feelings against them.
>
> The appreciation of my work by Messrs Wegg-Prosser and Strub was severely tested by my first report. I had become absolutely convinced that the grading of many of the prisoners was totally false. My report suggested entirely different grades for many, even including a handful of A's [anti-Nazis]. It caused a stir and I learned that within the PID I was being suspected of being a pro-Nazi. Wegg-Prosser assured me that he himself did not believe this but it was obvious that he doubted my judgement. One day, teams of PID officers descended on the camp and spent three days interviewing every single prisoner. At the end of it they not only came to the conclusion that I had been right but even obtained very similar percentages for each grade I had suggested in my report. This impressed my C.O. very much and I had almost unlimited freedom after that.

After the re-grading Sanders initiated a camp newspaper with the help of the Pioneer Corps company secretary, a conscientious objector, who did all the technical work. His role was to copy Sanders' articles, as well as those written by the German prisoners. Sanders nearly got into deep trouble for including in the newspaper an article written by a conscientious objector who criticised the dropping of the bomb on Hiroshima. Sanders had translated it into German and included it in the paper. The PID decided the article re-enforced for the prisoners the sense of real freedom of speech in Britain. The POWs, who had been brainwashed by the Nazi regime and were unused to freedom of expression and ideas, were encouraged by Sanders to join discussion groups in the camp. These conference-like meetings were introduced by Sanders himself as a way of moving the POWs beyond their totalitarian experience under Hitler. This was vital for when they were repatriated to a Germany which the Allies were reconstructing as a free, democratic society. Sanders comments:

> I also arranged smaller meetings without agendas in which the prisoners could raise and discuss whatever came into their heads. From that it was not difficult to get them to start discussion groups of their own. I tended to appoint the chairmen of organising committees with agendas and the taking of minutes and helped with the acquisition of necessary equipment. I used the official funds at their disposal and arranged the purchases.

Then Sanders received notification from the PID that the POW camp was to become a self-governing camp, which for them meant that they would be among the earliest groups to be sent back to Germany. That notification was accompanied by an order for Sanders to produce lists of prisoners according to their reliability and honesty: 'I did this by inviting about a dozen of those whom I trusted and knew well to provide me each with such a list of the men they knew personally. I worked on the assumption that it was in their interest to share their period of self-governing only with reliable people.'

Shortly afterwards Sanders was posted elsewhere, but, as he says: 'I had the definite feeling that I had fulfilled my task well beyond the duty routine. For three days I worked feverishly: closing my files, finishing my reports, handing over the routine etc. In the end I left without any particular goodbye scenes and, suddenly, pleased I was finished with it all.'

★★★

Another German POW camp, named No 9 POW camp, was located at Kempton Park Racecourse in Surrey, where five years earlier in 1940 the British government had interned male German and Austrian refugees. Eberhard Zamory, originally from Breslau, was stationed there as an interpreter. From there he was temporarily posted to Norway with five other ex-German refugees to supervise German troops that had surrendered. Conditions were not good in Norway. The German army continued to administer its own affairs because of the lack of sufficient numbers of British troops to oversee them. Zamory subsequently returned to England to continue his work at No 9 POW camp. Tony Hare (Anton Haas), who hailed from part of the defunct Austro-Hungarian empire, was also posted to this camp for special duties. The camp was an interrogation centre for German POWs captured on the front line. Hare's work at Kempton Park is described in his autobiography, *Spanning the Century*:

> From previous information we had some idea which German Divisions were in the area, and by learning all the numbers of the regiments and special battalions by heart, it was possible to call them out and make them fall in in the same sequence that they had been on the front line only some hours earlier. This gave the impression we knew a great deal about them and any questions during the preliminary negotiations that followed were frequently given freely and in a relaxed manner, particularly as they were simultaneously told about the hot shower and meal afterwards. The aroma of this meal was usually wafting across the interrogation huts at the time. The arrivals of these trains were very unpredictable and they had to be dealt with at once whether day or night. The result of this was a very strange psychological experience. For ten days we lived as if we were in Normandy, talking to prisoners who had been there some hours before, having constant detailed maps in front of us.[14]

During the interrogations, ex-refugees like Tony Hare often had to face entrenched anti-Semitism in the prisoners. Having escaped with their lives, they now faced those who would have them dead. Hare recalls:

> Prisoners were interrogated in a long hall where there were about a dozen tables in a line. Most of the Interrogation Officers in this room happened to be Jewish. A young German soldier made a statement about how terrible Jews were and proceeded to describe in detail what they looked like. 'Can you see one here?' asked the Interrogating Officer. The German looked around and

said, 'No I can't.' 'Have you ever seen one?' was the next question. 'No', said the soldier. 'Would you recognize one if you saw one?' 'Most definitely', was the answer. The German was about twenty-five and not particularly politically involved, but the hatred for these 'sub-human Jews' whom he had never seen was obvious.[15]

After Kempton Park, Hare was posted to a joint American/British unit which dealt with the interrogation of high-ranking officers or special prisoners. Some of his other work is narrated in Chapter 2.

★★★

The largest number of German POW camps was opened in the county of Essex. In May 1945, at the age of 18, Peter Sinclair (Peter Heinz Jacob, b. Berlin) of the Royal Fusiliers was posted to Laindon, near Basildon in Essex, to occupy an empty camp which was to be prepared for the arrival of the first 1,000 German POWs. The prisoners had been captured mainly in France; some had served in North Africa and on the Russian front. Their ranks ranged from private and staff sergeant to sergeant major. Sinclair remembers the day they arrived at Laindon railway station:

> They arrived by troop train, were immediately lined up in front of the station where I had the pleasure of receiving them. They had a British army escort. Suddenly a German NCO (a pilot) marched up to me, gave a military salute and said to me in German: 'We are all present and correct, sir.' This was my most poignant moment because six years earlier I had left Berlin on the Kindertransport for Britain. Now I was in charge.[16]

A thousand German POWs were marched into the camp and three days later they were allocated daily labour jobs on local farms or building sites. They returned to the camp at the end of the day. The camp had a hospital in one of the huts with a full-time doctor. Within a matter of months a number of similar German POW camps were opened – the first being at Chelmer Road, Chelmsford; then Hylands Park, also in Chelmsford; another at Rayleigh near Wickford in Essex; one in Southchurch at Southend-on-Sea; another at Great Wakering, also near Southend; and finally two in Tillingham near Bradwell-on-Sea. In total the camps housed around 4,500 German and about 120 Italian prisoners, all under the jurisdiction of Staff Sergeant Peter Sinclair who was based at the Laindon camp. Sinclair recalls:

I travelled between all the camps. All prisoners were sent out to work during the day. The camps had fences on the perimeter, but no barbed wire. There was nowhere really for them to escape. We only had one escapee – a Dutch SS fellow who got as far as Harwich but was caught. He was sent back to us and received 96 days detention. I interrogated each and every one of the POWs. On one occasion I was invited to go to No. 186 POW camp at Tilbury to carry out interrogations. I had a card index of 4,500 POWs which listed the name and unit of each POW. They were categorised. Lists as thick as telephone directories of wanted war criminals were issued to us and I had to check the names of our POWs against this list. I identified one such POW who was then under open arrest. He had been a private member of the SS. I had to register all SS members in our camps. There turned out to be about 150 SS in total in our camps.

One day I received an urgent telegram to return to Laindon camp because US intelligence were visiting. There was talk that Hitler might have escaped to Japan with high-ranking Nazis. We had submarine crews who had to be interrogated. The next morning, a Marilyn Monroe-type female driver in a luxurious limousine arrived at Laindon with a tall English Guards officer (Intelligence Sector) and a smaller Jewish US naval officer. It was my job to keep German submarine crews behind from work. I interrogated about twenty of them from various German submarine crews to see what they knew about the rumours.

There was a lot of talent in the camps. Sinclair organised lectures for the prisoners in their spare time. Some made artifacts using their carpentry skills. On one occasion, a delegation came to Sinclair and asked if they could build their own bakery: 'We arranged for flour and yeast to be delivered to the camps,' he says, 'and each camp had its own bread. They also did all their own cooking. The cakes were fantastic!' During their time in the camps, the men were exposed to ideas of democracy and freedom of speech. One of them, who had been taken prisoner at Falaise, admitted to Sinclair: 'We have all been duped by Hitler. We had believed in him.' But die-hard Nazis were still in evidence even after the war, as Sinclair explains:

One day we received at Laindon camp approx. fifty German submarine crews and airmen who were released by America and Canada. On morning parade they appeared with all their medals, swastikas and badges of rank. I addressed them in strict terms, telling them: 'I want your badges of rank and anything with a swastika to be taken off immediately.' One fellow asked to talk to me. He said that according to the Geneva Convention he was entitled to his badges of rank and medals with the swastika. I addressed them all again on the issue and said that it ill behoves them to mention the Geneva Convention considering the crimes that had been committed in the death camps. In any case, I continued, Germany was completely and utterly defeated and occupied by the Allies. I told them that the German army and navy no longer existed. If they didn't take off their badges and swastikas, they were not welcome in the camp. All except eight obeyed. The eight who refused were sent to a desolate camp at Wick in the north of Scotland.

In another incident we had a problem with the British Union of Fascists, who invited our German POWs to a garden party. The Commanding Officer issued them with passes without enquiring! I received a telegram to rush back from the home I was then visiting. Much to our embarrassment the incident was reported in the London Press that the German POWs went to a BUF party! The Germans however all walked out.

The German POWs certainly attracted the attention of some members of the British Union of Fascists. There was another incident when two BUF members tried to break into the Laindon camp: 'There was a commotion because some of our German POWs jumped over the fence. The BUF wanted to hand vitamins to these "badly treated POWs". In reality it was a cover for handing out Nazi literature. I arrested them and put them in our one-room jail. Both intruders were charged and fined £500 each plus costs for breaking Defence Regulations.'

Sinclair's commanding officer left him to carry out his responsibilities without interference. His duties were varied and interesting, and most work relating to POWs came his way – including pastoral issues:

I had a telephone call to say that a German POW would be sent to us and wanted to be billeted on a farm. He had served 96 days detention for fraternising and having an illicit affair with a WAAF. She was discharged dis-honourably and then gave birth to a son. In 1947 permission was granted for them to marry. I had the pleasure of taking the fellow to Highbury in London where they were married in the Registry Office. After the ceremony I escorted him back to our camp. Then I managed to find him work on a farm where his wife and child were allowed to stay so he had chance to be with them.

Sinclair felt no sense of revenge or bitterness towards the German POWs. He was determined to conduct himself with the utmost decency and took care over their welfare. Many ex-POWs were extremely grateful to him for his personal example. They sent letters to him once they had returned to live in Germany, and he has kept a bundle of these letters. In one, dated 27 April 1947, former POW Herbert Lehr told Sinclair: 'I am thankful for the decent treatment I have received and that you have considered the illness of my wife which enabled me to be repatriated in November 1946.'

Sinclair's exemplary work in the camps spanned over two years from May 1945 until November 1947. By the end of 1948, with one or two exceptions, all the prisoners were repatriated. All copies of the camp newspaper, which had been published every three to four weeks and edited by one of the prisoners, were latterly given to the Imperial War Museum.

★★★

A diary of life in POW camp 87, near Byfield in Warwickshire, has just come to light, written by ex-refugee Jussi Brainin who carried out interpretive duties there.[17] The diary covers the period from March to July 1946. Some extracts are reproduced below. In the summer of 1940, Brainin had been interned on the Isle of Man, and a separate diary records his experiences as an internee behind barbed wire. From internment, he enlisted in the Pioneer Corps.

In the 1946 camp diary, Brainin records insights into the thoughts of the German prisoners and also provides his own reflections of the time. The camp, less than two hours from London by train, held some 1,400 Germans and some Italians. Brainin outlines his duties:

> interpreting, censoring in and outgoing letters, evaluation of political currents among inmates, identification of troublemakers, political re-education, inspecting satellite camps, and visiting farmers who employ POW labour ... The Commanding Officer's principal concern was to run a strict regimen to ensure obedience. Anything to do with politics or re-education was of no interest to him. His role model, I suspect, was Colonel Blimp. This is how he defined his role: 'I don't mind if a man is a Nazi, as long as he works and behaves.' The German camp leader, an appointee of the Commandant, hailed from Bavaria. A Stabsfeld-Webel, equal to a staff sergeant. He was soft-spoken, anxious to co-operate, yet not submissive.

The day after his arrival at the camp, Brainin had to address the prisoners. It was only natural that going through his mind was the question: what atrocities have these men committed? Brainin wrestled with coming face to face with Nazis and possible war criminals:

> Scanning their drawn faces, I wondered what went on in their heads. What were they up to before they raised their arms in surrender? Herding Jews and other 'Untermenschen' into cattle wagons? How many lives have this lot on their conscience? What brutalities hide behind their gaunt features? How many shouted 'Juda verrecke' [death to Jews] and did their best to live up to the slogan? At the close of my address, during which I familiarised them with my origin and background, there was muted applause. Did some of them mean it or was it expedient to do so? The paradox of my role occurred to me time and time again. Here was I, an ex-enemy alien, expected to enlighten German soldiers, sailors and airmen about the British way of life and its institutions. They, I had no illusion, were interested in one topic only, when, oh when can we return home?

The diary entry for 13 March 1946 reads: 'After overcoming the objections of the CO, POWs who had no sign of life from their families were allowed an additional letter over and above their monthly allowance to help them trace their kin. I was called to one of our satellite hostels where one of the inmates was suspected of petty theft. For lack of evidence, no charge was laid. The visit though did reveal a messy, smelly billet. What happened to German tidiness?' Occasionally Brainin was required to escort newly arrived POWs from London to other camps. In his diary entry for 27 March 1946, he reproduces the memo from the CO of No 406 POW camp, Launceston in Cornwall, to the CO of the camp at Byfield:

> Staff Sergeant Brainin arrived this morning with a draft from your camp. He had taken over at Waterloo Station 240 POWs from other camps. He got them all sorted out in their respective parties with a list of numbers from each camp. He had a long wait for us at the station here owing to the early arrival of the train. He had everything in excellent order. I write this as you [might] like to know how extremely well this NCO has done with a large draft. He has been most helpful.

The diary contains philosophical reflections on the whole camp experience and inter-personal relations between the prisoners and their overseers:

'Human Relations', a byword for social workers, is of great importance in artificially created closed societies, such as a POW camp. A liveable climate depends on its occupants getting on with each other and how they relate to their custodians. An ambience of cordiality and of mutual respect is as essential for the smooth running of such a synthetic community, as are also discipline and material supplies. Such a collective is the sum total of each individual in it. Important as leadership is, the outcome, whether good or bad, depends on how all those involved inter-relate by harmonising or failing to do so. The Byfield POW Camp is a miniature community with all the characteristics of any human collective except the divide between inmates and warders: the very reason for a POW camp is not conducive to jovial, congenial relations between the two. Minor irritations are bound to get exaggerated by the captives, just as there is an inclination by the guardians to use their absolute powers absolutely. While the detention of enemy combatants at times of conflict is necessary, their continued incarceration after 'unconditional surrender' is an anachronism which inevitably creates additional strains and stresses.[18]

The diary entry for 30 March 1946 records the mindset of the German prisoners in the camp, prisoners who were struggling with the concept of freedom of speech and free-thinking. Deconstructing years of brainwashing by the Nazi regime was not straightforward:

Last night's weekly news review attracted a full house. This was not the case in the early days. Few attended, fewer participated in the subsequent discussion and fewer still dared to voice disagreement. Now they are getting quite good at arguing and even at dissenting. Speaking up is not only a safety valve for pent-up frustration, but it also provides an insight into their psyche. Besides concentrating on repatriation (their prime topic), they talk about collective guilt, the eastern provinces and their inhabitants' suffering, but not about the torment they inflicted on others. Their reasoning is still steeped in the ideology of the Third Reich. Goebbels' poison even now pulsates in their brain lobes. They marshal whatever they consider good in Germany and compare it with the worst elsewhere. Some of the recent domineering attitude is ever present. This results in a closed mind, making it difficult for them to understand another point of view.

New intakes continued to be brought into the camp. On their arrival Brainin was to read an address in German from the commanding officer:

> There is no need to stress to you as men of the German Armed Forces the importance of maintaining strict discipline. It is futile for a prisoner to escape. His chances of getting out of this island country are nil. He is bound to be brought back to this or some other camp for punishment. His escape would mean a restriction of privileges which prisoners in this camp enjoy. Any order given must be obeyed as promptly as if it has been given by your own officers. You are here for work and your pay will vary according to your output. If you show your willingness to co-operate you will be looked after well.

'Grudgingly,' Brainin says in his diary, 'I received permission to omit "Men of the German Armed Forces".'[19]

On 3 April Brainin went to collect a new intake of 200 Germans from the local station, some of whom had been sent from detention in America:

> The contingent consisted of two parts. One of them for camp 87. Somehow they got mixed up. Eventually after counting bodies and checking off lists, our lot finally moved off. Racing ahead in our van, I was ready in camp to receive the new boarders. All went well until the search of their kit bags began. What they contained was a surprise. Anything rationed or even unobtainable in the UK they had in abundance. You name it, Camels, Lucky Strikes, Philip Morris cigarettes, Kraft cheeses, toilet soaps, Chanel perfumes, Nivea cream and much more. Our Quartermaster, a shady cockney, quickly recognised an opportunity to 'impound', i.e. steal the tempting goodies. Alas, eventually, as a result of higher authority intervention, wiser counsel prevailed. Surely, carrying these riches with them was not their fault. For all we knew their American jailers wanted to show the wretched Germans how generous Uncle Sam is. Maybe they also had in mind to rub their British Allies the wrong way. In the end only their surplus blankets were impounded. Now, very likely, trouble between 'the haves and the have nots' will start. Yet, for the inmates to steal from each other is better than for their custodians to act unlawfully. The new arrivals look well fed, they are well clothed and chew gum continuously. They are also unanimous in praising their US captors and adopt some of the American disdain towards Britain.[20]

Two and a half months later, Brainin was still wrestling with the ingrained beliefs of those POWs he described as 'belligerent Nazis'. One in particular warranted an A4 page in his diary, a short extract of which reads:

> The 35 year old Luftwaffe Corporal fancied himself an intellectual, who liked to hear himself talk. There was no fanatical gleam in his eyes, nor any indication in his middle class appearance or behaviour pointing to a blind belief in Third Reich mythology. For all that, the moment he opened his thin-lipped mouth, there emerged a person who had no doubt about Germany's mission to rule Europe. Indeed the world. There was no dejection when he referred to Germany's defeat as 'a temporary setback'. 'Germany's hour will come,' he pronounced with a certainty as if it were as obvious as day changes into night …
>
> At times I felt like attacking his beliefs. But soon dismissed the wish to convince him of the error of his credos. Where does one start to convert a bigot for whom his fatherland can do no wrong, for whom both world wars of this century were lost by Germany as a result of betrayals, whose Bible is *Mein Kampf*, whose love is for a superior race he imagines to belong to and his hate is for anyone and anything non-German.[21]

In spite of the above, the majority of prisoners in the camp were quick to find *any* excuse to disassociate themselves from Germany's Nazi past. Brainin was, therefore, instructed to investigate the national status of the Germans in the camp. He made some interesting observations in his diary the following day:

> We have been instructed to look into the national status of the German POWs we hold. It turned out to be a revelation. The number of would-be Italians, French, Danes, Poles, Belgians, Dutch, Czech and Romanians was astonishing. Strange how at one time they were yearning to be part of the 'Greater Reich' [but have] now rediscovered their original ethnicity. To establish credibility for their non-German citizenship is a serious business. On achieving it depends the difference between early repatriation or continued internment. It means even a lot more – to be a member of a liberated people or be part of a defeated shunned nation. It strains one's credibility to hear a German-speaking South Tyrolean declare his love for Italy, or a middle-aged Alsatian proclaim his loyalty to France. There was also a Pole with a German name who genuinely spoke broken German. In 1939 he fought the German

invaders in the Polish army. Taken prisoner after a year, he was released only to be called up for the German army two years later. Once again, he was taken prisoner, this time in North Africa by the Americans. He was shipped to Texas. He landed now in our camp. He is anxious to become once more a Polish national.[22]

Towards the end of July 1946, Brainin left the Byfield camp to be demobbed. By then the camp was being largely administered by trustworthy POWs. On 21 July, the day that Brainin was leaving, the camp leader (a German) addressed all the POWs in a packed hall and paid glowing tribute to his leadership. That camp leader, whose name is never disclosed in the diary, told the gathering:

> Your departure means more to us [than an exchange of best wishes]. We lost a fair adjudicator who, as I can vouch, out of tolerance and convictions did more than his role demanded. Following his arrival, it soon became clear to me that we now have a go-between whom not only we could trust, but who was open-minded … [who] said I would rather sacrifice another day to wean a man away from evil dogma, than giving up a day too early … You encouraged discussion and no one who voiced contrary opinions was made to suffer for it … Even though there was, to start with, distrust you succeeded in gaining [the] confidence of the vast majority of the camp's population. In recognition of your unselfish activities I present you with a painting by one of our comrades … You got to know many of us, not everyone is bad. All of us are ready for peace.

★★★

In a similar capacity to Jussi Brainin, ex-Berliner Harry Brook (Heinz Brück) was posted to No 76 Camp (Merrythought Camp), Calthwaite in Cumberland (now Cumbria). It was part of a group of POW camps in the north of England which came under Northern Command and was the furthest north of all the German POW camps. Brook had been parachuted into Normandy just hours before D-Day with the 8th Parachute Battalion of the 6th Airborne Division. 'When I was dropped into France,' he commented, 'in the early hours of D-Day, half of my Parachute Regiment did not survive to see freedom and live a full life. They did not make it to the ground alive. I was lucky and survived.' When the fighting was over, Brook returned from Germany to a military base in Tilshead, Salisbury Plain. He was called into the CO's office because the army was looking for interpreters to deal with the influx of Germans being held in camps across Britain. Brook recalls: 'These German POWs fell into two main categories: first, those from temporary prison camps in Germany, France and Belgium who were brought to England for interrogation. Second, in 1945 a batch of POWs from Arizona, America, were brought to England. These turned out to be the most important POWs for our work.'[23]

The camp initially held Italians, with five out-camps in Westmoreland detaining around 500 German POWs, who were mainly naval personnel. Brook recalls:

> I lived in the Italian POW camp but was sent out on visits to the German camps. I was given a jeep and driver for the job. I had to get to know who they were, and they were then given manual labour tasks. My Italian driver was an ex-Italian fighter-pilot and an opera singer. He drove me around Cumberland at top speed in the jeep, as if he was in a plane and sang opera! This was the funny side of the work.

The time came when the Italians were shifted out of the camp to make way for a special convoy of a thousand Germans who arrived with a Military Police escort. They were the POWs who had been captured in either North Africa or Normandy and initially transported from America. Working with them was to have some unexpected consequences for Harry Brook, which included coming face to face with SS units he had fought in Normandy. It was a bilateral learning experience:

> I was introduced to their leader, a former submarine commander. I didn't like him at first, but I came to respect him and we became good friends. It turned out that many of these young POWs (of my age) had fought in the German 12 SS Divisions, called Hitler Jugend, whom we had confronted in battle in Normandy. As I got to know them, I learned a lot. It was a two-way learning process. I was prejudiced against anything Nazi initially – I had been thrown out of my country, with no formal education, lost my family and knew of the terrible atrocities and annihilation of Jews. It was natural to hate them. I assumed that these POWs in our camp were fanatical Nazis. But as I got to know them, I learned that they had been drafted into the SS units because of their date of birth. They were conscripted into SS Divisions and sent off to fight. This was a revelation to me. We embarked on what turned out to be

a mutual learning process. We learned together about the death camps – and we were equally shocked. Neither they nor I could believe what we heard and read. We knew about Auschwitz. News of other camps like Treblinka, Maidanek and Belzec came later. Before that, none of us knew and we were all equally shocked to the core. The German POWs immediately realised that they had been fighting a war which they were told, and believed, was an honourable war. That was the power of the Nazi-brainwashing. They had served far from the places of the death camps. They had been in Normandy and North Africa, so when they discovered the truth about the concentration camps in the East, they were shocked. They had acted as good soldiers but realised now that they had been deceived by their leaders. It was a huge traumatic shock for them. They felt betrayed. There was that double anger.

The consequence of learning about the concentration camps and the atrocities committed by their leaders led the German POWs to want to learn how they had been deceived by Adolf Hitler. That turned out to be one of the most significant re-education projects that Harry Brook carried out. It was an indispensable part of the denazification process. Brook recalls:

> The Political Intelligence Dept of the Foreign Office wanted to train German POWs to return to Germany to take over administration, teaching, police and security and all public offices. It wanted to re-educate a new generation with democratic ideas as a crucial part of the denazification process. It was a central part of rebuilding a country that had been under the control of Nazi ideology for twelve years, to rebuild a country free of Nazism. And that was quite a task.

It was Brook's job to interview and interrogate every inmate about his background:

> The majority told the truth. They were then graded A, B or C by the PID officers. I did not do the grading. I had to check their names against CROWCASS – the Combined Registry of War Criminals and Security Suspects. I didn't find anyone on that list. Anyone who was classified C, an unrepentant Nazi, was sent to another camp. There were two or three of them in our camp. Ninety percent of those in our camp were classified B, i.e. involved in Nazi activity but not war criminals. They hadn't done anything bad.

Another ex-refugee who carried out such work in a German POW camp was Herbert Salzbach. Harry Brook and Herbert Salzbach liaised frequently and visited each other to devise a suitable programme to re-educate the men. Brook explained:

First, we obtained a good library of books and discussed the subjects with the POWs. They did not know anything about the books which had been forbidden in Germany, so that was part of their re-education. Second, we held discussion groups which they were not used to. Third, we aimed to relieve their boredom in the camp with study groups. Amongst the POWs were experts in their field, including historians and teachers. They gave lectures on their subject. We started a camp newspaper to which any of the POWs could contribute. The in-topic at that time was the partition of India. Some of the POWs made me presents, e.g. a carved cigarette box. One of my jobs was to deal with in-coming mail for the POWs. They received heart-rending letters from their families who were in the Sudetenland and were being badly treated by the Czechs and Poles. It was news to me that the families of these POWs were also suffering in Germany, like my family had. They were very upset to be stuck in a POW camp in Cumbria with their families back home suffering.

Harry Brook bore no grudges for all that he had gone through and for what he had lost. Instead he made some poignant, thought-provoking remarks about his relationship with the prisoners:

The POWs came into the camp as enemies; they left as friends. It was a complete change brought about by the POWs themselves. We acknowledged that neither of us had committed atrocities. We realised that someone in a German uniform killed my family, but equally someone in British uniform killed some of their family (dropped the bomb on their town, etc), but we knew that it was not either of us who had done the killing. We therefore could not hate each other. We were not enemies. This made a profound change in my attitude to them. Today when I go to Germany, I bear no hatred for the people – they were not responsible for the atrocities of Nazi Germany. In 1997, when I visited Sonnenberg, I met German people. I met Max Weiss and we got talking about the war. It turned out that he had been a lieutenant in the Brandenburg Regiment in the Ardennes offensive. So was I, but in the Paras. It turned out that I was defending a bridge over the same river crossing that his company was attacking. We must have both been bad shots because we lived to tell the tale!

Was the denazification programme successful? Eric Bourne, mentioned earlier, concludes:

As a means of reconciliation, with already carefully selected Germans, it undoubtedly achieved some success. It brought prisoners face to face with what was, at the time, best in British life, politics and culture. It tried to show how a democratic state could function and what it could achieve, and it demonstrated that free expression and debate, and the liberty of the individual, were essential to the maintenance of a free society. For me personally, as a German refugee in a British officer's uniform, it was an unexpected, revealing and memorable experience. It certainly gave me a clearer insight into the mentality of Germans who had followed Hitler so blindly. It has largely determined my attitude towards a new generation of Germans who today try to practise the principles which Wilton Park sought to uphold, and it made me conscious of having played a small part in a worthwhile, if unusual, educational experiment.

These are Harry Brook's words on the success of the process:

The denazification process was a success in terms of our re-education programme. Yes — it is true that not all Nazi war criminals were caught, and some lived out their days in freedom in South America. But, the denazification process at every level led to a free democratic Germany which still functions as such today. Anti-semitism and discrimination against Jews is now outlawed in Germany. That's what I fought to achieve, and have lived a full life in the knowledge that I did my part in the downfall of Hitler and contributed to a free Europe in every sense of the word.

Notes
1. CSDIC also had mobile units working in North Africa. After D-Day, they worked on the European mainland too.
2. Quoted from an article, 'They Bugged the Nazis', in the *Jewish Chronicle*, 17 April 2009. Screenwriter Adam Ganz, the son of the late Peter Ganz, who worked at this centre, produced a play called *Listening to the Generals* for Radio 4.
3. See Sonke Neitzel, *Tapping Hitler's Generals*.

4. Interview with Adam Ganz in the *Jewish Chronicle*, 17 April 2009.

5. Information supplied by Peter Ganz's son, Adam Ganz.

6. His brother Lewis Gann (Ludwig Ganz) was also in the British forces and served in British intelligence in Berlin at the end of the war.

7. Fritz Lustig, unpublished memoirs, pp. 82–3.

8. Article entitled 'Wilton Park: A Very Special POW Camp', by Fritz Lustig in the journal of the Association of Jewish Refugees, August 2009.

9. Information supplied to the author by Fritz Lustig. See also Oliver Hoare (ed.), *Camp 020: MI5 & the Nazi Spies*.

10. Correspondence with the author.

11. Correspondence with the author.

12. See Gillman & Gillman, *Collar the Lot: How Britain Interned and Expelled its Wartime Refugees*; and Cresswell, *Living with the Wire: Civilian Internment in the Isle of Man during the two World Wars*.

13. Correspondence with the author.

14. Tony Hare, *Spanning the Century*, p. 106.

15. Ibid., p. 108.

16. Profile based on interview with the author.

17. Kindly lent to the author by his daughter, Carole Angier, who plans to deposit a copy at the IWM.

18. Diary entry, 11 June 1946.

19. Diary entry, 2 April 1946.

20. Diary entry, 3 April 1946.

21. Diary entry, 19 June 1946.

22. Diary entry, 4 April 1946.

23. This profile is based on extensive interviews with the author.

Nine

CIVILIAN LIFE

The time came for the enemy aliens to be demobilised, after what had been for many at least six years of active service in the British forces. They faced an uncertain future. The majority did not have British nationality. They were under no illusion that life could ever be the same again – they could not realistically return to Germany or Austria because there was nothing to go back to. But equally, they did not want to anyway. With the trauma of being thrown out of their country of birth and with the murder of their families in the Holocaust, the pain remained deep within. How could they trust the nation, albeit newly democratised? What of the older German man and woman walking through the streets – had they been Nazis? The ex-refugees saw Britain as their home and began to apply for British nationality, which was granted. A few decided to make America or Palestine their home instead.

The issue of identity is an interesting one. If these veterans are asked when they began to feel British and no longer German or Austrian, their answers are pretty consistent – they began to feel British several years before they actually gained British nationality. Peter Sinclair said: 'I began to feel British at boarding school when I joined the cadet corps in about 1943. I felt at home the moment I arrived in England and this had to do with the kindness of the people.' For Colin Anson of the commandos, putting on the British army uniform was the beginning of feeling British: 'I was very proud of the brass buttons which I diligently polished all the time I had them. Being in British army uniform was enormously important because, although we were all German-speaking comrades, it was not yet a metamorphosis into being a British soldier, but it was *the* first step on the way to feeling British.'

Walter Eberstadt felt great attachment to Britain, which had become his home in spite of serving abroad for several years:

> Military government wanted me to stay beyond the time when I was due to be demobilised. It was tempting. Was it possible I had rediscovered *Heimat* [homeland] feelings for Hamburg and Germany? I had an influential and interesting job. Apparently my work was well thought of. I was promised a promotion with more pay. I could see ways of ultimately leveraging my NWDR [German radio station] experience into a civilian career in broadcasting or journalism without starting at the bottom. But in fact I had had one wish from the day I joined the army – to be demobilised the day it was my turn. I wanted to get home. England had become my country, even if the wretched British had not yet troubled to naturalise their loyal enemy aliens. In particular I wanted to go back to Oxford and get a degree.

Eberstadt fulfilled his dream. He went on to become a financial writer and emigrated to America where he worked as an investment banker on Wall Street. He is chairman of the World Policy Institute, a trustee of New School University and a director of the American Council on Germany.

None were under any illusion about the difficulties that faced them in civilian life. Clive Teddern wrote:

> What of the future? What of the past? I have to adjust to the fact that everything I knew and loved has gone. What is there to make Civvy Street attractive? I signed on for another year. But life did not stop. I could not spend the rest of my life in the army. I had to face reality. Did I really want to? It had to be done. York Station: a train called LMS takes me south. I am a civilian. No, I'm not, not yet. I am still in uniform with my civvies incarcerated in a cardboard box in the luggage rack. I am on demob leave until February. Time to find a place to live, a job. A job with prospects and a future. Time to sever mental ties. Surely people will open their doors to ex-soldiers? Land fit for heroes to live in and all that. I have all kinds of ideas, few of them feasible. But will I have friends, companions, the kind of relationships I had in the army when most of the thinking was done for me? Or is it going to be a rat-race as some people predict. Does it help that I am the rat with medal ribbons? I try to be hopeful but I feel lonely, abandoned and apprehensive. Nobody knows me and nobody cares. Everybody is excited. Tomorrow, Princess Elizabeth, the future Queen is getting married.[1]

Gideon Behrendt wrote:

> I was 21 years of age, without much happiness to look back on, and as an occasional thought, not much to look forward to. What kind of a future did I expect to have? I still had two years to serve in the army. And after that? What would I do? Where would I live? Back in Germany? Out of the question. It would be like living in a spiritual graveyard. Of course, rubble could be cleared, houses could be rebuilt, but those masses of faceless people 'who had never been Nazis', those thousands of unseen tattoo-marks under hidden armpits who would remain hidden among the millions of fellow travellers, those that had once 'only' been shouting themselves hoarse, cheering 'their Führer'. No. My homeland, *meine Heimet*, had been taken away from me long ago. I had no home anymore. Should I try to build one with a future in England? Hardly, although I was entitled to stay on the island that had given me refuge; I knew I could apply for and receive British nationality, but at the same time I knew at heart I could never become an Englishman, even if I lived in England a hundred years.[2]

In his autobiography *Grey Dawns*, Harry Rossney makes that same distinction about being British but never becoming English.

These men and women had come to Britain prior to 1939 with virtually nothing. They left the army with nothing except money for a demob suit. They had to find a place to live and employment. They began to think about the future and a family life. The younger ones amongst them had had their education cut short under the Nazi regime, had come to Britain, fought for the country that saved them, but were demobbed with no formal qualifications. Finding employment was not going to be easy. Harry Brook, who was demobbed as a staff sergeant in January 1947, commented: 'When I came out of the army, I had a hell of a time because my education had been dislocated by Hitler. I had no formal qualifications. I was a poorly paid common labourer for three years until I was able to get a good job.' It was often a lonely time, as Willy Field recalls:

> When I first came out of the army, I was very lonely for the first 3–4 weeks. The Finchley Road in Swiss Cottage [London] was a place I could wander around and meet people I knew from army days, or other refugees. The Finchley Road was often colloquially called Finchley Strasse! Some of the bus conductors would call out 'Swiss Cottage austeigen!' at the station.

Around the corner was the famous Continental restaurant the Cosmo, owned by ex-Austrian refugees, which was the main meeting place along with the Lyons teahouse for the refugees. The Cosmo was where I met a lot of my old friends again. The food was really excellent – good German and Austrian cuisine.[3]

Many ex-refugees from the army helped each other and began their own small, humble businesses. What is so striking about these veterans is that, having come out of the army with virtually nothing to their name, the majority went on to build up highly successful businesses and enterprises – as the snapshot list of profiles below shows. Amongst them are distinguished academics, others in public services, politics, the arts, the film industry and journalism. It is not possible to compile a complete list of their achievements here, just an insight into what they did.

***

After demob in 1947, Leslie Brent began his studies in Zoology at Birmingham University, with the help of a Ministry of Education grant. He then completed a PhD in Immunology under the supervision of Professor Peter Medawar. Brent joined Medawar's small research team whose work led to Medawar's Nobel Prize in Physiology and Medicine in 1960. Brent held the post of Professor of Zoology at Southampton University from 1965–69, and then Professor of Immunology at St Mary's Hospital Medical School, London.

Peter Ganz, who had eavesdropped on the atomic bomb scientist at Trent Park, went on to become a professor in German at Oxford University and was subsequently decorated by the German government for services to Anglo-German relations. Ernest Goodman, of the Coldstream Guards, emigrated to America in the 1950s and became a professor of political science. Sir Ken Adam, the only known German fighter pilot in the RAF, had a distinguished international career in the film industry. He was the production designer for over seventy films, amongst them *The Ipcress File*, *Barry Lyndon* and *Sleuth*, plus the well-known *Dr Strangelove* with the American director Stanley Kubrick. He is applauded for designing the sets for the first seven James Bond movies, with the exception of *From Russia with Love*, and the much-loved car in *Chitty Chitty Bang Bang*. His contribution is eloquently described by Daniel Snowman in the book *The Hitler Emigrés*:

if you wanted a colourful evocation of another time or place, a burst of imaginative technological innovation, plus a big dollop of visual humour, Ken Adam was the set designer to go for. Did your film script have scenes set in the secret Pentagon War Room (*Dr Strangelove*) or Fort Knox (*Goldfinger*), or require an extravagantly customised car (*Goldfinger, Chitty Chitty Bang Bang*), yacht (*Thunderball*) or speedboat (*Moonraker*) – or a fleet of nuclear bombs or space rockets? You could rely on Ken to dream up a stylised creation far more memorable than the real thing. Was your villain's vast headquarters concealed inside an extinct volcano (*You Only Live Twice*), the interior of a submarine tanker (*The Spy Who Loved Me*) or a city in space (*Moonraker*)? Just the thing for Ken Adam to design – and if necessary to destroy in a series of spectacular terminal explosions.[4]

Sir Ken Adam was awarded two Oscars; one for his work on *Barry Lyndon* and the other for *The Madness of King George*. In December 1995 he was awarded an OBE for services to the film industry. The Royal College of Art bestowed upon him an honorary doctorate in June 1995, as did the University of Greenwich in July 2000. He was knighted by Her Majesty the Queen in the 2003 Birthday Honours for services to the film industry and German–UK relations.

Lord Claus Moser, who also served in the RAF, has an eminent post-war career of public service. He held academic posts at the London School of Economics and Wadham College, Oxford and was also in charge of government statistics for many years, and in banking at Rothschild's. In the arts world he was chairman of the Royal Opera House (1997–2002) and the British Museum. The Rt Hon. Sir Michael Kerr (b. Berlin) became QC, Lord Justice of Appeal, treasurer of Lincoln's Inn and president of the British-German Jurists Association. Ken Ambrose became an MEP. John Mendleson (Jacques Mendelsohn, b. Berlin) was elected Labour MP for Peniston. Ex-commando of 3 Troop Paul Streeter became director of the Institute of Commonwealth Studies; fellow of Balliol College, Oxford; and then professor at Boston University and senior consultant of World Bank.

Four of Sigmund Freud's grandsons served in the British forces in the war, as mentioned in various chapters throughout this book. In civilian life they made their contribution to the arts, media and business. Lucian Freud, albeit only in the Merchant Navy for nine months, has become one of the greatest living artists. His eldest brother Stephan took up a career in publishing. The other brother Clement became a successful broadcaster, writer and wit. Only their cousin Anton Walter Freud felt that he had not achieved his full potential in civilian work, partly due to his refugee roots. He worked for the British Oxygen Company, then British Nylon Spinners, followed by British Hydro-Carbons. Although he died a British citizen, having lived over sixty years in Britain, he still felt an outsider. Being uprooted from Vienna deeply affected his identity and feeling of acceptance. He once said: 'In a way, it's not what you feel – that doesn't count. It's what others think. And their first impression wouldn't be "Oh, another Britisher". One is an outsider and one has to stay an outsider until one dies. But it doesn't worry me too much.'

A number of veterans interviewed for this book started their own businesses or worked for other companies. Peter Sinclair became director of an import company. After 1959 his work took him to Germany, Russia and Hungary: 'We had the sole distribution of Soviet Glassware,' he comments. 'We imported china, glassware and fancy goods from all over Europe. The import company was called "Loewenstein and Hecht", founded in Berlin in 1888, transferred to UK in 1926. The group became a public company in 1963.'

In 1957 John Langford started a textile business at 1 Hanover Street in Mayfair, which became a well-known international company, John Langford of London, making shirts. Peter Eden's first job was with Milverton Fashions, a clothing company with offices in Langham House near Oxford Circus. During the 1950s he traded with an Austrian from the army days, Henry Keith. Together they founded a successful company called Olympic (later Metro Leisureware) which became the leading supplier of ladies' separates. In 1963 Eden bought the first of many hotels which he named Hyde Park Towers Hotel. In the late 1960s he bought another, which he named the Eden Park Hotel, again near Hyde Park. At the height of his career he owned fourteen restaurants and several hotels.

Personal contacts were vital at this time. Willy Field came across an older friend, Kurt Morgenroth, who had been with him in internment in Australia and then the Pioneer Corps, but was invalided out of the army when a concrete mixer fell on his leg. Morgenroth had returned to London and learnt the trade of watchmaker. He started importing watches from Switzerland and began a mail-order business. By chance he met Willy Field one day and asked him to join him at his premises in London's Gray's Inn Road. Field took up work for him on an initial wage of £10 a week. The business became successful and expanded until it had several jewellery shops in London and elsewhere in the country. He was eventually made a partner and worked in the trade for twenty-two years:

> In 1969, the business was taken over by a public company. This changed everything. I didn't like it at all once it had become a public company. I left and started up on my own, selling advertising gifts. Eventually I became the sole UK agent for a company called Gundlach, which traded in diaries and advertising gifts. I finally retired from there at the age of 80 in 2000.[5]

Ex-Vienneser S. Gruber obtained an engineering degree at Bradford. After a spell at Jowetts Motorcars and J.W. Roberts Leeds on railway engines and coaches, he joined Spooner Industries in Ilkley, Yorkshire. As their export manager for the Central and Eastern Europe area west of the Rhine and south of the Alps, he opened their offices in Vienna in 1959. When the group expanded he was appointed export director of the new sub-sidiary in Manchester in 1969. He eventually became product manager at Spooner Industries, with offices again in Vienna, where he retired in 1983. Consciousness of his roots and what had happened to him in the war was to surface even in the workplace. Gruber explains:

> The Managing Director had soon assessed me correctly and very early in our relationship he took me to one side and said, 'Herr Gruber, I would like to tell you that I have been a member of the NSDAP – the Nazi party'. I replied: 'Herr NN, if you have not committed a crime for which you feel guilty, I am not interested in what you have been, but only in what you are and think now.' That summed it up.

Gruber's attitude is one of forgiveness which seems to permeate many of the veterans to the Nazi past of their country of birth. The same is true of ex-commando Colin Anson. A few years ago, whilst travelling by train with his wife through Austria, he came unexpectedly face to face with the Luftwaffe pilot that probably caused his near-fatal head injuries off Sicily in the summer of 1943:

> In our carriage there was an older man with a young boy. It turned out to be grandfather and grandson. The grandfather was explaining in German about the mountains we were passing through. Alice and I found it very interest-ing and started to join the conversation in German. Then we talked about

holidays, different countries and travel. He said that he had been in Sicily. And I replied: 'Yes, me too, but that was only during the war.' He then said, 'Ah, I was in the Luftwaffe, a Stuka pilot.' I was surprised and admitted that I had been hit by a Stuka. One thing led to another and it transpired that he remembered an operation over Sicily in which he and his mates had had to attack Allied shipping in Augusta Bay. His memory was so accurate: 'But,' he said, 'a smokescreen had been laid and obscured most of the ships – with the exception of one, so we concentrated our fire on that one ship that was laying the smoke screen.' It was the moment when I realised that he may well be the very pilot who had dropped the bomb that wounded me! He was terribly embarrassed and I had to console him and explain: Why should I resent it? It was his job. It was his duty. Today I would not hold it against anyone for having been a Nazi. What else should they have done?[6]

A number of ex-refugees turned their hand to publishing, including Robert Maxwell, mentioned in Chapter 7, and George Clare. The latter became chief executive for international affairs of the Axel Springer publishing empire. Geoffrey Perry, who had arrested Lord Haw-Haw, established a highly successful business publishing *Family Circle* and *Living*. After selling his company to Thomsons, he became head of the Thomson Organisation's magazine division. Subsequently he bought *Business Traveller* magazine and expanded the title into a group of five magazines, now published in Britain, USA, Germany, the Middle East and the Far East. Away from publishing he served first as a prison visitor and subsequently as a magistrate in South Westminster, where he became a deputy chairman of the bench. His brother Peter also had a successful professional life, devoted to the development of British vocational education and training, mainly as director of the British Association for Commercial and Industrial Education. He was actively involved in the training of instructors and in public debates, leading to the Industrial Training Act of 1964. This in turn led to an invitation to serve on a number of government committees, and being appointed OBE at the Queen's Birthday Honours in 1969. He has written several books and published his PhD thesis, *The Evolution of British Manpower Policy*. Britain's membership of the EEC led to his appointment as a British representative on some of its vocational training committees.

For Britain's enemy aliens, the subsequent decades were concentrated on building up a livelihood, making a home life and supporting their families. Many married ex-refugee girls, others English girls. Family life for them has taken on an extra special dimension because many lost their own parents and extended families in the death camps. They have had children and now, in many cases, grandchildren and great-grandchildren. Through their own survival their bloodline lives on in spite of Hitler's attempt to wipe out European Jewry. Ernest Goodman sums up their situation at the end of the war:

> After the war some of us stayed with our regiments until our demob numbers came up. Others became translators and interrogators who were urgently needed as soon as the Allied armies reached Germany. Whether at home or on the continent, wherever we were, we wandered among ruined buildings and homeless people. We wondered what was a normal life in a normal world? However, we knew that the world was now free and that those who came through were proud of the years they had given so that they and future generations can live and prosper in peace.[7]

Notes

1. Clive Teddern, *Boy with a Suitcase*, p. 98.
2. Gideon Behrendt, *The Long Road Home*, p. 89.
3. Interview with the author.
4. Daniel Snowman, *The Hitler Emigres: The Cultural Impact on Britain of Refugees from Nazism*, p. 293.
5. Based on interview with the author. See also Helen Fry, *From Dachau to D-Day*.
6. Helen Fry, *German Schoolboy, British Commando*, pp. 169–70.
7. Correspondence with the author.

POSTSCRIPT

Historians have debated the success or otherwise of the denazification process. It was never going to be possible to capture and bring to justice *all* the Nazi war criminals, but for the enemy aliens who worked in denazification, whether abroad or in Britain, they argue that failure to capture all the perpetrators does not mean the process as a whole was a failure. The greatest success lay in restoring democracy to Germany in such a short space of time. That democracy lives on sixty-five years later. With other colleagues in the forces, these veterans had their own unique part to play in that process, and one that largely made use of their fluency of German. Seventy or more years after their flight from the country of their birth, these veterans often still have a trace of a German accent, in spite of seven decades of life in Britain. It is something that bothered Walter Freud during his lifetime. He was especially sensitive to his German accent which he never really shed, in spite of taking numerous elocution lessons at various points in his life. He, like many refugees from Nazism, adopted England and felt terribly grateful to Britain for saving him from certain death. The past is ever present in the minds of these men and women. They continue to reflect on the past and how it has shaped their lives. They still debate how far ordinary Germans knew about the events of the Holocaust and the crimes committed in the death camps. In his autobiography, *From Dachau to Dunkirk*, Fred Pelican, who lost over forty members of his family in the death camps, succinctly wrote:

In the course of my duties with the war crimes investigation branch, I hardly ever came across a German who admitted having supported Adolf Hitler. The excuse usually was that they had been forced to follow Nazi ideology or found it convenient to go along with the madness. The facts are quite contrary to their unpalatable lies; Nazism poisoned their minds and they allowed themselves to be manipulated by a gradual process from being a people of great culture to being savages of the worst kind. Is it not remarkable that millions of people passed through Germany en route for extermination camps, starved, beaten, gassed and burned to death, yet nobody noticed anything? They heard about concentration camps but had no idea what went on inside the camps. Of course, I knew differently, having lived among them when the masses attended big rallies at Nuremberg with effigies, hysteria and adulation offered up to a mad Machiavellian. The Nazis debauched an entire civilization, and this fact must be indelibly imprinted in every decent person's mind.

These men and women still hold deep inside the pain of their loss. None could escape some kind of psychological damage which still surfaces sometimes in their dreams or quiet moments. They were the lucky ones who survived the war – survived the death camps and were able to fight back. At the end of the war many had the satisfaction of bringing in the most wanted Nazi war criminals. Given all that they have been through, these veterans could be forgiven for harbouring resentment for their past suffering, but many are philosophical about the need to forgive but never forget. In spite of the scars, they do not hold anger or hatred for Germany. They fought to defeat the evil of Nazism, not of Germany as such.

Remembrance plays an important part in the lives of these veterans in their retirement. They believe that through education of each generation lies the hope that history will never again repeat itself. Some veterans like Willy Field return each year to Germany to give talks to school children there. In 2001 he made an emotional re-visit to Dachau concentration camp with a group of school children from Bonn; the first time he had been back to Dachau since his release in April 1939. His reactions can be read in his biography *From Dachau to D-Day*. What does it mean for these veterans to remember today? The annual November Remembrance Sunday, when wreaths are laid at the Cenotaph in London and other war memorials around Britain, has an added dimension for these particular veterans. Ernest Goodman, who served on the front line with the Coldstream Guards, comments:

The poppies for me mean sacrifice for a cause. They are a reminder of the hardship of war, the trenches and of those who fell. To me they mean Flanders and the thousands who were left there and those who grieve for them. Of course my generation also thinks of the Second World War and those who

fought and died in the various theatres of that war. I have had the privilege
of participating in a Remembrance Sunday Parade and it moved me very
deeply as I thought of those who died so that future generations may live and
prosper. One word sums it up: Sacrifice.

Ernest Goodman, like thousands of other veterans, is exceedingly humble
about his contribution to the war. He survived, but was wounded in action
and nearly died. He, like so many, was prepared to make the ultimate sacrifice and lay down his life to free Europe from Nazism. He is reluctant
to take any praise for his part in the liberation of Europe, but we today
owe our freedom to the selfless sacrifice of men and women like Ernest
Goodman. Ken Ward (Karl Würzburger), who fought on the front line
with the 1st Tank Regiment, recently sponsored a *stolperstein* (a memory
stone) set into the pavement outside his family home in Frankfurt in
memory of his parents. On 18 October 2006 he returned to Frankfurt for
the special ceremony:

> It was a very emotional time. I stood in front of the house where I grew up.
> As the stones were being laid, a piece of music was played which my father
> [Siegfried Würzburger] had composed called *Passacagli und Fuge*. My parents
> had not survived. They were deported from Frankfurt to the Lodz Ghetto
> where they perished. At the laying of those stones, the ceremony was attended
> by my school friend Heinz-Jochen Stiege. He had joined the Hitler Youth
> in 1933 and during the war served as a fighter pilot flying a Messerschmitt.
> When we met up again in the 1950s, we exchanged stories on what we had
> done in the war. He assured me that he had only fought on the Eastern front.
> Was that the truth or was he covering up as Germany had lost the war? He
> was not the same man of my childhood. Although we still see each other and
> communicate with each other now, the present friendship is quite different
> from the time we were best friends at school.

In a unique gesture of benevolence, Ken Ward sponsored an extra *stolperstein* in memory of Arnd Freiherr von Wedekind (b. 1919), a non-Jewish
anti-Nazi who was executed for his views. On 3 September 1943, exactly
four years to the day that war broke out, von Wedekind was killed by the
Nazis in Plötzensee Prison, Berlin. Nearly seventy years after Ken Ward left
Germany with the Kindertransport, he thought not only of his own loss
and suffering, but placed a permanent memorial to a man who would have

otherwise been forgotten. This is the importance of remembrance. Every year ex-commando Colin Anson watches on his television set the annual remembrance service at the Royal Albert Hall. Seventy years later, it still has the power to move him: 'The ceremony in the Royal Albert Hall is rather lengthy, but at the end, in that moment of silence when the petals descend from the dome, they are all there: I see their faces. There's Robbie and there's Max. And that gets me every time.' Colin Anson is referring to his comrades of 3 Troop who died on the battlefields of Normandy with their respective commando units.

Failure to defeat Nazism was never an option in the minds of Britain's enemy aliens. Many have since discussed how they did not expect to survive the war, especially those involved in front-line fighting and operations behind enemy lines. By the end of the war, they had distinguished themselves in all disproportion to their numbers. Without them, the war would have lasted longer and the task of reconstructing post-war Europe would have been impossible in such a short space of time. Post-war obligations lasted longer than the war itself. The ex-refugees remained loyal to Britain, were granted British citizenship and went on to distinguish themselves in public life. Ernest Goodman succinctly sums up the story of Britain's enemy aliens who served king and country:

> Wherever one meets refugees today who fought as members of the great Allied liberation armies, one senses the pride of a people who were part of a glorious time when civilisation was given another chance. Wherever they live today, they will tell you of that time when they had the honour of fighting for King and a democratically governed and free country.

Lest we forget. This book is a tribute to those refugees who fought, then rebuilt post-war Europe.

BIBLIOGRAPHY

Papers and Archives

The Imperial War Museum; The Association of Jewish Ex-service Men and Women (AJEX); The Association of Jewish Refugees; The Freud Museum, London; The Jewish Military Museum; The Library, Belsize Square Synagogue, London; The Public Record Office, Kew; The Royal Logistics Corps Museum; The National Army Museum; The Tank Museum; The RAF Museum, Hendon; and The North Devon Record Office. The National Archives, ref: WO 208/3779 (The Last Will and Testament of Adolf Hitler) and WO 208/3781 (Investigations into the last days and death of Adolf Hitler). The Sworn Statement of Rudolf Höss, IWM, ref: 05/14/1.

The British Officer Told me to Write my Story, unpublished report written by Nazi war criminal Leopold Falkensammer, interrogated by Walter Freud, original typed copy in the Freud family private archive, a photocopy held by the author.

Books and Memoirs

Alexander, John. *A Measure of Time*, privately published, 2000, copy in Belsize Square Synagogue library, London

Ambrose, Kenneth. *The Suitcase in the Garage: Letters and Photographs of a German Jewish Family, 1800–1950*, unpublished memoirs

Ambrose, Tom. *Hitler's Loss: What Britain and America Gained from Europe's Cultural Exiles*, Peter Owen, 2001

Arton, Michael. *One Day in York*, copy lent to the author

Behrendt, Gideon. *The Long Road Home*, privately published memoirs, Israel, 2005

Bentwich, Norman. *I Understand the Risks: The Story of the Refugees from Nazi Oppression who Fought in the British Forces in the World War*, Victor Gollancz, 1950

Berghahn, Marion. *Continental Britons: German-Jewish Refugees from Nazi Germany*, Berg Publishers, 1988

Bernstein, Jeremy. *Hitler's Uranium Club: The Secret Recordings at Farm Hall*, Copernicus Books, 2001

Brainin, Jussi. *Internment 8 July–26 October 1940*, unpublished diary, copy to be deposited at the IWM

——. *Prisoner of War Camp 87 Diary March – July 1946*, unpublished, copy to be deposited at the IWM

Cesarani, David & Bardgett, Suzanne. *Belsen 1945: New Historical Perspectives*, Vallentine Mitchell, 2006

Clare, George. *Berlin Days 1946–47*, Pan Books, 1989

——. *Last Waltz in Vienna: The Destruction of a Family 1842–1942*, Pan Books, 1990 edition

Compton, David Michael. *Life Story of a 'Friendly Enemy Alien' Paratrooper Pathfinder*, unpublished memoirs, lent to the author

Cresswell, Yvonne. *Living with the Wire: Civilian Internment in the Isle of Man during the two World Wars*, Manx National Heritage, 1994

Dale, Stephen. *Spanglet or By Any Other Name*, privately published memoirs, 1993

Eberstadt, Walter Albert. *Whence We Came, Where We Went*, W.A.E. Books, 2002

Flanagan, Ben (ed.) with Joanne Reills & David Bloxham. *Remembering Belsen: Eyewitnesses Record the Liberation*, Vallentine Mitchell, 2006

Fournier, Gérard & Heintz, André. *If I Must Die ... From Postmaster to Aquatint*, France, OREP Editions, 2006

Frayling, Christopher. *Ken Adam: The Art of Production Design*, Faber & Faber, 2005

Freud, Anton Walter. *Before the Anticlimax: with Special Operations Executive in Austria*, unpublished memoirs, copy in the Freud Museum and Imperial War Museum

——. *An Austrian Grandfather*, unpublished memoirs, copy in the Freud family possession and the Freud Museum, London

Freud, Clement. *Freud Ego*, BBC, 2001

Freud, Martin. *Glory Reflected. Sigmund Freud – Man and Father*, Angus & Robertson, 1957

Friedlander, Gerhart & Turner, Keith. *Rudi's Story: The diary and wartime experiences of Rudolf Friedlander*, Jedburgh, 2006

Fry, Helen. *German Schoolboy, British Commando*, The History Press, 2010

——. *Freuds' War*, The History Press, 2009

——. *From Dachau to D-Day*, The History Press, 2009

———. *Churchill's German Army*, paperback, The History Press, 2009

———. *The King's Most Loyal Enemy Aliens: Germans who Fought for Britain during the Second World War*, Sutton Publishing, 2007

———. *Jews in North Devon during the Second World War*, Halsgrove, 2005

Gill, Alan. *Interrupted Journeys*, Simon & Schuster, 2004

Gillman, Peter & Gillman, Leni. *Collar the Lot: How Britain Interned and Expelled its Wartime Refugees*, Quartet Books, 1980

Goodman, Ernest. Unpublished memoirs

Gottlieb, Amy Zahl. *Men of Vision: Anglo-Jewry's Aid to Victims of the Nazi Regime 1933–1945*, Weidenfeld & Nicolson, 1998

Grenville, Anthony. *Continental Britons: Jewish Refugees from Nazi Europe*, The Jewish Museum, London, 2002

Haines, Joe. *Maxwell*, Guild Publishing, 1998

Hare, Tony. *Spanning the Century: The Story of an ordinary Man in Extraordinary Circumstances*, The Memoir Club, 2002

Hoare, Oliver (ed.). *Camp 020: MI5 & the Nazi Spies*, Public Record Office, 2000

Holden, Rolf. *One of the Lucky Ones*, unpublished memoirs

Jeffreys, Diarmuid. *IG Farben and the Making of Hitler's War Machine*, Bloomsbury, 2008

Langford, John. Unpublished memoirs

Lasker-Wallfisch, Anita. *Inherit the Truth*, St Martin's Press, 1996

Leighton-Langer, Peter. *X Steht für unbekannt: Deutsche und Österreicher in den Britischen Streitkräften im Zweiten Weltkrieg* ('X Means Unknown: Germans and Austrians in the British Fighting Forces in the Second World War'), Verlag, Berlin, 1999

———. *The King's Own Loyal Enemy Aliens*, Vallentine Mitchell, 2006

Leon, Gary. *The Way it Was*, The Book Guild Ltd, 1997

Levy, Isaac. *Now I Can Tell*, privately published, 1978

———. *Witness to Evil*, privately published

Lustig, Fritz. Unpublished memoirs

———. 'Wilton Park: A Very Special POW Camp', article in the journal of the Association of Jewish Refugees, August 2009, pp. 4–5

Lynton, Mark. *Accidental Journey: A Cambridge Internee's Memoir of World War II*, The Overlook Press, 1995

Manchester, William. *The Arms of Krupp*, Michael Joseph, 1969

Masters, Peter. *Striking Back: A Jewish Commando's War Against the Nazis*, Presidio Press, 1997

Neitzel, Sonke. *Tapping Hitler's Generals*, Frontline Books, 2007

Pelican, Fred. *From Dachau to Dunkirk*, Vallentine Mitchell, 1993

Perlès, Alfred. *Alien Corn*, George Allen & Unwin Ltd, 1944

Perry, Geoffrey. *When Life Becomes History*, White Mountain Press, 2002

Perry, Peter J. *An Extraordinary Commission: The Story of a Journey Through Europe's Disaster*, published by the author, 1997, distributed by T.J. Gillard Print Services, Bristol

Rogers, Garry. *Interesting Times*, privately published autobiography, 1998

Rossney, Harry. *Grey Dawns: Illustrated Poems about Life in Nazi Germany, Emigration, and Active Service in the British Army during the War*, The History Web Ltd, 2009

———. *Normandy 1944: Recollections*, privately published, copy in the author's possession and the Imperial War Museum

———. *Personal Recollections during War-Service Abroad 1944–46*, privately published, copy in author's possession

Rothman, Herman (ed. Helen Fry). *Hitler's Will*, The History Press, 2009

Sanders, Eric. *From Music to Morse*, The History Web Ltd, 2010

———. *Emigration ins Leben. Wien-London und nicht mehr retour*, Czernin, Wien, 2007

Stent, Ronald. *A Bespattered Page? The Internment of 'His Majesty's most Loyal Enemy Aliens'*, Andre Deutsch, 1980

Streat, Norman (trans.). *The Sacrifice We Are Now Making … Letters from one of His Majesty's Most Loyal Enemy Aliens, July – November 1940*, unpublished, copy in the author's possession

Teddern, Clive. *Boy with a Suitcase*, unpublished memoirs lent to the author

Trevor-Roper, Hugh. *The Last Days of Hitler*, Pan Books, 2002 edition

Ward, Kenneth. *And then the Music Stopped Playing*, Braiswick, 2006

Warner, Fred. *Personal Account of SOE Period*, unpublished memoirs, copy in the Imperial War Museum and courtesy of Eric Sanders

INDEX

6th Airborne Division 79, 80, 113, 162

Abrahams, Karl 40
Adam, Ken (Klaus Adam) 21, 171–2
Alexander, Howard 40, 44-45, 46, 86
Allied Military Government
    see Military Government
Altengamme concentration camp
    65–7, 69
Alvensleben, Rudolf von 64
Ambrose, Ken 105–6, 172
Anderson, Herbert 91, 127
Anschluss 112
Anson, Colin 10, 27, 29–30, 31, 34, 35,
    101–2, 168, 174, 180
Ardeatine Cave massacre 57, 80–1
Argentina 16, 64
Arnott, Alfred 111
Arnott, Max 111
Atomic bomb scientists 144–5, 171
Attlee, Clement 114
Auschwitz concentration camp 13, 16,
    20, 26, 28, 39, 41, 42–4, 45, 69, 72,
    73, 75, 84, 91, 92, 120, 164
Auschwitz Trial 72, 91
Austria 9, 11, 13, 14, 17, 19, 40, 55, 57,
    62, 74, 77, 79, 80, 81, 82, 85, 94, 109,
    110, 111, 112, 131, 143, 146, 168, 174

Bad Oeynhausen 62, 64, 75, 111, 118
Barr, Hans 51
Beck, Walter 111
Behrendt, Gideon 11, 28, 31, 128, 170
Belgium 10, 17, 19, 24, 43, 46, 84, 103,
    104, 122, 123, 145, 163
Belsen concentration camp 11, 19–20,
    21–5, 28, 43, 44, 45, 60, 84, 85, 86,
    90, 93
Belsen Trial 44, 84–5, 86, 134
Bennett, George 91
Benson, Freddie 54
Berger, Richard 54–5
Berlin 12, 13, 16, 19, 20, 21, 26, 27, 28,
    32, 33, 34, 39, 41, 71, 75, 76, 77, 80,
    83, 86, 91, 94, 95, 100, 101, 102, 103,
    104, 105, 106, 108, 110, 114, 117,
    118, 119, 120, 122, 123, 124, 125,
    126, 131, 134, 140, 141, 146, 148,
    154, 162, 172, 179
Best, Werner 49–50
Blair, Capt 111
Blake, Peter 97
Bletchley Park 18, 142, 144
Bonn 10, 15, 26–7, 90, 178
Bourne, Eric 148–50, 166
Brainin, Jussi 157–8, 160–2
Braun, Charles 80

Bremen 25, 46, 76, 97, 123, 136

Brent, Leslie 121, 171

Brett, David 123–4

British-Austrian Legation Unit
(BALU) 111–3, 150

British Army of the Rhine (BAOR)
9, 13, 62, 86, 110, 113, 121

British Bombing Survey Unit 105, 106

British Control Commission
see Control Commission

Broad, Perry 72, 92–3

Brook, Harry 15, 162–4, 165, 166, 170

Brown, Ernest 110

Brussels 45, 108, 110, 118, 123

Bryan, Roger 83–4

Bryant, George 111

Buchenwald concentration camp 21,
43, 145

Burnett, Richard 104

Byfield camp (Camp 87) 157–9, 162

Carsten, Francis 110

Carynthia, Austria 55

Chelmsford 154

Churchill, Winston 13, 57, 113, 114,
144, 148

Clare, George 117–8, 131, 175

Cohen, Ernest 113

Cohn, Wilhelm 113

Cologne 27, 58, 90, 104, 105, 110,
129, 134

Combined Services Detailed
Interrogation Centre (CSDIC)
143, 146

Commandos 10, 17, 27, 34, 35, 168
3 Troop 17, 19, 44, 73, 91, 101, 103,
118, 127, 180

Compton, David Michael 91

Control Commission 9, 13, 58, 77, 91,
101, 103, 110, 127, 128, 131, 140

Counter-Intelligence (British) 14, 97

Cuba 60

Dachau 15, 35, 40, 43, 51, 57, 83, 101,
111, 178

Dale, Stephen 19, 33, 126-127

Danish Jews 49, 61

Denmark 49, 50, 55, 56, 75

Dickson, Max 73

Dönitz, Admiral Karl 48, 100

Dorffmann, Leo 110

Drew, Harry 103

Dunera, troopship 111, 130

Eberstadt, Walter 12, 21, 60, 133–5,
136, 169

Eden, Peter 90–1, 173

Education of German POWs 14, 21,
103, 134, 143–66

Eisenerz massacre 77–8, 79

Engel, Dr Hans 24–6

Envers, John 103

Essen War Crimes Trials 90

Esser, Hans 52–3

Falkensammer, Leopold 65–9, 70

Farben, I.G. 70, 73, 102, 116

Farm Hall, near Cambridge 144–5

Farnborough, Lt Col. 113

Fast, Walter 111

Field Intelligence Agency Technical
(FIAT) 101–2

Field, Leonard 131

Field Security Service 29, 35, 39,
46, 73, 75, 90, 103, 111, 114, 127,
131

Field, Willy 10, 15, 23, 26, 32, 170–1, 173, 178

Fisher, Eric 121

Flensburg 14, 38, 39, 46, 48, 49, 111, 136, 137

Flick, Friedrich 101

Flossenburg camp 43

Frankfurt 12, 27, 32, 34, 35, 72, 91, 101, 102, 122, 179

Freud, Clement 118–9

Freud, Sigmund 13, 17, 73, 118, 172

Freud, Stephan 119

Freud, (Anton) Walter 13, 17, 51, 55, 64, 65, 67, 69, 72, 73, 173, 177

Ganz, Peter 145–6, 171

German scientists 101–2, 108, 117, 120, 144–6

Gillard, Fred 115–6

Goebbels, Joseph 34, 38, 47, 60, 98–9, 100, 159

Goldberg, Sidney 32

Goldman, Martin 19

Goodman, Dennis 63–4

Goodman, Ernest 171, 176, 178, 179, 180

Göring, Hermann 47, 76, 84, 98, 118, 135

Greece 19, 43, 77

Grese, Irma 44, 86, 87, 88

Gruber, S.H. 79–80, 82, 174

Hachenberg, Sgt Hans 83

Hahn, Otto 144, 145–6

Hamburg 12, 13, 24, 25–6, 33, 39, 43, 51, 63, 64, 65, 69, 70, 71, 72, 74, 75, 76, 84, 87–8, 91, 95, 96, 103, 120, 127, 128, 131, 132, 133, 135, 136, 137, 139, 169

Hameln Prison 13, 36, 44, 56, 72, 87

Hanover 105, 113, 120, 121, 122, 127, 139, 148

Hardman, Rev. Leslie 19

Hare, Tony 85, 153–4

Harris, Ian 118

Haw-Haw, Lord
    see William Joyce

Heide 39, 75

Henley, Peter 116–7

Hereford, John 107–8

Herz, Rudi 120

Hess, Rudolf 76, 84

Himmler, Heinrich 13, 34, 38, 41, 46–8, 51, 60, 64, 70, 80, 85, 98, 99, 100

Hirsch, Walter 32

Hitler's Last Will & Testament 14, 98–100, 109, 181

Holden, Rolf 21

Horn, Leo 108

Horwell, Arnold 20

Höss, Rudolf 13, 20, 39–44, 75, 83, 84, 181

Howard, William Ashley 16

Ilfracombe 146

Intelligence Corps 9, 23, 27, 35, 39, 40, 58, 63, 90, 131, 146

Internment 53, 63, 89, 97, 99, 119, 145, 149, 157, 161, 173

Interpreters 9, 35, 42, 58, 83, 94–109, 110, 111, 163

Interpreters Corps 9, 96, 110, 111

Interrogation of POWs 10, 14, 16, 18, 23, 29, 30, 35, 39, 44, 49, 51, 54, 57, 63, 69, 70, 73, 75, 76, 94, 95, 96, 99, 111, 114, 119, 122, 143, 147, 153–4, 155, 163

Iserlohn 100, 101, 108
Italy 10, 17, 19, 29, 57, 77, 80, 91, 101,
    119, 121, 141, 161

Jackson, Fred 40
Jepsen, Gustav 13, 55–6
Johannmeier, Willi 100–1
Johnson, Peter 104
Joyce, William (aka Lord Haw-Haw)
    14, 131–2, 137

Karrell, Rudy 119–20
Kennard, Robert 111
Keynes, Capt. 111
Kiel 26, 39, 40, 91, 94, 95
Kildare, Les 140
Kindertransport 32, 40, 122, 154, 179
Klagenfurt, Austria 19, 80
Klein, Dr Fritz 23, 36, 86, 87
Knight, Jack 57, 81
Kramer, Josef 20, 84–7, 135
Kristallnacht 54, 120
Krupp, Alfried 74
Krupp, Gustav 73, 74
Krupp industrial company 73–4, 115–6

Lahde-Weser concentration camp 75
Laindon, Essex 154–6
Landsberg, Herbert 22–3
Langford, John 13, 113–5, 173
Lasker-Wallfisch, Anita 45, 86
Lasky, Major (Laszky) 111–2, 113
Latimer House 18, 143, 146, 147
Lausegger, Gerhard 54–5
Leighton-Langer, Peter 16
Leon, Gary 95–6
Levy, Rev. Isaac (Harry) 19
Leyton, Henry 114

Lincoln, Ken 29
Loibl Pass concentration camp 80
Lorenz, Heinz 97–9, 100–1
Luftwaffe pilots 21, 32, 88, 89, 100, 107,
    146, 161, 174–5
Lüneberg Heath 23, 24, 48, 121
Lustig, Fritz 143, 146–8
Lynton, Mark 33, 46–8, 49, 95

MacGarrety, Ernest 97
MacKay, Charles 40
Mauthausen 79, 80
Maxwell, Robert 100–1, 141, 175
Media (denazification of) 131–42
Merrythought Camp (Cumbria) 162
Merton, Michael 91, 113
Military government 10, 27, 35, 62,
    90, 91, 104, 110–30, 133, 134, 138,
    169
Minsk 27, 28, 121
Moore, Gerry 27, 39, 44
Mortimer, Henry 94
Moser, Claus 106–7, 172
Murdoch, Capt. 50

Nazi War Criminals 10, 11, 13, 35,
    38–61, 62, 64, 74–5, 81, 83, 94, 103,
    166, 177, 178
Neuengamme concentration camp
    24, 43, 51, 62–4, 65, 71, 77, 84, 87
Neumann, Theo 111
Newspapers (denazification of)
    131–42
Nichols, Gerald 103
Normandy 10, 16, 17, 24, 32, 103, 107,
    122, 153, 162, 163, 164, 180
Norton, Edward 114
Norton Fitzwarren POW camp 150

Norvill, Major 111
Nuremberg Trials 23, 39, 49, 51, 73, 74, 76, 83–4, 101, 103, 109, 135, 144

Oakfield, Bill 84
Ohlendorf, Otto 76
Oliver, Sgt 131
O'Neill, Sgt Major Oscar 44
Oppenheimer, Rudi 23

Parker, Ralph 46, 97
Pelican, Fred 51–3, 65, 69–72, 81, 177
Perry, Geoffrey 13, 19, 32, 131–2, 136, 141, 175
Perry, Peter 12, 34, 124
Philipp, Werner 104–5
Pioneer Corps 11, 13, 16, 17, 20, 22, 23, 26, 35, 40, 73, 80, 83, 84, 85, 91, 93, 96, 104, 111, 113, 119, 120, 123, 124, 126, 130, 131, 140, 144, 146, 150, 152, 157, 173
Pohl, Oswald 13, 20, 43, 50–1
Poland 40, 41, 43, 77, 85, 111, 129
Pollitt, E. 140
Potsdam conference 13, 113–4, 115
Priebke, Erich (SS officer) 57
Pringle, Reginald 111
Prisoners of war 14, 16, 17, 18, 29, 30, 31, 32, 35, 39, 57, 59, 65, 67, 68, 71, 104, 124, 133, 143–67
Prisoner-of-war camps 143–67

Radio Hamburg 131–3
Rainer, Gauleiter 80
Ravensbrück concentration camp 87
Rawdon, Sgt 110
Recklinghausen 52, 53, 58
Reitlinger, Major 94

Renow, Capt. 113
Reppin, Paul 77
Rhodes, Capt. 111
Roberts, Henry 97, 99
Rogers, Garry 22, 58–9
Romberg, Major 113
Rosney, George 26
Rossney, Harry 11, 14, 27, 170
Rothman, Herman 14, 82, 91–2, 97–8, 99
Royal Air Force 17, 21, 51, 77, 84, 89, 90, 105, 106, 107, 120, 171, 172
Royal Armoured Corps 17, 22, 27, 39, 44, 111, 140
Royal Army Medical Corps 24
Royal Army Service Corps 121
Royal Electical & Mechanical Engineers 80, 121
Royal Engineers 93, 111, 120, 127
Royal Marine Commando 17, 73, 101, 103, 118
Royal Navy 16, 17, 32
Russia 9, 76, 109, 114, 173

Sachsenhausen concentration camp 19, 33, 35, 40, 41, 120, 126
Salzbach, Herbert 165
Sandbostel 24–5
Sanders, Eric 111, 112, 150–2
Schnek, Friedrich 111
Schweiger, Eric 50
Scientists
    see German scientists
Sely, Kaye 131
Shaw, Sgt 114
Sherwood, Michael 16, 27, 122
Sicily 10, 17, 19, 101, 174, 175
Simms, Fred 77–8

Sinclair, Peter 16, 154–7, 168, 173
Skorzeny, Otto 57
South America 38, 60, 166
Spain 57, 60
Spandau Prison 114
Special Operations Executive (SOE)
    17, 19, 33, 50, 55, 74, 75, 87, 91, 94,
    101, 111, 126
Speer, Albert 38, 83, 102–3
Spier, Alfred 110
Stade 119, 120
Stenham, Henry 96–7
Stewart, Stephen 75, 85–6, 87
Stuart, Geoffrey 103
Summerfield, Alfred 94

T Force 116, 120, 131, 132
Teddern, Clive 87–9, 169
Terezin
    see Theresienstadt
Tesch, Bruno (arrest of) 71–2
Tesch & Stabenow 13, 62, 66, 69–70,
    71, 72
Tessmann, Colonel SS 77
Theresienstadt 26, 28, 43, 73, 84
Thomas, Michael 110
translation work 62, 83, 111, 115, 116
Trent Park 143–4, 145, 146, 171
Trevor-Roper, Hugh 14, 100
Tyrol, Austria 54, 161

Vienna 64, 73, 79, 80, 83, 91, 110, 111,
    112, 113, 115, 117, 118, 121, 131,
    140, 173, 174

Waller, Sgt 73
Wallich, Walter 131
War Crimes Group South-East Europe
    57, 79, 80, 81
War Crimes Investigation Unit 35, 51,
    55, 62, 74, 81, 82
War Crimes Tribunals 72, 74, 83–93,
    94, 119
War criminals, Nazi 10, 11, 13, 35,
    38–61, 62, 64, 74, 75, 81, 83, 94, 103,
    166, 177, 178
Ward, Ken 122–3, 179
Warner, Fred 74, 75, 76–7
Wayne, Peter 94
Weikersheim, Capt. Prince Franz 139
Westmoreland POW camp 163
White, Allan 127–8
Wieselmann, Ft Sgt 77
Wilton Park 18, 143, 145, 146–9, 166

X-Troop
    see Commandos (3 Troop)

Zamory, Eberhard 153
Zeltweg airfield 17